FIGHTING
FOR THE
BUCKS

FIGHTING
FOR THE
BUCKS

THE HISTORY OF THE
ROYAL BUCKS HUSSARS
1914–18

E.J. HOUNSLOW
FOREWORD BY PROFESSOR IAN BECKETT

The Buckinghamshire Military Museum Trust

This book has been produced in association with the Buckinghamshire Military Museum Trust. The Trust preserves the heritage of the local military units raised in the historic county of Buckinghamshire in England from the 1500s onwards, including the militia, yeomanry, volunteers, Territorials and Home Guard. The Trust preserves uniforms, flags, weapons, equipment, documents, paintings, and photographs relating to the amateur military forces raised in Bucks since the 1500s. Intended mainly for home defence against foreign invasion – from the Spanish Armada to Napoleon and Hitler – these citizen soldiers were just as significant for their high visibility in the local community, involving a far wider section of society in military affairs than the small regular army, which was often out of sight and out of mind serving overseas. The Trust's collections reflect this dual military and social function.

For further information on the Buckinghamshire Military Museum trust
see www.bmmt.co.uk

Cover illustrations: Front: Royal Bucks Hussars charge at El Mughar.
(J.P. Beadle, reproduced courtesy of the Bucks Military Museum) *Back, left:* Bucks Hussars resting during the Palestine campaign (Bill Cowell); *right:* A British tank destroyed outside Gaza. (Bill Cowell)

First published 2013
by Spellmount, an imprint of The History Press
The Mill, Brimscombe Port
Stroud, Gloucestershire, GL5 2QG
www.thehistorypress.co.uk

© E.J. Hounslow, 2013

The right of E.J. Hounslow to be identified as the Author
of this work has been asserted in accordance with the
Copyright, Designs and Patents Act 1988.

British Library Cataloguing in Publication Data.
A catalogue record for this book is available from the British Library.

ISBN 978 0 7524 9899 7

Typesetting and origination by The History Press
Printed in Great Britain

CONTENTS

Foreword by Professor Ian Beckett   6

1 Introduction   9
2 Early days   15
3 Bucks Yeomanry   17
4 The start of war and the origins of the Gallipoli Campaign   35
5 Suvla Bay, Gallipoli   44
6 Egypt   69
7 Crossing the Sinai Desert and the battles for Gaza   81
8 General Allenby and the Third Battle for Gaza   95
9 Turkish retreat and the capture of Jerusalem   113
10 The sinking of HMT *Leasowe Castle*   138
11 France   146
12 Peace   153
13 Those who fought with and alongside the Royal Bucks Hussars   165

References   182
Notes   185
Index   189

FOREWORD

Since the revival of popular interest in the First World War at the time of the fiftieth anniversary, there has been a great deal of attention paid to the 'New Armies' of Kitchener volunteers in 1914, especially the 'Pals Battalions' that were mostly raised from urban areas in the Midlands and the North. By contrast, there has been far less awareness of the Territorial Force, the successor to a far older 'amateur military tradition' stretching back at least to the fifteenth century and, in some respects, to the Anglo-Saxon kingdoms. It is true that there have been studies of Territorial infantry battalions in recent years, but the county yeomanry regiments have attracted little notice. In part, this reflects the fact that their service was not on the Western Front but at Gallipoli, in the Western Desert and in Palestine, though several returned to France and Flanders in a dismounted role later in the war. As we now approach the centenary, John Hounslow's study of the Royal Bucks Hussars is thus especially welcome.

I particularly appreciate it as both John and I grew up in Buckinghamshire villages at about the same time. Like John, I was very aware of the many Great War veterans of the Bucks Battalions and the Royal Bucks Hussars still living around me. Although my father and his generation had fought in the Second World War, that earlier global conflict seemed to hold more significance for so many of my grandfather's generation among whom I grew up. Among the sixteen war dead commemorated on the memorial in Whitchurch Parish Church are five from the Bucks Battalions and three from the Royal Bucks Hussars. Of the latter, two were killed at Gallipoli on the same day – 21 August 1915 – while the third was my cousin's maternal grandfather. Many years later I have seen, too, their graves or names on memorials to the missing in foreign fields. Far too late, in the 1980s, I was privileged to interview the few Royal Bucks Hussars who were still alive. Fortunately, as John's splendid book shows, there are sufficient archive sources remaining to do justice to a regiment that, like the other yeomanry units, was unique to itself, not least in its mingling of the very wealthy, like the Rothschilds – one of whom lies still in Palestine – with the farmers and farm labourers, the jockeys, and the mounted policemen. Some of the records come from the collection of the Buckinghamshire Military Museum Trust, of which I have the honour to be Secretary, and which preserves the memory of all the auxiliary forces of the historic (pre-1974) County of Buckinghamshire.

I am delighted to have been invited to contribute the foreword to John's book. It is a diligently researched and very worthy tribute to a regiment that I hold dear. More to the point, it is a very necessary contribution to the historiography of the yeomanry, the Territorials and the Great War. We need far more studies like it.

Professor Ian Beckett
University of Kent

Bill Cowell aged 19 and recently enlisted in the Royal
Bucks Hussars. (Bill Cowell)

1

INTRODUCTION

There were the flies, the heat, the noise of battle and the alien landscape, but for the young men of the Royal Bucks Hussars they were not the greatest problem. The worst thing was fear, and not just fear of being killed or maimed, although that was real enough: it was also fear of the unknown, of letting your mates down and not knowing how you will perform in battle.

One of the men was a 20-year-old youth called Bill Cowell, and today was to be his first experience of coming under fire. He wasn't alone; it was the first combat experience for the vast majority of the soldiers with him. They were too young to have fought the last time the Royal Bucks Hussars had gone to war. That had been in South Africa against the Boers at the beginning of the twentieth century. This day, at 3.30 in the afternoon on 21 August 1915, was different. This was part of a world war, not just a colonial fight against an ill-equipped and weaker opposition. As they sheltered behind the small hill, the soldiers knew that they would soon be ordered to march forward in an assault against an enemy entrenched in hills over 2 miles away overlooking the coastal position where they waited.

The date of 21 August 1915 was to be engraved many times on war memorials. The next few hours proved to be the first and last experience of war for so many of these young men. They were waiting to go into battle on a long, mountainous peninsula jutting out into the Aegean Sea. It was called Gallipoli, a place name which, until the Allied invasion, most had never heard of, but which now figures large in the national consciousness of Australians, New Zealanders, the French, Turks and, of course, the British.

Bill Cowell and his comrades were originally recruited from farms in and around Buckinghamshire. In peacetime many had been neighbours and had known each other well, but now they could do little to help each other except perhaps to grin nervously and whisper good luck. Their orders were to keep the lines and their discipline as they advanced, and not to stop to help comrades who were hit or wounded.

In order to reach the enemy positions they first had to march across a dried-out salt lake followed by a large flattish plain overlooked by hills on which were situated Turkish artillery, machine guns and snipers. These were to take a heavy toll of the young soldiers and most of those who died that afternoon did so having never seen the enemy they were attacking. It was ironic that their first experience of battle was as infantry soldiers; having been trained as cavalry troops, they would have expected to ride into battle. When they had enlisted, these young men would have dreamed of going to war as cavalry soldiers, on horseback, with swords in hand. The reality was to be very different.

Bill Cowell survived the day unscathed, and this book tells his story and that of his fighting comrades in the Royal Bucks Hussars. It tells how and why they arrived at Suvla Bay in Gallipoli and what happened there and in the other theatres of war; how Bill Cowell was one of those lucky ones who eventually returned to the farm and took up his normal life again. He was my grandfather, so this story is part of my family story.

This is a history book deliberately narrow in its focus. It concerns itself solely with the Bucks Hussars rather than the Great War as a whole. It concentrates on the actions in which the Bucks Hussars were involved and, although it is inspired by my memories of my grandfather, it is impossible from official records to pick out one person unless they are an officer or of special distinction. Bill Cowell was neither of these and I am therefore dependent on photographs he took, family history and private sources, letters etc., to piece together the whole story. Britain was still a hierarchical society and particularly so in the military. Whilst official records and regimental diaries frequently refer to officers by their names, they refer to the other ranks as simply 'O/R'. A further difficulty for all who try to study this part of our country's history is that many of the soldiers' records were kept in London and unfortunately fell victim to the Second World War when they were destroyed in the Blitz.

Britain had always relied on an extremely small professional standing army so that in times of great national emergency, when the size of the peacetime army would not suffice, the country relied on allies, mercenaries and the proverbial butcher, baker and candlestick maker – the ordinary man in the street – to fight our national battles.

Bill Cowell was just such a man – a tenant farmer, as his father had been before him. It is hard for us who live in the twenty-first century to understand what these young men went through during the four years beginning in the summer of 1914. Bill Cowell and his friends, along with many other young men of his generation, were participants in truly extraordinary events. The peaceful Edwardian age in which they had grown up exploded into an orgy of killing – put simply, everything that they were brought up to understand and cherish was changed by the next four years. Bill Cowell was aged 20 at the outbreak of war and it was to provide him with the most dramatic of educations.

All of the inventions and mass industrialisation that had taken place over the past fifty years were subordinated into the one objective of slaughter. The European nations embarked on a war which they appeared helpless to prevent. A complex system of treaties and alliances, which had been designed to keep peace in Europe through a balance of power, proved to have exactly the opposite effect. It dragged some reluctant nations into a world war and ensured others were forced to pick sides in order to protect their own interests. No war prior to 1914 had seen killing on this scale and the young men of Britain could not possibly anticipate what awaited them. Far more importantly, those in power – the chiefs of staff, the politicians and the generals tasked with actually fighting the war – were all equally unprepared. In his famously outspoken diaries published after the war, David Lloyd George comments:

> How was it that the world was so unexpectedly plunged into this terrible conflict? Who was responsible? Not even the astutest and most far-seeing statesman foresaw in the early summer of 1914 that the autumn would find nations of the world interlocked in the most terrible conflict that had ever been witnessed in the history of mankind: and if you came to the ordinary men and women who were engaged in their daily avocations in all countries there was not one of them who suspected the imminence of such catastrophe. Of those who, in the first weeks of July, were employed in garnering their hay or corn harvests, either in this country or on the Continent of Europe, it is safe to say that no one ever contemplated the possibility that another month would find them called to the Colours and organised in battle array for a struggle that would end in the violent death of millions of them, and in the mutilation of many more millions. The nations slithered over the brink into the boiling cauldron of war without any trace of apprehension or dismay.
>
> The outbreak of war found this country totally unprepared for land hostilities on a Continental scale. Our traditional defence force has always been our Navy, and this weapon has been kept efficient and ready at all times. But our Army, mainly used for policing our widely scattered Empire, was a small, highly trained force of professional soldiers, excellent for their normal tasks, but lacking both the numbers and the equipment for large-scale fighting against European armies.[1]

Lloyd George's memoirs, like all political autobiographies, are self-serving. Written in retrospect with all of the wisdom that brings, and coupled with his almost demonic hatred of the military, the politician castigates the military machine for its unpreparedness and training procedures based on wars which had been fought in the past rather than the war to come. It is true that one of the key criteria of great military leaders is combat experience, but there must be a caveat attached which is that training, tactics and strategy derived from that experience should be relevant to the war about to be fought rather than that which preceded it. All too often Britain, with its huge empire, had fought battles and minor wars to hold onto its colonial possessions, which provided plenty of combat experience and ensured a ready supply of battle-hardened senior military officers who had earned their spurs. The problem is that experience and those lessons learnt did not necessarily transfer seamlessly into a full-scale European, or indeed, a world war. Technology moves on, as do the strategy and tactics of war. Unfortunately, because British military experience had been limited to these colonial wars carried out far from the prying eyes of the press and usually against a foe far less technologically advanced than Britain, the learning curve for all involved in the Great War was to prove extremely steep.

Further difficulties for the Army were caused by the political desire to keep peacetime defence budgets to a minimum. At the start of the twentieth century, Britain put most of its defence eggs in the Royal Navy's basket. Britain had two major imperatives: first, to protect the British mainland, for which command of the English Channel was paramount; second, to keep the links to the rest of the Empire open, for which wider control of the high seas was vital. Most of the defence budget was therefore taken up with Admiral 'Jackie' Fisher's dreadnought-class battleships. With the Royal Navy seen as the key element in this homeland defence strategy, the Army inevitably came a distinctly poor second in the distribution of resources. There was another reason for this lack of investment in the Army. British politicians considered, quite correctly, that the main threat was from Germany and therefore the first, and perhaps most important part of the British defence lay in the hands of the French Army. It was considered far preferable to reinforce the French with a British Expeditionary Force and to fight on their territory than to consider the alternative of having what would today be described as an independent deterrent. In short, Britain was part of a complex defensive international coalition and was contributing the minimum number of ground forces to ensure their credibility.

This is not to say that some good work was not carried out in the years immediately preceding the Great War. The Boer War had seen the experiences of our armies incorporated into standard operating procedures as promulgated by the then Secretary of State for War, Richard Haldane. The British armies also owed a lot to a junior lieutenant general who worked closely with the politicians on the reforms of the army. His name was Douglas Haig and he was to figure prominently in the war to come. However, despite these reforms, which were undoubtedly necessary and timely, the central point remained that the last time Britain had fought a truly continental war was in the first decades of the nineteenth century, when Arthur Wellesley (Lord Wellington) had faced Napoleon Bonaparte. Probably the only lesson still relevant from that war was the overriding need to keep international coalitions together when facing a common foe.

If most of the military and political leaders were unprepared, some members of society did have premonitions of war. In 1896, A.E. Houseman wrote the following prophetic words in his masterpiece 'A Shropshire Lad':

> On the idle hill of summer,
> Sleepy with the flow of streams,
> Far I hear the steady drummer,
> Drumming like a noise in dreams.
>
> Far and near and low and louder
> On the roads of earth go by,
> Dear to friends and food for powder
> Soldiers marching, all to die.
>
> East and west on fields forgotten
> Bleach the bones of comrades slain,
> Lovely lads and dead and rotten;
> None that go return again.
>
> Far the calling bugles hollo,
> High the screaming fife replies,
> Gay the files of scarlet follow:
> Women bore me, I will rise.[2]

In writing about such a traumatic period of our history it is tempting to move into colourful emotional prose which would perhaps have been an embarrassment to those who fought. Following a spell in a dug-out situated in front of the 'front line', the famous poet Wilfred Owen wrote home to his mother to describe his emotions, fears and terror during the period when he and his platoon sheltered in no-man's-land whilst the Germans did their best to drive them out. In his description Owen uses the word 'sheer' to describe the experience, an unconventional and yet graphic way of describing the fear. But the powers to describe raw emotion in such ways would be far beyond the vocabulary of the ordinary soldier.[3]

Today, with the wealth of published First World War poetry, we are perhaps inclined to imagine that all regiments marched off to war with the resident poet/artist in their ranks or that the ordinary soldier was capable of revealing the true emotions felt during the abnormal experience of total war. This was not the case, and most contemporary accounts display the stilted, emotional denial of a Victorian/Edwardian male upbringing. The accounts written by the soldiers are also produced, at the very least, some days after the events they describe, often after the war itself. The mind has had a chance to settle, the nerves to repair and thus the language is frequently more prosaic and matter of fact than the events may warrant.

Nevertheless, soldiers' accounts still offer the best description we have and I have tried whenever possible to use the words of the actual combatants to describe the actions. Readers will have to use their imagination to understand really what it must have been like for these young men, how they felt, and what their emotional state was.

2

EARLY DAYS

For me, the story of the Great War began one summer's day in the late 1950s when I spotted a peculiar-looking, wobbly flower pot adjacent to the farmhouse at Dodley Hill Farm just outside Swanbourne. When I asked, it turned out to be my grandfather's steel helmet brought back from the war. In a gentle and amused fashion he explained how he had come by it. It was hard at the age of 7 to reconcile the image of a kindly, white-haired, old gentleman with that of a soldier going to war. He was one of those rare adults who had an instinctive rapport with young children. He went up a notch or two in my estimation when he explained that he had been a soldier who had gone to war on a horse and finished up as a machine gunner.

For a 1950s boy this was truly manna from heaven. At that time, we were surrounded by memories of two world wars; indeed the Second World War had only been over some seven years when I was born and most boys' comics and books deified 'our soldiers' whilst at the same time demonising the 'Hun' or 'Boche' as the German soldiers were described. I was the only boy in my family, with three elder sisters. We lived some way from the nearest village and I spent a lot of my early days running around by myself in an imaginary world fighting German and Japanese soldiers. In that imaginary world it was only me against the enemy and it was my job to fight them off. When my grandfather allowed me to take the helmet home it became my treasured possession and, though it was several sizes too large, I wore it with pride.

But how different was the England of 1894, the year of Bill Cowell's birth? It was a peaceful age when the wars that involved Britain were fought far away in parts of the Empire that were just names on the map. They did not affect the ordinary man in the street unless he had a family member who was in the military.

Bill Cowell was born into a farming family that lived and worked in a small part of North Buckinghamshire which borders the east and south-east of Buckingham. Nash, Addington, Winslow, Swanbourne and Verney Junction were the village names where Bill grew up. The area is not dramatic: it has no significant hills, no mountains, no great rivers or lakes; what it does have is a quiet and dignified beauty of its own. It is intrinsically English and understated. The war was to take the men of Bucks to places that were very different, but Buckinghamshire was a homely place to remember and letters home show the fond memories that helped the soldiers whilst serving their country overseas.

The year 1894 saw Queen Victoria moving into the final stages of her sixty-year reign over a huge swathe of the world. This was a time when the United Kingdom was one of the super powers both militarily and commercially. In North Buckinghamshire, which had never been at the cutting edge of progress, most people were employed in agriculture or the industries that lived indirectly off the proceeds of agriculture. Bill Cowell's father was a tenant farmer who at one time had worked as farm steward to Lord Wyfold and, although he now worked in Buckinghamshire, the family had originated from Essex. Bill was the second youngest of six children.

In July 1913, Bill Cowell made the decision to join the Territorials. He enlisted in the Royal Buckinghamshire Hussars Yeomanry, a mounted regiment (cavalry regiment) of the Territorial Force. This decision can probably be explained by an autobiography of one of the officers of the Bucks Hussars, Lieutenant Colonel (The Honourable) Fred Cripps (Lord Parmoor), who mentioned that he ensured that tenants' sons were aware of and, if possible, joined the yeomanry.[4] Lord Wyfold's estates were adjacent to those of Lord Parmoor and it seems quite possible that suggestions as to the desirability of yeomanry enrolment were made.

Whatever the reason behind this decision it was unlikely to be a direct response to rumours of war. There were signs of forthcoming conflict in Europe throughout the latter part of the nineteenth century and the early years of the twentieth: Prussia invading France some forty years earlier, the gradual decline of the Austro-Hungarian and Ottoman empires and the unification and militarisation of Greater Germany. However, I suspect these events did not figure in everyday conversation in North Bucks.

Surely, even if there was a certain amount of moral pressure from the Lord of the Manor, the attraction of charging around on a horse at weekends, wearing a soldier's uniform and the opportunity to get hold of military weapons would be of considerable interest to any red-blooded young man. Bill Cowell was 19 when he signed up for the yeomanry, an age when many young men are far more interested in cutting a dash with women than in distant boring talk of possible unrest in Europe.

It is fairly certain that Bill Cowell would not have travelled outside of England prior to the mobilisation of the army. However, the next few years would have certainly sated any wanderlust that he may have had. Indeed, as far as I am aware, after the armistice and demobilisation he never ventured abroad again. He was 20 when war broke out and almost immediately he volunteered for overseas duty as the terms under which he had enlisted with the yeomanry only required him to serve in his home country.

3

BUCKS YEOMANRY

Yeomanry regiment units were originally formed in the eighteenth century as instruments of repression and to protect the country from invasion. If there was one thing the British ruling classes feared worse than a revolutionary Frenchman, it was their own tenants in revolt. The French were at least separated by 22 miles of salt water which was firmly under the control of the British Navy, but control of the seas could do nothing about preventing the spread of ideas, and what the British ruling classes feared most was the spread of revolutionary ideas and sedition. A home defence force, therefore, loyal to the Crown and with a stake in the status quo, was an attractive proposition to the government of the day, especially if it could be formed cheaply.

The Royal Buckinghamshire Yeomanry (motto: 'Yeomen of Bucks, strike home') was formed in May 1794. King George III was on the throne, William Pitt the Younger was Prime Minister and earlier, in 1793, the government had legislated to allow for the inclusion of voluntary yeomanry units within the coastal defence militia. Britain undoubtedly felt threatened by the French, who had gathered an army of over half a million men, but, as already stated, the threat of revolutionary propaganda was of more significance to the reactionary British Government. France was, after all, the nation that had executed its legal ruler, King Louis XVI, and such ideas threatened the British way of life. The irony of the fact that the French had borrowed the idea of regicide from the British would have been lost on Pitt's government. They felt more secure having armed personnel in every county, especially when they were recruited from the conservative core of society. Arming such men, who had a vested interest in maintaining the status quo, men who owned and farmed the land, fitted in with the mood of deep conservatism.

Buckinghamshire was not slow to act following Parliament's mandate to recruit volunteer yeomanry cavalry units which could be called on by the king or by the lord lieutenant to defend the country against invasion or, if necessary, to subdue any civil or revolutionary disorder within the country.

Bill Cowell (second left) and colleagues at camp on Salisbury Plain. (Bill Cowell)

In May 1794 a subscription was opened for home defence and over £5,000 was pledged within the first month, although the majority of the money came from the Marquess of Buckingham. He had more reason than most to wish for security, having just spent a large fortune on renovating and modifying his Buckinghamshire home, Stowe House.

Yeomen were typically small landholders and tenant farmers, originally defined as those with an income of greater than £100 p.a. They were usually men who hunted regularly and were used to horse-riding. Their military training was, however, likely to be more haphazard as many of the yeomanry regiments had been maintained by the largesse of the local lord. The Bucks Yeomanry were formed following a public meeting convened on 3 May 1794 at Aylesbury Town Hall. The meeting was followed by the publication of a resolution.

How these yeomanry forces were to be used is shown in the following events. Contemporary reports of Luddite riots in Nottinghamshire describe extensive use of the yeomanry, including calling out of regiments some distance from the scenes of disorder. In November 1811, both the Bucks and the Nottingham Yeomanry were called out to prevent Luddites destroying the cotton looms in Sutton and in Ashfield, and several times the troops confronted and dispersed what contemporary accounts refer to as 'dangerous mobs'. It was the job of the lord lieutenant of the county to decide whether or not the yeomanry should be called out.

The second and even more famous event in the history of the yeomanry forces was to provide a smear on their name, especially amongst the poorer

The Royal Bucks Hussars muster for war, 10 August 1914. (Mike Holland)

A fully kitted-out yeoman's horse from the Royal Bucks Hussars on Salisbury Plain. (Bill Cowell)

classes. The so-called 'Peterloo massacre' of Monday 16 August 1819 was to provide a deep well of hatred against yeomanry forces which lasted for many years. From the end of the eighteenth century through the revolutionary wars with France and the early nineteenth century, Manchester and its surrounding cotton towns had been a centre of radical thinkers and those wishing to see reform of British political institutions. In August of 1819 the leading members

A Squadron from the Royal Bucks Hussars taken before the outbreak of war. (Bill Cowell)

of these freethinking reformers invited Henry Hunt to address an open-air public meeting aimed at bringing pressure on Parliament for reform and universal suffrage. Both the organisers and Hunt went to great lengths to stress that this was to be a peaceful meeting.

Nevertheless, the local gentry and, importantly, the magistrates were concerned that this meeting was a possible spark which would inflame revolution, much as had been seen recently in France. The comparatively newly formed yeomanry troops gave the forces of law and order a tool which they fully intended to use in bringing the meeting to a speedy conclusion. Local magistrates signed the requisite orders and the Manchester, Salford and Cheshire Yeomanry troops were called out, in addition to regular troops from the 15th Hussars and the Royal Horse Artillery.

By 11.00 a.m. it was estimated by eye-witnesses that some 50,000 people had gathered in St Peter's Field and following the speakers' arrival the press of people was such that the authorities ordered the arrest of the speakers. The yeomanry were ordered to disperse the crowd so that constables could arrest the main speakers, but when the crowds linked hands in an attempt to thwart the arrest, the yeomen panicked and began to hack and slash at the unarmed crowd with their cavalry sabres. The situation rapidly deteriorated, worsened by the fact that the army had sealed off the exits from the public space, presumably to prevent the speakers escaping.[5]

The regular army wrongly interpreted the disturbances as an assault on the yeomanry, and the Hussars were therefore ordered into the field to disperse the crowd. The 15th Hussars formed themselves into a line stretching across the eastern end of St Peter's Field and charged into the crowd, but at the same time the Cheshire Yeomanry charged from the southern edge of the field. As foot soldiers had blocked the main exit route into Peter Street, the crowd simply had nowhere to escape. Now out of control, the yeomanry troops slashed indiscriminately at the crowd with their sabres. One officer of the 15th Hussars was heard trying to restrain the Manchester and Salford Yeomanry by shouting, 'For shame! For shame! Gentlemen: forbear, forbear! The people cannot get away!' By the end of the day there were eleven dead and over 600 injured, and the yeomanry's reputation was badly besmirched.

The terms under which the yeomanry forces were formed, however, make it clear that such demonstrations as those at Peterloo were exactly what the yeomanry forces were created to suppress. The Bucks Yeomanry declaration reads as follows:

> That we the Gentlemen, Clergy, Freeholders, Yeomen and substantial inhabitants of the County of Buckingham, desire to take this public mode of expressing our zeal and willingness to exert ourselves at all times by whatever legal and constitutional means we may, in defence of our King and Country.
>
> That in the present very important moment we deem it to be peculiarly useful and meritorious, voluntarily to stand forward in the support of such measures as may best contribute both to the internal and external security of the free and happy Country.
>
> That considering the local circumstances of the County of Buckingham and the augmentation actually making to its Militia, it seems expedient to adopt the most practical part of the fourth proposition from among those plans of defence which have been communicated to the meeting.
>
> That the Gentlemen, Yeomen and substantial Inhabitants of the County be accordingly invited to enrol themselves in their several respective neighbourhoods into different troops of men armed and mounted on horseback attached to the Central Body, to be known by the name of THE ARMED YEOMANRY OF THE COUNTY OF BUCKS under command of the Lord Lieutenant.[6]

Recruitment began shortly after this meeting, with the 'substantial inhabitants' signing up to the following terms and conditions:

> We whose names are hereunto subscribed, being freeholders, Yeomen, or substantial Inhabitants of the County of Bucks, in pursuance of an Act of Parliament entitled An Act for the encouragement and disciplining of such Corps or Companies of men as shall voluntarily enrol themselves for the defence of their Towns, or Coasts, or for the general defence of the Kingdom during the present war, do voluntarily enrol themselves to form a body to be called the Armed Yeomanry of the County of Bucks for the internal defence and security of the Kingdom during the present war on the following conditions:
>
> 1st To receive no pay unless when embodied or called out, but to attend, mounted on a serviceable gelding or mare to be approved of by the

Commanding Officer of each Troop, and not less than fourteen hands high, for the purpose of meeting at such times and places as shall be fixed by such commanding Officer with the approbation of the Field Officer commanding the whole Body.

2nd   The times and places of meeting to be fixed on such days and such hours as may interfere the least with the other occupations of the persons composing the respective Troops.

3rd   The Corps to be subject to be embodied within the County by special direction from His Majesty on appearance of invasion and to be called out of the County by the like Authority from His Majesty in case of actual invasion.

4th   To be liable to be called upon by order from His Majesty or by the Lord-Lieutenant, or by the Sheriff of the County for the suppression of riots and tumults within the country.

5th   In all cases when embodied, or called out as above to receive pay as Cavalry and to be subject to the provisions of the Mutiny Bill.

6th   Each person attending on the day of meeting to wear a uniform to be provided at the expense of the County subscription together with arms and accoutrements.

7th   Each troop to consist of not less than fifty men (officers included) to be under the particular command of the officers belonging to it whilst assembled in their respective districts but the whole body to be under the general superintendence of the Field Officers; if six troops or more, three Field Officers, if four two Field Officers if two only one Field Officer.

Captain	I	Corporals	3
Lieutenants	2	Trumpeter	I
Qr Master	I	Farrier	I
Sergeants	3	Privates	38

8th   Persons desirous of furnishing a substitute may do so, on condition that he be a man of good character having a fixed residence within the county, that he is accustomed to riding, that he is not a person likely to enlist in the Army, Navy or Militia, and that he be approved by a majority of those persons who compose the Troop in which he is to serve.

9th   The substitutes to be equipped and mounted in the same manner as those who serve for themselves, and their clothes and horses to be provided at the expense of those persons by whom they are brought forward.

10th   Whereas several gentlemen who offer their personal service may be desirous of rendering further assistance towards the formation of this body by furnishing men and horses to make up the complement of any Troop, Persons so brought forward and furnished with horses may be accepted on the same conditions as the substitutes above mentioned.

Above: Officers of the Royal Bucks Hussars. Standing (left to right): Lt T.C. Smith, Captain E. Pauncefort-Duncombe, Captain L.E.W. Egerton, Major A. Grenfell, Captain G. Gardiner, Lt J. Bogue, Captain E. Rothschild, Lt G.B. Pearson. Sitting (left to right): Major G.W. Swire, Major J.P. Grenfell, Col C.A. Grenfell, Major W.E. St John, Major F. Cripps. On the ground (left to right): Lt C.L.C. Clarke, Lt H.L. Jones, Lt F. Lawson, Lt A.G. de Rothschild, Captain T. Agar Robartes, Lt P. Barker, Lt J. Crocker Bulteel. (Bucks Military Museum)

Left: Frank Lunnon, a farmer from Bourne End in Buckinghamshire. (Mike Holland)

It being understood to be the wish of the Yeomanry enrolling themselves in this Troop and in the Newport Pagnell Troop that the two Troops may occasionally meet to support each other in case of riot or disturbance within their respective Hundreds we hereby agree to consider ourselves as forming one united squadron for that purpose, and every Yeoman shall be at liberty to attend to be exercised in whichever of the two Troops shall be the most convenient to him, giving notice of such intention to the two Commanding Officers of the Troops. And, as it is necessary to regulate the ranks of the commissioned and non-commissioned officers serving in the two Troops, it is understood that they take rank and command in the following order, viz:

Captain Marquess of Buckingham, Captain William Praed, Lieutenant Mansell, Lieutenant Pigott, Second Lieutenant Higgins, Second Lieutenant Talbot, Quartermaster Gooch, Quartermaster Gray, Sergeant John Henry Talbot of Olney.[7]

This document was signed at Stowe House on 21 April 1795 and over 300 men had enlisted by the end of that month. In 1803 war broke out again with revolutionary France and recruitment to the yeomanry increased such that the Bucks Yeomanry became a full-scale regiment. Earlier, the Defence of the Realm Act of 1798, known as the *Levée en Masse* Act, placed a duty on counties (via the lords lieutenant and their deputies) to list all men aged between 17 and 55, except clergymen, Quakers, school masters and the infirm. The list would be categorised into four classes: unmarried men under 30 with no living children under 10 years of age; unmarried men aged between 30 and 50, with no living children under 10; married men between 17 and 30 with no more than two living children under 10; and those not included in the previous classifications. They would then be trained, armed and eligible to be called out anywhere in the British Isles in the case of invasion.

By late 1803, there were three yeomanry regiments in Buckinghamshire, collectively known as the 1st, 2nd and 3rd regiments of the Buckinghamshire Yeomanry, a nomenclature which may indicate that Buckinghamshire men lack imagination or that they are simply straightforward. The three regiments

4th Troop C Squadron prior to leaving for Egypt. Fred Lawson is in the centre, second row from the front. (Mike Holland)

A Squadron meet in Newport Pagnell. (Mike Holland)

lasted until 1827, when the 1st and 3rd were disbanded; the 2nd Regiment was only kept in existence by private funding from the Duke of Buckingham. In 1845 Queen Victoria conferred the title 'Royal' on the regiment and changed the unit's name to The 2nd Royal Bucks Regiment of Yeomanry. The yeomanry increased enormously and reached its peak, numbers wise, and between 1803 and the Haldane reforms of the Territorial Force of 1907, there was to be a number of ups and downs in which the generous support of the Duke of Buckingham and Chandos remained constant and vital to the survival of the Bucks Yeomanry.

In December 1899 the Bucks Yeomanry supplied volunteers to fight in the Boer Wars. Under Lord Chesham and alongside the Berks and Oxfords, the regiment saw a number of engagements with the enemy. As a result of its experiences in the Boer War, the regiment was reorganised and officially became the Royal Buckinghamshire Hussars Imperial Yeomanry. The training was also changed to emphasise the scouting, reconnaissance and dismounted infantry duties which were to be vital in the battles to come. At the same time there was a conscious decision that the Royal Bucks Hussars should not lose the ability to supply the shock tactics of the 'charge' if and when conditions required.

Most of the officers came from the very top rungs of county society. Indeed, membership of the yeomanry was counted as an integral part of fitting into county life. When the Rothschild family moved to Buckinghamshire, they soon took prominent positions in the Bucks Yeomanry to cement their position in county society. Of course, such people were not dependent on the army for a career or income and as such were not renowned for taking all aspects of military discipline seriously. It was not necessarily uppermost in their minds. One of Bill Cowell's commanding officers was the Rt Hon F.H. (Fred) Cripps, later to be the 5th Baron Parmoor, and even the most cursory examination of

Jack on pack horse

Bill Cowell's elder brother, Jack, jumping on a pack horse. (Bill Cowell)

A typical hunter which was to serve the Royal Bucks Hussars so well in Palestine. (Bill Cowell)

his autobiography, *Life's a Gamble*, is sufficient to convince that he was not a man who took any aspect of his life entirely seriously.[8]

Lord Longford was the Brigadier General of the Yeomanry Brigade, which consisted of the three regiments (Bucks, Berks and Oxon) and Col Fred Cripps tells a story in his autobiography of how, during one of the general's inspections, he asked the young F.E. Smith (later Lord Birkenhead) how much corn was required for a horse's daily ration. The young officer immediately asked the same question to his sergeant who replied, 'Ten pounds of oats'. When the general complained, stating that he had asked the question in order to see whether or not Smith knew the answer, the unabashed lieutenant replied, 'Quite so – and I asked the sergeant to see if he knew the correct answer.'[9]

Such tales, whilst amusing, added to the image that the yeomanry were playboys who were not fully trustworthy, and it is not surprising that the rather straight-laced Lord Kitchener never considered yeomanry regiments fit for service in the harshest of theatres. When coupled with the fact that the terms under which the yeomanry signed up (home service only), this gave Lord Kitchener ample reason not to send yeomanry regiments to the Western Front at the outbreak of the First World War. He was not the only person to hold such views; an eminent professor in military history is quoted by Lt Col Cripps as stating that 'there was not a volunteer unit in the country which would not go to pieces in action'.[10]

When Bill Cowell joined the Bucks Hussars, the Army, together with the yeomanry regiments, had just gone through an enormous reorganisation. Richard Burdon Haldane was a barrister who, when the Liberals came to power under Campbell-Bannerman in late 1905, became Secretary of State for War. He set out to reform the Army in all aspects and with Lieutenant General Douglas Haig assisting him, he was to drive through probably the most thorough reform that the British Army has ever been subject to. Standard operating instructions were drafted. Known as Field Service Regulations Part II, the document set out how the Army should fight in the field, the ethos of the 'decisive battle' and the importance of allowing the 'man on the spot' to command and make tactical decisions.[11]

The drafting of Field Service Regulations was not prescriptive in setting down what officers should do in each and every situation. What they did do was to set down a common approach and give a framework for the training of officers which would allow the newly created forces necessitated by the First World War to fight and prepare for war in a structured way. They presaged the 'all-arms battle' which, when refined by the harsh experiences to come, would see the British Army emerge victorious.

For the first time, the yeomanry were properly amalgamated into the British Army as part of the new Territorial Force. The defence budget now funded the training and administration of the yeomanry and, vitally, the regulations laid down the role of mounted troops in a modern battlefield which, thanks to better artillery and the advent of machine guns, was becoming an increasingly hostile environment. It may seem antiquated to our twenty-first-century eyes to allocate such a key role to cavalry troops. This, coupled with the fact that much of the drafting was the responsibility of General Haig who, to say the least, emerged from the First World War with a reputation somewhat of the curate's egg variety, would seem to imply that military planners were some way behind the game. However, it should be remembered that the internal combustion engine was still, relatively speaking, in its infancy and could not be relied upon to carry troops across rough terrain. At the start of the twentieth century it still made perfect sense to rely heavily on mounted troops. The battlefield then, as now, would be dominated by the side that had the ability to get troops in sufficient numbers to the right areas. In the early years of the twentieth century, mounted troops were still one of the best ways of achieving this.

The Territorial Force saw the army integrate the county forces, thus providing a way of quickly extending the relatively small regular army when required. However, integration into the regular army and training for officers in regular army institutions did little to dampen the spirit of the yeomanry and they continued to see their part-time army obligations as some glorious extension of fox hunting and amateur point-to-point races. The Territorial Force consisted of fourteen infantry divisions and fourteen mounted yeomanry brigades, which amounted on paper to some 270,000 men.

Thus, at the outbreak of hostilities in August 1914, there was, for the first time, at least a blueprint laid down as to how the army would go to war. Field Service Regulations Parts I and II (Operations and Organisation and Administration, respectively) formed the basis of all British and Imperial Army planning. They made possible the huge expansion of the army that took place. In addition, Haldane's reforms of the Territorial Force codified what a yeomanry regiment should consist of and what training they should receive. From the promulgation of Orders in Council under the Territorial and Reserve Forces Act of 1907, a yeomanry regiment would be centrally funded to consist of twenty-five commissioned officers and 450 other ranks. The regiment would be 475 strong (at full complement) with provision of 304 horses for training purposes (this was reinforced by officers bringing their own hunters etc.). The non-commissioned ranks included such specialised trades as saddlers and blacksmiths. Amongst the officer posts were a veterinary officer and two medical officers. Some of the instructor posts were permanent employees paid from the public purse and the minimum training requirements were then laid out in some detail in the Regulations for the Territorial Force and for County Associations, 1908.[12]

This structured approach ensured that by early 1914 the Royal Bucks Hussars had been fully integrated into the Territorial Force. The regiment consisted of a Regimental Headquarters and three squadrons, A, B and C. The regiment was commanded by a Lieutenant-Colonel with a Major second in command.

Each of the three squadrons consisted of just over 100 soldiers when fully established and each was commanded by a Major with a Captain as Second-in-Command. In addition, there was a Squadron HQ including a Sergeant-Major, a Quartermaster Sergeant, with additional troopers fulfilling roles essential to the HQ such as drivers.[13]

Entry requirements and training necessary for military service were all set down in the Regulations for the Territorial Force and County Associations, 1908. These regulations set out that new yeomanry recruits should stand a minimum of 5ft 3in tall and weigh a minimum of just over 8 stone. This was hardly a prepossessing example of British manhood; luckily recruiting mainly from farmers meant that the yeomanry had the pick of British society with the best diet and probably the healthiest lifestyle, and the average yeoman was certainly somewhat bigger that the minimum requirement set down in the regulations.

The 'other ranks' recruits were then expected to complete twenty drill sessions within the first year, plus an annual training camp and a specific course in musketry. At the completion of his first year a yeoman would be able to ride competently, to shoot accurately over 300 yards, to maintain his equipment whilst out in the field and to have a basic understanding of what was expected of him in a military context. The 1908 Act of Parliament, which brought the Territorial Force into being, specified that all mounted recruits should have a minimum of eighteen days' training per annum.

For officers joining yeomanry regiments there were compulsory written and oral exams to be undertaken within the first year of service. These included cavalry training, combined training, tactical handling of troops, and care of arms, the mechanics of the rifle and elementary musketry practice. For promotion from 2nd Lieutenant to Lieutenant a further examination had to be successfully negotiated, which included sketching maps in the field, tactics and military engineering, and tactical managing of small numbers of troops in the field. The King's Regulations were also covered, plus military law and the general organisation of the British Army. The last compulsory written paper was the history of the British Army and the questions were set from J.W. Fortescue's *History of the British Army*. This was a weighty series of volumes, the first of which was published in 1899, though the twentieth and last did not appear until 1930, so I am unsure how many volumes had to be studied in the early 1900s by the unfortunate candidates.

In short, although the yeomanry forces in the early part of the twentieth century still enjoyed a good time and perhaps did not always take life seriously, there were the beginnings of a professional reserve force. When war came, the yeomanry regiments were competent horsemen who could operate their arms in an appropriate manner and, once they gained experience under fire, fit in with their full-time military colleagues.

Troops mounted up in Hamilton Camp. Bill Cowell is far left. (Bill Cowell)

At the time of Bill Cowell's enlistment, July 1913, the regiment was com-manded by Lt Colonel H. Lawson (Lord Burnham), the proprietor of the *Daily Telegraph*. Training, mostly at weekends, was held in the grounds of Stowe House, then owned by Lady Kinloss, the title of Duke of Buckingham and Chandos having died out in 1889 when the 3rd Duke died without a son. His daughter, however, inherited the title of Lady Kinloss and, whilst not living in Stowe House, allowed the yeomanry use of the extensive grounds for train-ing purposes.

Other officers serving at that time included several members of the Grenfell family, Captain John Crocker Bulteel, several members of the Rothschild family, Lord Rosebery's younger son Neil Primrose and Coningsby Disraeli, the nephew of Benjamin Disraeli. They frequently trained with both the Berkshire Yeomanry and the Oxford Yeomanry. The Oxford Yeomanry were commanded by the Duke of Marlborough and included Winston Churchill and F.E. Smith later Lord Birkenhead amongst their officers. War exercises between the Oxfordshire Yeomanry and the Bucks troops were keenly contested events and were a vital part of the training effort.

At the outbreak of the First World War, in August 1914, the Royal Bucks Hussars were mobilised and trained at Hamilton Camp on Salisbury Plain and in Norfolk. They were attached to the 2nd (South Midland) Mounted Division.

The training undertaken reflected the nature and traditional responsibili-ties of light cavalry troops. It was based on a view of the nature and duties of warfare that was, sadly, to prove unrealistic for many of the troops in the forth-coming war.

Cavalry were the eyes and ears of an army and reconnaissance was one of their main duties. However, when the infantry and the artillery had broken enemy formations, or where the enemy was less than securely dug in, the charge and the pursuit of the enemy were still expected to be an integral part of cavalry duties. The other factor which weighed heavily in favour of the horse was that cavalry officers were long considered the elite and occupied many of the higher echelons in the War Office, and thus were responsible for most strategic decisions.

The Marquess of Anglesey had been responsible for the most authoritative history of British cavalry and his book lists the daily requirements of a hunter on campaign as being 18lb of hay, 8lb of corn and a minimum of 5 gallons of water. Thus the logistical requirements of the Bucks Yeomanry would have been considerable just to keep the horses fit for duty. This of course discounts all the other requirements, such as blacksmiths, veterinary experts etc. Whilst all of this was essential in order to get the soldier to the battlefield, once he was there what became critical were his weapons.[14]

As a private, Bill Cowell would have been armed with the Short Magazine Lee-Enfield rifle and a sword, whilst officers and sergeants carried a sword and a Webley pistol. No bayonets were issued to cavalry troops. All of the yeomanry mounted regiments were also equipped with a machine gun section which utilised the French-designed Hotchkiss machine gun. However, the British Enfield Rifle company was given rights to build a .303 calibre version which became the standard cavalry machine gun. It was officially designated the 'Hotchkiss Mark I', a relatively light weapon which was air-cooled and thus not dependent on precious water supplies. With a maximum range of 4,200 yards and weighing only 27 lb, it was the ideal weapon to support fast-moving cavalry troops. The manual for the gun recommended pausing after firing about 300 rounds of continuous fire to let the barrel cool down, but also stated that, in emergency situations, up to 1,000 rounds could be fired without pause through the single barrel, causing no significant harm to the gun.

British Army tactics, however, relied on rifle drill and even cavalry regiments were expected to be able to dismount and fight as infantry if needed. Fifteen aimed rounds per minute at 300 yards plus an acceptable degree of accuracy was still considered essential for all troops, including cavalry troops. An important part of Bill Cowell's early training was therefore marksmanship.

The Short Magazine Lee-Enfield rifle or, in British military parlance, the SMLE Mk III, was the main weapon of the British Army. It arrived at its name from the designer of the rifle's bolt system – the American James Paris Lee – and the factory in which it was designed – the Royal Small Arms Factory in Enfield. The 'short' refers to the barrel length, which for reasons of ease of use, was shorter than the original design, known, unsurprisingly, as the 'Long' Lee-Enfield.

The rifle utilised .303in calibre ammunition which was standard for the British Army, and was also used for the Hotchkiss and Vickers machine guns.

The Royal Bucks Hussars meet prior to the outbreak of war outside the pub! (Mike Holland)

It was accurate up to 550 yards but could kill up to nearly 1 mile. Bill Cowell and fellow members of the Bucks Hussars would have practised with the rifle on ranges of 300 yards in order to gain their marksman badges. It was an iconic weapon. It is reputed that over 17 million have been produced and it was to be used as the main British Army rifle up until the 1960s. Indeed, a modified sniper variant was used until the 1990s. It can still be found in service today with the Indian Police Force and is probably the longest serving military rifle in history.

The rifle weighed nearly 9lb and was close to 4ft long. Whilst cavalry troops were on horseback it was held in a leather scabbard secured to the side of the saddle on a webbing strap. It was envisaged that, when firing the weapon, the troops would be dismounted, either prone or standing at the fire step of a trench. There was to be no 'wild west' firing from the saddle.

If the Lee-Enfield had one weakness, it was that the firing mechanisms were susceptible to dirt and grit. Therefore, keeping your rifle clean in the sandy environment of Palestine and the Sinai Desert was of paramount importance. When not in battle, the Royal Bucks Hussars learned very rapidly that it was essential to cover the firing mechanism with cloth in an effort to keep out fine sand which would, if allowed to do so, rapidly clog up the rifle. The butt of the Lee-Enfield had a space inside it where cleaning material could be kept.

The rifle was one of the British Army's great success stories. With its bolt action and a ten-round magazine, experienced marksmen could manage twenty to thirty aimed rounds per minute. Just prior to the outbreak of the First World War an instructor at the Hythe Musketry School set a world record when he placed thirty-eight rounds into a 12in target at 300 yards within 1 minute.

Whilst the average soldier could not hope to emulate that feat, so fast and accurate was British rifle fire that, early on in the war, the Germans were sure they were up against machine guns when they attacked British infantry battalions. The theory was that a cavalry regiment should be able to dismount and fight as well as an infantry regiment should circumstances demand.

Last, but not least, of the weapons used by cavalry was the sword. The 1908 cavalry pattern sword was widely acknowledged to be the finest cavalry sword ever made, and the Palestine campaign of 1916–18 represented its swansong as a British Army weapon. Other ranks such as Bill Cowell were issued with their swords by the army, whereas officers were required to buy their own.

The design of cavalry swords had been the subject of great debate in the army, which boiled down to two schools of thought – the 'slash and cut' theory versus the 'thrust and stab' theory. With the introduction of the 1908 sword, the debate was settled with the 'thrust' theorists victorious. The 1908 sword was a design which was optimised for thrusting. The blade had a thick 'T' cross-section, thicker than a traditional sword design, making it stiffer and thus more resistant to buckling when thrust into the human torso. The blade ended in a sharp point. The large, sheet steel bowl guard gave considerable protection to the hand. The grip was a semi-pistol configuration which meant that the handle was at a slight angle from the blade, but when held out in front of the rider the sword blade formed a straight line with the rider's arm. As well as protecting the soldier's hand, the large hand guard and the relatively large grip ensured that the centre of balance remained near the hand, thus easing the task of holding it straight out at arm's length.

The sword was probably not the key element in a full-blooded charge as the shock value stemmed from the momentum of the combined horse and rider. With the force of a fast-moving horse and rider behind it, a well-aimed sword thrust would certainly impale an enemy soldier, probably right up to the hilt. If this happened, and it seems to be rather an unlikely feat, then the rider concerned would have difficulty in dragging the blade out of the body, leaving him at best disarmed or at worst unhorsed or with a broken wrist.

To complete his weaponry, a yeoman soldier had his horse. Cavalry was still considered to be an enormously important part of any successful army – the earlier distinction between light and heavy cavalry had by now disappeared and all British Army cavalry were mounted on hunters, all over 14 hands tall (some 6ft at the shoulder). When ridden by a 6ft burly farmer armed with a sword and rifle, they presented a formidable sight to any potential foe. Cavalry should really have had no part to play in the age of the machine gun and repeating rifles, and though the First World War was essentially the swansong of horses on battlefields, cavalry did play its part. Firstly, mounted troops could cross the killing zone more quickly than infantry, and by minimising the time exposed to machine gun and artillery fire, which was zeroed in on a particular zone, casualties were lessened. Secondly, in desert or rocky conditions where defenders could not adequately dig in, the charge still had an enormous psychological effect on defenders and there would be several instances in Palestine when Turkish formations broke and ran when faced by a determined charge.

At the start of the First World War the UK military possessed some 25,000 horses but only eighty motor vehicles. In a war that was to introduce mechanisation to international warfare this seems an enormous imbalance, but certainly as far as the battles to come in the Middle East were concerned, the number of horses needed to increase dramatically. During the two weeks following the declaration of war a further 165,000 horses were requisitioned. Animals were also purchased from the USA, New Zealand, South Africa, India, Spain and Portugal.

The ideal horse for the purposes of the cavalry was a thickset, strong hunter/thoroughbred of approximately 14–15 hands in height and aged 3 to 12. These horses had to be strong as the average cavalryman's weight was 12 stone and his equipment, saddle, ammunition, etc. usually weighed another 9. To counter this, the yeomanry were instructed to dismount and walk with the horse whenever possible.

They were trained as rapidly as possible by British soldiers called 'roughriders'. When they were ready, the horses were formed into squadrons and sent to war. During the war the need was so great that a specific organisation, the British Remount Service formed originally in 1887, had to be rapidly expanded and re-equipped to cater for the enormous increase in demand. It was fully engaged with buying and ensuring appropriate breeding of horses. It became a major multinational business and a leading player in the international horse trade, supplying horses not only to the British Army, but also to Canada, Belgium, Australia, New Zealand, Portugal, and even a few to the US.

4

THE START OF WAR AND THE ORIGINS OF THE GALLIPOLI CAMPAIGN

The British Army that existed in 1914 could not win the war, not even when combined with the other Allies, and the British Government knew this, although it was not a fact they wished the public to know. The Army was simply not large enough to fight a prolonged land battle on the European continent, but the conundrum facing the politicians was where to look for military success and what could be done to convince voters that they were up to the job. Asquith made an unusual political move right from the outbreak of the war by appointing a soldier, Lord Kitchener, as Secretary of State for War.

Lord Kitchener was by any standards an eccentric character. When posted to Cyprus as a young Royal Engineer officer in the 1870s, he arrived with a pet bear, which he lived with in a small house in Nicosia. It seems almost unnecessary to mention that he was unmarried and remained so throughout his life. He had been engaged, but his fiancée died. He adored hunting during his youth and imported fox hounds and foxes into Cyprus so that he could pursue his hobby. Although he loved all forms of hunting, he was notoriously bad at it, thanks to a squint in one eye and severe myopia in the other. When serving in India he was nicknamed 'Bang, Damn' by his fellow officers.

Though he enjoyed fox hunting, he was quoted as saying 'man shooting is the finest sport of all; there is a certain amount of infatuation about it, the more you kill the more you wish to kill'.[15] He was a deeply religious man who despised all non-Christian religions, which he classified as 'foreign'. Despite this he was a fluent French, Arabic and Turkish speaker. All in all, he was probably ideally suited to be Secretary of State for War.

From the start, Lord Kitchener disagreed with the prevailing view that this was to be a short war and set about systematically putting the army into a position where it could wage a major war over a prolonged period.

Above all, Kitchener knew that modern war needed manpower. He both started and starred in a campaign to recruit the millions of young men required for twentieth-century war. In recruiting what came to be known as Kitchener's

New Armies, he tended to ignore Haldane's previous Army reforms which anticipated the Territorial Forces, including the Royal Bucks Hussars, as being the first port of call in any wartime expansion of the Army.

It is unclear whether or not Lord Kitchener trusted the yeomanry, whether he thought that they could not possibly supply the numbers required or whether he was concerned with the terms and conditions under which they were recruited (home service only); whatever the reason, he ignored the obvious step of incorporating the Territorial Force into the Army in France. It has to be said that there was some evidence from the Boer War that yeomanry troops at that time were not of the highest calibre. Indeed, the standing joke was that the 'IY' on the cap badge, which stood for 'Imperial Yeomanry', should really stand for 'I Yield'. This is probably more than a little unfair, however, for whilst the yeomanry did not cover themselves in glory, nor did the rest of the Army. Lord Kitchener concentrated on building the New Army from the plentiful supply of volunteers who responded to the now famous advertising campaign built around his image and his reputation.

Whatever Kitchener's motives, his wish to mount a massive recruitment drive was absolutely correct. He knew that he needed to plan for vast numbers. Twentieth-century total warfare required manpower in unimaginable numbers. When Edward III invaded France in 1346, he fought the battle of Crécy with some 16,000 troops. In 1415 Henry V invaded France with some 11,000 troops, but fought the Battle of Agincourt with some 8,500. The Duke of Marlborough fought the Battle of Blenheim in 1704 with 40,000 troops, of which just 16,000 were British troops, the rest being mercenaries and allies.

By 1815, at the Battle of Waterloo, the Duke of Wellington commanded 68,000 troops consisting of both the regular army and a mixture of mercenaries and allies. He was joined towards the end of the battle by another 50,000 Prussians under the command of Blücher, thus making a total allied strength of just under 120,000. Britain sent some 400,000 troops to the Crimean War in 1853, but all of these numbers were to be dwarfed by what was required for the impending war. Anybody who has attended a major sporting occasion will be able to imagine an army of, say, 68,000, as commanded by the Duke of Waterloo, but 5 million: that is a completely different scale of number, which defies most imaginations, and yet this is the number eventually mobilised by Britain.

During those first terrible weeks, even holding the German forces to a line east of Paris was going to prove an extremely difficult task and at times it seemed to be beyond the Allies' capabilities. At the outbreak of hostilities the German Kaiser had described the British Expeditionary Force as 'a contemptible little army'. The many years for which the British defence policy had been reliant on the navy and the payment of monies to allies and mercenaries to assist in fighting their land battles were coming home to roost. The size of the problem facing Britain and France was considerable and the overriding problem was numbers. At the outbreak of war, Britain had 11,000 regular army officers, about the same number of Territorial Army officers and some 240,000 troops in the regular army with what should have been some 300,000 territorial troops. It was estimated that the Territorial Force was 60,000 short of a full complement, which meant Britain had a total armed force of just over 500,000 trained soldiers. The British Expeditionary Force which left for France soon after the outbreak of war consisted of some 160,000 men. The remainder of the Army and the Territorial Force remained in the UK as the Home Defence Force.

In September 1914, at the Battle of the Marne, Britain and France finally brought the German forces to a halt. The first month of the war had seen a continuous German advance almost to Paris, but at the River Marne the French and British forced the first reverse in what had been, until then, continuous German success. There then followed what was later described as the race to the sea. Both armies tried to sidestep the other by moving northwards, hoping to outflank them and gain access to the others' rear, thereby engaging in a war of movement. When this also failed to achieve any decisive advantage, the war on the Western Front settled down into stalemate. Trenches stretched from the English Channel, across Belgium, eastern France and all the way to the Swiss border.[16]

During the first year of the war nothing would be developed in the way of tactics or strategy to challenge the dominance of defensive tactics with machine guns, deep dug defences backed up by barbed wire, and heavy artillery. There appeared to be no way to attack and gain a significant advantage without horrendous casualties. A war of attrition required massive recruitment and training and all of this took time. Democratically elected politicians, however, do not like long-term planning and the British Cabinet soon began to look for opportunities to achieve military successes which could be put into action quicker and cheaper than looked likely in France.

Several plans were floated; Admiral Jackie Fisher initially advocated a landing of troops from naval ships to attack Germany from the rear. Lloyd George fancied an expedition into Salonika, but it was the fertile imagination of the First Lord of the Admiralty (Winston Churchill MP) that attracted the greatest interest and was to lead to the Dardanelles campaign and the landings on Gallipoli.

Winston Churchill, as First Lord of the Admiralty, was naturally keen that the Royal Navy should play a part in winning an advantage for Britain and the Allies. He won the support of the Secretary to the Committee on Imperial Defence, Maurice Hankey, and eventually the influential support of Lord Kitchener for a campaign aimed at driving Turkey out of the Central Powers and out of the war. The initial plan was for the Royal Navy to force a passage through the Dardanelles into the Sea of Marmaris to threaten Constantinople and thus force Turkey out of the war. By January 1915 Churchill, who by now had also won the acquiescence if not the backing of his First Sea Lord 'Jackie' Fisher, argued strongly within the Committee of Imperial Defence for a naval operation in the Dardanelles, which was finally agreed on 28 January 1915.

The majority of the blame that has subsequently been placed on Winston Churchill for the Dardanelles campaign needs to be looked at carefully. In 1915 Britain was a long established and sophisticated democracy with a history of collegiate decision making. To blame one individual, however persuasive, is to misread what happens in cabinet-style government. The facts are that the War Council made the decision jointly to force a passage through the Dardanelles and when that failed, it was the same War Council that agreed the decision to land the army on the Gallipoli Peninsula. At various times during the debates which took place on this campaign, there were varying degrees of support and opposition from various members of the full cabinet, the war cabinet and what became known as the Dardanelles Committee. What is absolutely certain is that it split the politicians from the majority of the military, leaving Lord Kitchener with an awkward foot in both camps. This split, of what were reckoned to be the military realities and the political imperatives, persisted throughout the war.

The fact that this was the first war fought by a democracy with almost universal male suffrage is just one of the characteristics that made the First World War the first truly modern war. Subsequently, when David Lloyd George took over as Prime Minister, the problems worsened. He had a very low opinion of the military in general, and Field Marshal Haig in particular, and this was to be a theme that ran right through the campaign. This distrust of the military, and their insistence that the war could only be won in France by grinding the German Army down by attrition, was to have a profound effect on the campaigns in Gallipoli and the Middle East, which is where the Bucks Hussars were bound and where they saw the majority of their war service.

At the outbreak of war, Turkey had initially adopted a neutral position, but was extensively courted by both Germany and Britain. Indeed, Britain arguably had a stronger reason than the Central Powers to woo Turkey as the Ottoman Empire butted up against Egypt which, in turn, put it in close proximity to the Suez Canal, Britain's main link to the Empire.

Prior to the Crimean War, Britain's foreign policy had from time immemorial been driven by one principle: ascertain which side France was on and then side with the other lot. Turkey had a similar view of foreign policy, but instead of France, their *bête noire* was Russia. Given that Russia was firmly in the Allied camp, it was probably inevitable that Turkey would throw in their lot with the Central Powers. However, this decision was made more certain when Britain, having entered into a contract with Turkey to build and supply two dreadnought-class battleships, reneged on the deal. To make matters worse, Turkey had already paid most of the monies and they had only managed to find the foreign currency needed by public subscription! Whatever the rights and wrongs, the First Lord of the Admiralty made the decision and the battleships were never delivered. By November 1914, Turkey was at war with the Allies and from that moment on, with Britain increasingly concerned about the Suez Canal that linked her to her Empire, some sort of military action against Turkey became inevitable.

The assault on the Dardanelles began on 19 February 1915 under the command of Vice Admiral Sackville Carden, and continued without any great success until the middle of March. It proved impossible to get the ships through the narrow sea straits because of mines and coastal gun batteries and it became obvious that action would have to take place with troops to suppress the Turkish artillery batteries. Hence the Gallipoli landings. What had started as a naval-only action was to become a full-scale amphibious landing on a hostile shore and, to make matters worse, there was no element of surprise. The Turks and their German advisers knew they were coming and had plenty of time to prepare.

General Sir Ian Hamilton was offered, and accepted, the command of the Mediterranean Expeditionary Force (MEF) and was tasked with the job of putting the troops onto the beaches and, hopefully, taking control of the peninsula so that the Royal Navy could proceed up the Dardanelles with mine sweepers unimpeded by hostile enemy fire. General Hamilton was one of the British heroes from the Boer War. He was highly regarded and considered to be highly intelligent in an army sometimes suspicious of those who were too clever. He was an extremely brave soldier. His record in South Africa proved that, but by the time he took command of the MEF he was 61 and had been side-lined for some time, being seen as too closely linked to Liberal politicians and, perhaps, lacking the drive and ruthlessness to take command in France.

Whatever his military talents, General Hamilton had undoubtedly been handed something of a poisoned chalice by his old commander-in-chief, Lord Kitchener. The troops landed at five separate beaches on 25 April 1915 but from the very start, things did not go as planned, despite the amazing courage of the troops. By the summer of 1915, the Gallipoli front was reaching a critical stage with the troops still bogged down in beach heads overlooked by Turks who continued to hold the high ground. The original landings at beaches 'x', 'w', 'v' and 's', in the very southern tip of the peninsula, had advanced some 2 miles but had failed to take the village of Krithia, despite three attempts which had been long and bloody affairs and had severely depleted the Allied forces. Hamilton also had the problem of not being able to rotate troops from the front line to a rear rest area, such as existed in France. At Gallipoli all of the troops, wherever they camped, were effectively on the front line and subject to artillery fire.

The Australian and New Zealand forces, who had originally landed north at 'z' beach, were in an even worse position. There was virtually no beach at Anzac Cove and the troops were dug into the steep sided ravines which ran down to the sea from the high ground where the Turkish forces had them pinned down. The original intention was that they would cross the peninsula and command the heights, thus impeding any Turkish reinforcement of the south. They had gained a foothold on the first plateau but at no point around Anzac Cove were they more than 2,000 yards inland.

Progress without significant reinforcement seemed impossible. Equally, the 'status quo' was also impossible as the Allied soldiers on the beaches and the lower slopes were under more or less constant heavy fire. This is the exact situation that military leaders on the Western Front in France had prophesied and feared. The group of military leaders who believed that war could only be won on the Western Front were known as the 'Westerners' and they argued, not without logic, that opening any other military front would inevitably draw resources from France; a view with which the French allies concurred.

The situation had become critical by the summer of 1915 and Hamilton was now in the position of pleading with the authorities in London for additional resources. The liberal government at that time was also in a very weak position. Its support within the electorate was weakening and several PR disasters were not helping. Recently, journalists had received briefing from military sources about problems with both the quantity and the quality of the ammunition being shipped to France. This, coupled with the lengthening casualty lists, was beginning to rebound on the government and the public were beginning to question its fitness for office. Inevitably, with governments in such a position, things always go from bad to worse, and it was during this period that Admiral John Fisher chose very publically to resign over the issue of Gallipoli. He had never been a keen supporter of the campaign but had allowed himself to be carried along by Winston Churchill's enthusiasm. When he had finally had enough and resigned, citing Gallipoli as the reason, the public felt they had lost one of their great naval heroes and, as is usual in such cases, blamed the government.

The upshot of all of this political turmoil was the formation of a coalition government with the Liberals and Conservatives forming a new cabinet. The price that the Conservatives demanded for propping up the government was the sacking of Winston Churchill, and so the Gallipoli campaign lost its strongest political supporter. As Prime Minister, Asquith would have liked also to clear out Kitchener, but he had become the public face of the war; the man who appeared to be above politics, adored by the public, Kitchener's strength was such that Asquith felt bound to keep him in post as Secretary of State for War. The new 'Dardanelles Committee', as the War Council was called, decided to continue plugging away and to agree the request to reinforce Hamilton's forces. He was granted three extra divisions from the 'new army' and two divisions from the territorials. It is likely that this decision stems from Lord Kitchener's support. He had initially been a 'Westerner' but had latterly been converted to, at the very least, lukewarm support for the Gallipoli project.

Hamilton could now begin to plan for a renewed offensive in August. His plans aimed at a breakout from Anzac Cove, an amphibious landing of troops at Suvla Bay and routing the Turkish Army from the high ground which was enabling them to dominate the battlefield. He also desperately needed to get troops across the peninsula to the eastern shore in order to be able to cut the Turkish internal transport links and thus isolate the Turkish soldiers, preventing progress of Allied forces from the southerly tip of the peninsula. One further attack was planned to try and link the Suvla landings to Anzac Cove. The Dardanelles Committee agreed to Hamilton's request for additional troops on 13 August.

The need to augment the forces in Gallipoli had always been foreseen as a strong possibility and, when added to Britain's need to protect their Middle Eastern interests, would result in the deployment of the yeomanry brigade to Egypt. However, before that could happen, the yeomanry forces had to be trained and fitted out.

The Royal Bucks Hussars were initially mobilised on 5 August 1914. The call ups had resulted in A Squadron mobilising at Buckingham, B Squadron at Aylesbury, C Squadron at High Wycombe and D Squadron at Chesham. The four squadrons were taken to Reading to organise themselves and there they were joined by a machine gun section under the command of Major A.M. Grenfell. The regiment was under the command of Lieutenant Colonel C.A. Grenfell and during the ten days they were at Reading they reorganised into three squadrons – D Squadron troops were re-allocated to the three other squadrons.

The regiment was already incorporated into the 2nd South Midland Mounted Division, which in turn was part of the 2nd Mounted Brigade. The troops were moved within the second week of the war to the east coast. From Reading, the Bucks Hussars were sent by train to Bury St Edmunds where, initially, they were billeted around the Great Saxham area.[17]

By 31 August, the regiment was stationed at Churn, adjacent to Cromer. They were to spend their time training, and skills such as map reading, fire discipline, marksmanship and route marching were the order of the day. Alongside these was the question of who would go to war. As previously explained, the yeomanry terms of recruitment did not require them to serve overseas, but to be of any use in the war they would obviously be needed overseas. The Bucks Hussars were asked by their officers who would volunteer to go overseas. Anecdotally, Captain Cripps stood his squadron with their backs against a wall and asked all of them who did not wish to volunteer for overseas duty to take one step backwards! Whatever methods were employed, an extremely high proportion of troops volunteered.

Of course, not all did so and the process of filling the vacancies began. For the first time the essentially 'Bucks nature' of the Bucks Hussars began to be diluted. To fill the gaps left by those who felt unable to volunteer, Newmarket jockeys,

SS *Menominee* described by most as a 'nightmare voyage'. (Bill Cowell)

Metropolitan Police and *Daily Telegraph* employees were brought in. They obviously brought with them varying degrees of equestrian skills and perhaps differing views on life to the traditional Buckinghamshire rural outlook.

These initial stages of the First World War for the Bucks Hussars had an element of 'Dad's Army' about them. Not all the men had full uniforms, the horses provided by the Army were unsuitable and the armaments provided were obvious 'seconds'. Nevertheless, the regiment trained hard and from contemporary accounts they acquitted themselves well. Reports from some of the surviving members who were interviewed during the latter part of the twentieth century indicated that they were fully employed with military training, riding, physical exercises including boxing, and the unending care for the horses.

Finally, after eight months, their orders for overseas deployment arrived. The long spell of being in limbo came to an end and the Bucks Hussars were finally going to war. They sailed from Avonmouth on 5 April 1915 and arrived at Alexandria in Egypt on 19 April, having sailed on the hired transport *Menominee*, described by some of the aristocratic officers as a 'cattle vessel'. During the voyage they stopped at Gibraltar and Malta, although it appears from contemporary accounts as if the troops were not allowed ashore during transit. Certainly it cannot have been pleasant for Bill Cowell and his colleagues, not least because of the ever-present threat of U-boats, which required the vessel to extinguish all lights every night. In his autobiography, Cripps of the Bucks Hussars refers to the voyage as a 'nightmare', and it is true that there were large amounts of sickness, both equine and human. Quite a few of the horses died during the voyage from septic pneumonia caused by the lack of ventilation in the holds where they were stabled. One man interviewed after the war stated that the ship was constantly followed through the Mediterranean by sharks which fed on the horse carcasses thrown overboard.

Major Fred Lawson wrote to his wife in a letter posted from Gibraltar that they had already lost three horses by that stage and that 'the boat is packed with

1700 men and 600 horses on quite a small boat and the discomfort for the men is considerable.'[18] On arrival in Alexandria on 19 April, the Bucks Hussars were moved overland to the Citadel Barracks in Cairo. In what was probably good training for later battles, they arrived during one of the hottest spells that Egypt had experienced for several years.

The Bucks Hussars remained in training in and around Cairo at the Citadel Barracks until, in early August, orders for their deployment arrived and the soldiers were dismounted and infantry equipment was issued, including bayonets. On 15 August they set sail as part of the 2nd Mounted Yeomanry Division, leaving their horses in Cairo with some of the older and often married members of A Squadron. The intention was to bolster the forces that had become bogged down in Suvla Bay. They were joining the battered 29th Division which had been moved up from the Helles landing zone. The Bucks Hussars supplied some 250 soldiers and ten officers. In total, the Berks, Bucks and Oxon Yeomanry made up some 800 troops and about thirty officers. Among the troops who embarked for Gallipoli was Bill Cowell.

5

SUVLA BAY, GALLIPOLI

The Royal Bucks Hussars disembarked in Suvla Bay at about 11.00 p.m. on 18 August 1915. The landing itself was made via landing craft from the ship anchored out in the bay. The landing craft came under Turkish shell fire on their way into the beaches, resulting in the Royal Bucks Hussars' first official war casualties since the Boer War. They were required to dig in and an experienced NCO was attached to help them with their infantry duties. On 21 August they marched some 8 miles across the loose sand of Suvla Bay before mustering in relative safety, protected from direct shell fire, behind the hill of Lala Baba.

The plans for the British forces in the Suvla Bay area were to attempt to drive the Turks off the high ground immediately surrounding the landing ground and then subsequently link up with the Anzac troops who were holding beachheads south of the bay. The troops could then move inland to cut off the southern tip of the Gallipoli Peninsula, with Suvla Bay providing a beachhead for the navy to resupply the troops ashore. That at least was the plan, but it required some complex manoeuvres from the troops attacking up from Anzac Cove. It required energetic, hands-on command from the officers landing at Suvla; above all, it would require aggressive action during the first precious hours whilst the element of surprise existed. The three high command objectives of the August campaign were to:

break out northwards and east from Anzac Cove, capturing the high ground of Hill 971 and Hill 60;
secure Suvla Bay as a base for supporting the Allied position; and
move east towards the Dardanelles and thus disrupt the Turks' internal lines of communication.

These objectives were set against the background of ultimately destroying the Turkish coastal defences and allowing time and safety for the navy to clear the Dardanelles and for ships to enter the Sea of Marmaris and thus threaten Constantinople.

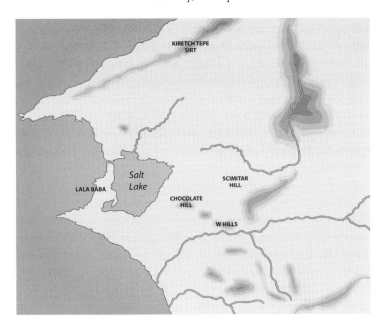

Suvla Bay, the area fought over by the Bucks Hussars.

There seems to be general agreement that the three objectives outlined above were possible and, given the surprise initially achieved on the first landings on 6 and 7 August, should have been successful. However, this would have required vigorous leadership and, in the appointment of General Stopford, this was one thing with which General Hamilton was not blessed. It would be difficult to conceive a worse choice for overall commander and this was further compounded by General Hamilton's laidback, hands-off style of management. It is probably fair to say that Lord Kitchener must accept his share of the blame as he was only too aware of what he was saddling Hamilton with when Stopford was appointed.

Lieutenant General Sir Frederick Stopford was described by the illustrious military historian J.F.C. Fuller as having no conception of what generalship meant and, indeed, he was appointed despite having seen little combat and never having commanded men in battle. In addition, he plainly lacked energy and enthusiasm (he had retired in 1909, aged 61). He was appointed solely because of his position on the list of seniority. Hamilton had requested one of the more energetic commanders from the Western Front; his choice would have been either Lieutenant General Julian Byng or Lieutenant General Henry Rawlinson, who were both experienced and extremely capable Western Front corps commanders. Sadly for Hamilton, and for thousands of young British soldiers, both of his original choices were junior to Lieutenant General Sir Bryan Mahon, who was already commander of the 10th Division and had made it clear that he would only answer to a senior officer. Byng and Rawlinson were ruled out and Stopford was selected purely because of seniority and availability.

When the troops landed at Suvla Bay on 6 and 7 August, it did indeed come as a surprise to the Turkish Army, which was desperately short of reserves in the area. What was needed was an immediate and energetic push into Kiritch Tepe to the north of the Bay and onto the Anfarta Ridge to the east. Instead, with Stopford completely lacking the drive and determination to hammer home the position and the advantage, there was complete inertia. A famous war correspondent who was embedded with the troops at Gallipoli, Ellis Ashmead-Bartlett, wrote, 'The British had simply landed anew and dug another graveyard.' Colonel Aspinall, a member of General Hamilton's HQ staff, was sent ashore on 8 August to check what was happening and to report back to the Commander-in-Chief. What he found was simply incredible and he was so worried that he approached General Stopford in his HQ on a ship offshore. He reports his conversation as follows:

> General Stopford greeted me by 'Well Aspinall, the men have done splen-
> didly and have been magnificent'. 'But they haven't reached the hills, Sir'
> I replied. 'No' he replied 'but they are ashore!' I replied that I was sure the
> Commander-in-Chief would be disappointed that they had not yet reached
> the high ground covering the Bay, in accordance with the orders, and
> I impressed on him the urgent importance of moving forward at the earliest
> possible moment, before the enemy's reinforcements forestalled him on the
> hills. General Stopford replied that he quite realised the importance of losing
> no time but that it was impossible to advance until the men had rested. He
> intended to make a fresh advance on the following day.[19]

Colonel Aspinall was so dismayed with both his interview with Stopford and what he saw on shore that he sent a telegram to Hamilton stating:

> Just been ashore where I found all quiet. No rifle fire, no artillery fire and
> apparently no Turks. IX Corps resting. Feel confident that golden opportuni-
> ties are being lost and look upon the situation as serious.[20]

Colonel Aspinall's summary and his fears were absolutely correct. In his diaries, Hamilton states that he never received Aspinall's report, but this was not significant as he met Aspinall on his way into Suvla Bay the day after the landings took place. By this stage, despite Hamilton's efforts, it was too late to inject some urgency into the landings. The Turkish forces had not wasted the reprieve granted by Stopford's lethargy and had managed to rush reinforcements onto the hills. The opportunity had gone. On 13 August even the ever-optimistic Hamilton seems to have lost heart. He writes in his diary:

There is no way out. Whether there is any good looking back even for one moment, God knows; I doubt it! But I feel so acutely, I seem to see so clearly, where our push for Constantinople first began to quit the rails, that I must put it down right here. The moment was when I asked for Rawlinson or Byng, and when, in reply, the keen, the young, the fit, the up-to-date Commanders were all barred, simply and solely that Mahon should not be disturbed in his Divisional command. I resisted it very strongly: I went so far as to remind K (Kitchener) in my cable of his own sad disappointment at Bloemfontein when he had offered him a cavalry brigade and he returned instead to his appointment in the Sudan. The question that keeps troubling me is, ought I to have fought it further; ought I to have resigned sooner than allow generals old and yet inexperienced to be foisted on me.[21]

Jack Churchill, Winston's brother, was on General Hamilton's staff and wrote to his brother after the initial battles at Suvla about the performance of the 10th, 11th and 53rd Divisions. He wrote:

We are all trying to understand what has happened to these men and why they are showing such extraordinary lack of enterprise. They are not cowards – physically they are as fine a body of men as the regular army. I think it is partly on account of their training. They have never seen a shot fired before. For a year they have been soldiers and during that time they have been taught only one thing, trench warfare. They have been told to dig everywhere and have been led to expect an enemy at one hundred yards range. From reading all the stories of the war they have learned to regard an advance of 100 yards as a matter of the greatest importance. They landed and advanced a mile and thought they had done something wonderful. Then they had no standard to go by – no other troops were there to show them what was right. They seemed not to know what they should do. Was it right to go on so far – might they be cut off or suddenly walk into a trap? Was an occasional bullet only a sniper or was a hidden trench bristling with rifles waiting for them? The 10th and 11th had nothing to go by. They showed extraordinary ignorance. A shell burst near a working party – at least half a mile away. Officers and men stopped working, rushed to the low beach cliffs and lay down taking cover! A landmine exploded and the men near all lay flat and remained there thinking they were being shelled! I have just heard that the 53rd are no better. A few shots sent them retreating pell mell from Chocolate Hill! Blaming the senior officers must be left to the people who can give effect to their opinions. But there is no doubt that these Divisions were completely out of hand.[22]

On 14 August – only a week after the landings – Lord Kitchener wrote to Churchill stating that he intended to sack the generals in charge of the landings.

Generals Stopford, Hammersley and Lindley were relieved of their commands and General Mahon resigned, but it was all too late. The vital moment in which victory may have been possible was passed and would not reoccur.

What happened next was blind stupidity or pig-headedness from the British commanders and for this, Hamilton has to accept much of the responsibility. He reinforced failure by bringing up a war-weary 29th Division from Helles and the 2nd Mounted Division which included the yeomanry regiments from Egypt. The young men who sacrificed their lives in that long march across the Salt Lake and the Suvla Plain, and who died unimaginably horrible deaths in the trenches around Chocolate Hill, did so with no realistic possibility of success.

What was asked of the reinforcing Allied forces at Suvla was the capture of a group of hills: Scimitar Hill, Chocolate Hill and the 'W' Hills. These should have been captured on day one of the campaign and could have been taken with ease, as at that point they were virtually undefended. The new attacks were scheduled to commence on 21 August. The 29th Division was commanded by Major General W.E. Peyton and beneath him, commanding the 2nd South Midland Brigade, which consisted of the Bucks, Berks and Dorset Yeomanry regiments, was Brigadier General, the Earl of Longford. In his pep talk to his officers, Brigadier General Longford told them, 'Don't bother ducking, the men don't like it and it doesn't do any good.'

The 29th Division was to attack Scimitar Hill. The 2nd Mounted Division was in reserve near Lala Baba on the far side of the Salt Lake. This attack was the largest mounted by the Allies at Gallipoli. It was absolutely vital for any meaningful intervention to drive the Turkish forces off these heights commanding Suvla Plain. What was mercifully unknown to the yeomanry soldiers massed by the shore was that the opportunity to beat the Turks, if there had ever been one, had been in the first week of August when the initial landing took place. The inertia in the command during the first days of August had meant that the advantage of surprise had been lost entirely and by 21 August it was all too late, and they were to pay the price of the delay with their lives. The initial attacks went in from the 29th Division, but by late afternoon it was obvious that the yeomanry would have to be called into action.

The yeomanry marched from the cover of Lala Baba across the Salt Lake (dried in the intense summer heat) and over some 1.5 miles of open scrubland before assaulting the Turks dug in around Chocolate Hill. Contemporary records indicate that the scrub was set on fire by both Turkish and British artillery during the march across the plain. Young men wounded by shrapnel and unable to escape were burnt alive. The yeomanry marched through the dead and wounded colleagues of the previous assault, but it was clear from all accounts that not once did they lose their discipline nor their determination to do their utmost to get to grips with the enemy.

The Royal Bucks Hussars shelter behind the hill at Lala Baba prior to marching across the Salt Lake, 21 August 1915. (Mike Holland)

I cannot imagine what it was like during that march across the Suvla Plain. It is impossible for anybody who did not participate to know what Bill Cowell and his comrades felt and what they were thinking during the hour or so of hell it took to cross that plain under gunfire. This was warfare from the history books: marching forward towards the guns as Wellington's and Marlborough's armies had done in times gone by. It had overtones of the Charge of the Light Brigade, albeit at a slower pace. It is impossible to read the stories and not feel admiration for the discipline and courage of the civilian soldiers. Months before, they had worked on peaceful farms; now death was all around them, randomly striking down their friends. Bill Cowell and the yeomanry were not found wanting when the call came. He was surrounded by his friends and fellow farmers from Buckinghamshire, men he had known all of his short life and had trained with, but nothing could prepare them adequately for their first time under fire.

Many young men from Buckinghamshire died on that day – their first under fire. Percy George, a farmer's son aged 21, died in the assault, as did Frank Wood, just 22 and from Whitchurch. Both were pupils of the Royal Latin School in Buckingham. I had walked past their names many times during my school days, never realising that they were comrades-in-arms of my grandfather. For all I knew, he could have been marching a few yards from them as they fell. Now their names are commemorated on the Helles Memorial along with all the other young lads from Buckinghamshire, Dorset, Berkshire and Gloucestershire, and of course those from Australia and New Zealand.

Twenty-one out of twenty-eight yeomanry officers were killed, including Brigadier General Lord Longford. He had advanced the whole way under the strongest machine gun and artillery fire armed only with a map and a walking stick. He was finally killed on the slopes of Chocolate Hill by close-range rifle fire. One of the soldiers, Frank Lunnon, interviewed many years after the war, stated that they went up Chocolate Hill and attacked the Turks holding the summit armed only with bayonets. His only comment was, 'Mercifully, I did not remember anything about that.' Surely nothing could be more traumatic for a young soldier than the experience of hand-to-hand fighting with bayonets, especially for those engaged in their first day of battle.[23]

Lt Col Cripps was arguably one of the luckier officers in that he was wounded early on, hit in the right knee and in the chest. In his autobiography he quotes an extract from the *Royal Armoured Corps Journal* Vol V No 1:

Quite soon a few puffs of smoke appeared above them, gradually increasing in number as the Turkish guns opened up on this promising target. Fortunately for the leading regiments, the enemy shrapnel concentrated on the middle of the column, where the Warwickshire Yeomanry and the Gloucestershire Hussars suffered considerable casualties; as did the Hertfordshire Yeomanry, who lost their Colonel, Gurney Sheppard, with his servant, who stayed with him to save him from the burning scrub, which was sending clouds of smoke drifting across the plain.

When finally the tail of the Division reached the shelter of Chocolate Hill and, breathless and with relief from their ordeal, sat down in groups under its slopes, all eyes were turned on a small but dramatic spectacle.

Among the wounded was Major Cripps of the Bucks Hussars, hit in the leg and unable to move. As the Westminster Dragoons came by, Lieutenant

Ferguson, a forty year old officer, for whom court martial appeared to hold no terror, handed over his troops to his sergeant and went to Cripps's help. Their two figures could now be seen in the distance, staggering slowly arm-in-arm across the plain, outlined against the dust and smoke. Their progress seemed interminably slow, their chances of survival remote, and everyone's hopes were wrapped up in their fate; gradually they came nearer and, when at last they reached us, Cripps slowly produced a large cigar case from his pocket, took out a large cigar and lit it. Then a mighty cheer went up.[24]

The reference to a court martial alludes to the instructions to all troops that they were not to stop to help wounded friends, but carry on advancing.

Lt Col Cripps subsequently wrote about his medical evacuation as follows:

… from the clearing-station I was taken to a hospital ship, operated on there and transferred to an ordinary transport. I was only semi-conscious, but this was merciful, for if I had been in a normal state I should have found conditions unbearable. I found myself lying on deck in a tightly packed row of severely wounded soldiers. We were all wearing our uniforms and there was nothing between the deck and ourselves. There were 800 of us in that slow-moving ship. Her progress was necessarily slow as she could not fly the Red Cross flag. The Captain was with good reason fearful of submarines. A terrible responsibility rested on Officers in charge of these hospital ships, especially when at sea and exposed to a ruthless enemy. It took us three weeks to reach England, and during that weary and dangerous time there were only two doctors and two nurses to attend to us. There were no hospital orderlies, no anaesthetics and only the ordinary military rations of bully beef and biscuits. I must say, however, that during the week in which I had been wounded there had been some 47,000 casualties in Gallipoli – and Gallipoli was only a side-show in the First World War. All this proved far too great a strain on medical resources … I was lying between a sergeant-major and a private of the 29th Div. The sergeant-major had been shot in the stomach and after three days on board he died with his head on my chest. We were packed in like sardines in a tin: a day or two passed before it was possible to heave the body overboard. Among other very bad cases on board was an Officer, a friend of mine, who was lying close to me. He was strangled during the night by his neighbour on the other side who had been shot in the head and screamed out that he had caught and killed a Turkish spy. My knee had become badly septic and I was operated on twice: I was given a piece of rope to bite on instead of an anaesthetic. Others were in the same unfortunate position. The private on the other side of me had his arm amputated without any anaesthetic. Undaunted, he just sat up, put his arm behind his back and said to me 'Lord, it do make I sweat!' A Spartan indeed …[25]

Major Fred Lawson wrote to his father after the advance and described it as follows:

> Ashmead's account of the attack, less the purple patches, is fairly accurate. The whole scheme was changed at the last moment. The other Brigadiers went astray and the only Brigade which reached its objective was ours.
>
> Longford knew where he wanted to get and walked straight there at the head of his Brigade under very heavy fire with his walking stick in his hand. He was told that the other Brigades would be there before him and he need not wait for them as they had a shorter way to go. In point of fact, only about two troops of them ever got beyond our advanced trenches. Our Brigade took the trenches on Hill 70 at some loss and remained in them. They were enfiladed and withdrew below the crest of the hill, but remained on the hill. At 2 o'clock in the morning they received orders to retire and the show was over. They did extraordinarily well. They went where they were meant to go and took the trench at the point of the bayonet. Unfortunately the Brigade lost all their officers who were on the hill and the remnants were brought back by Young, our MG officer, who had gone up when he could get his guns no further.[26]

Later on in the same letter Lawson refers again to the confusion on the hill and refutes the suggestion that the brigade had been beaten off the hill, but had rather been ordered to retire. This was obviously a sore point with the soldiers who were there, and Lawson describes it:

> There was general confusion as to who ordered them to retire but the general opinion seems to be that the Officer commanding the Inniskillings, on their left, ordered them to retire.[27]

Scimitar Hill, or Hill 70 as it is sometimes referred to, was undoubtedly captured briefly by the yeomanry forces. Typically, in the fog of war and in the midst of such a close-quarter fire fight, there remains uncertainty as to whether they were driven off or killed by the defensive fire from the Turks higher up the spur, or whether they were ordered to retire by one of the few remaining officers. In the end it matters little. To add to the horror of being under constant enemy fire, the undergrowth ignited, burning and killing many of the wounded.

The 2nd Mounted Division's performance, their conduct and courage under fire, totally refuted Kitchener's opinion of 'part-time soldiers'. They advanced, marching in extended formation, straight across the salt lake, under fire the whole way. They were advancing across flat ground overlooked by Turkish artillery and machine guns that were looking down on what in modern military parlance is described as a 'target-rich environment'. In short, it was like shooting rats in a barrel. The Turkish gunners simply could not miss.

The remains of Dick Turner's wallet hit by a bullet or shrapnel (lower left-hand corner) on the march across the Salt Lake. (Mike Holland)

Brigadier General the Earl of Longford had led the yeomen with incredible personal bravery up to the British front line held by the remnants of the 29th Division. Having reached the temporary, comparative safety of these positions, the Berks and Bucks Yeomanry were rallied and taken forward again by Lord Longford in an attempt to take the summit of Scimitar Hill/Hill 70.[28]

They briefly held the position on or near the top of the hill and, when forced to retreat temporarily by enfilading fire from Hill 112, they attacked for a second time and the hill was recaptured before being lost for the final time. A further attack of the 11th Division towards the W Hills was also held up by the strong Turkish defences. It was during this confused last offensive late in the evening of 21 August that Lord Longford was killed, as was Lt William Niven (Berks Yeomanry), father of the Hollywood actor David Niven.

General Sir Ian Hamilton later commented on the action of the yeomanry forces in his third dispatch to the chiefs of staff as follows:

> At 3 p.m. an advance was begun by the infantry on the right of the line. The 34th Brigade of the 11th Division rushed the Turkish trenches between Hetman Chair and Aire Klavak, practically without loss, but the 32nd Brigade, directed against Hetman Chair and the communication trench connecting that point with the south-west corner of the Ismail Oglu Tepe spur, failed to make good its point. The brigade had lost direction in the first instance, moving north-east instead of east, and though it attempted to carry the

communication trench from the north-east with great bravery and great disregard of life, it never succeeded in rectifying the original mistake. The 33rd Brigade, sent up in haste with orders to capture this communication trench at all costs, fell into precisely the same error, part of it marching north-east and part south-east to Susuk Kuyu. Meanwhile the 29th Division, whose attack had been planned for 3.30 p.m., had attacked Scimitar Hill (Hill 70) with great dash. The 87th Brigade, on the left, carried the trenches on Scimitar Hill, but the 86th Brigade were checked and upset by a raging forest fire across their front. Eventually pressing on, they found themselves unable to advance up the valley between the two spurs owing to the failure of the 32nd Brigade of the 11th Division on their right.

The brigade then tried to attack eastwards, but were decimated by a cross fire of shell and musketry from the north and south-east. The leading troops were simply swept off the top of the spur, and had to fall back to a ledge south-west of Scimitar Hill, where they found a little cover.

Whilst this fighting was in progress the 2nd Mounted Division moved out from Lala Baba in open formation to take up a position of readiness behind Yilghin Burnu. During this march they came under a remarkably steady and accurate artillery fire. The advance of these English Yeomen was a sight calculated to send a thrill of pride through anyone with a drop of English blood running in their veins. Such superb martial spectacles are rare in modern warfare. Ordinarily it should always be possible to bring up reserves under some sort of cover from shrapnel fire. Here, for a mile and a half, there was nothing to conceal a mouse, much less some of the most stalwart soldiers England has ever sent from her shores. Despite the critical events in other parts of the field, I could hardly take my glasses from the Yeomen: they moved like men marching on parade. Here and there a shell would take toll of a cluster; there they lay; there was no straggling; the others moved steadily on; not a man was there who hung back or hurried. But such an ordeal must consume some of the battle-winning fighting energy of those subjected to it, and it is lucky indeed for the Turks that the terrain, as well as the lack of trenches, forbade us from letting the 2nd Mounted Division loose at close quarters to the enemy without undergoing this previous too heavy baptism of fire.

Now that the 11th Division had made their effort, and failed, the 2nd South Midland Brigade (commanded by Brigadier General Earl of Longford) was sent forward from its position of readiness behind Yilghin Burnu, in the hope that they might yet restore the fortunes of the day. This brigade, in action for the first time, encountered both bush fires and musketry without flinching, but the advance had in places to be almost by inches, and the actual close attack by the Yeomen did not take place until night was fast falling. On the left they reached the foremost line of the 29th Division, and on the right also they got as far as the leading battalions. But, as soon as it was dark, one regiment pushed up the valley between Scimitar Hill and Hill 100 (on Ismail Oglu Tepe), and carried the trenches on a small knoll near the centre of this horseshoe. The regiment imagined it had captured Hill 100, which would have been a very notable success, enabling as it would the whole of our line to hang on and dig in. But when the report came in, some doubt was felt as to its accuracy, and a reconnaissance by staff officers showed that the knoll was a good way from Hill 100, and that a strongly-held semi-circle of Turkish trenches (the enemy having been heavily reinforced) still denied us access to the top of the hill. As the men were too done, immediate assault, and as the knoll actually held would have been swept by fire at daybreak, there was nothing for it but to fall back under cover of darkness to our original line. The losses in this attack fell most heavily on the 29th Division. They were just under 5,000.

I am sorry not to be able to give more detail as to the conduct of individuals and units during this battle. But the 2nd South Midland Brigade has been brought to my notice, and it consisted of the Bucks Yeomanry, the Berks Yeomanry, and the Dorset Yeomanry. The Yeomanry fought very bravely, and on personal, as well as public, grounds I specially deplore the loss of Brigadier-General Earl of Longford, K.P., M.V.O., and Brigadier-General P.A. Kenna, V.C., D.S.O., A.D.C.[29]

Other eyewitnesses were situated on one of the hills overlooking the Salt Lake:

From Two Tree Hill we had a magnificent view of the dismounted, or rather unmounted, Yeomanry as they moved out from Lala Baba and began their march across the Salt Lake in open formation. This was sometime between 3.30 and 4.00pm. On the Karakol Dagh, Hamilton and his staff were also watching. It was a sight to behold. There were five brigades, each nearly 1,000 strong, marching in extended order – wave after wave – with about seven paces between each man. They stretched from just below the Cut to the scrubby ground south of the Salt Lake, a distance of 2,000 yards. And they presented such a target as artillerymen dream of. They marched steadily, like an army of soldier ants that cannot be deflected, and almost as soon as they came into the open from the bivouacs behind Lala Baba, shrapnel began to thin them out.[30]

Lt Harold Davis of the Gloucester Hussars was also part of the 2nd Mounted Brigade marching on that day. He later recorded his impressions:

The first shell I remember seeing burst a little over to my left nearly smashing an ambulance party with stretchers – the next thing I saw was one of our staff captains double up then run towards the ambulance to be attended to – then

Splott Road Hospital, Cardiff, where Bill Cowell was invalided back to the UK from the Dardanelles. (Bill Cowell)

our Colonel dropped with a bullet through his jaw. After that shells and bullets began to burst and spit amongst us properly and we knew we were copping it hot and strong. First one poor fellow would double up and fall then another poor chap would collapse all in a heap. I suddenly found out that we were all at the double though as far as I had heard, no order had actually been given. There are one or two more incidents which still stand out in my mind – one was the bursting of a shell a little to my right scattering bullets right through us. It was from this shell that most of the casualties in my troop were made and I distinctly remember ducking under a piece of it which ricked from the sand, sang just over me hitting someone on the left flank and smashing his rifle which was held up in front of his face to protect him – he came through unhurt. Another thing I remember was getting caught with some part of my equipment in some bushes and how bad tempered I got (to say the least of it) because I thought it would prevent me keeping up with my pals. I also remember how fearful the desire seemed to want to lie down behind each bush or tuft of grass to take useless cover. In fact most of us did start to get down in one place where the shells were falling the thickest but I think it was more through fatigue than anything else. However we had hardly touched the ground when our Adjutant, running from the rear, yelled, 'Come on boys, it's worse if you lie down!' So off we went again until we reached the safety of cover of Chocolate Hill. This was our baptism of fire which had to be done in cold blood because the enemy were absolutely invisible and we had no chance to get our own back in any way.[31]

The attempts to capture the high ground failed; even though the attempt upon Scimitar Hill by 29th Division initially succeeded in dense fog (which rendered artillery support ineffective), that too was ultimately repelled by Turkish fire from the hill's far slopes. With the troops unable to drive the Turks off the high ground, both sides dug in and the next day the attacks were renewed. Eyewitness Major John Gillam of the 29th Division commented:

> We did not attack at dawn and so the 88th have not been in action. We are as we were – yesterday's battle is not to be recorded as a victory for us. Machine guns again from right, left and centre fired from behind great boulders of stone and hidden hillocks covered with gorse, and wave after wave of our men were mown down as if with a scythe. Twice we captured the Burnt Hill [Scimitar Hill], but twice were driven off, and Burnt Hill remains Turkish. The Yeomanry were unable to get to grips with the enemy; but for gallantry in that march from Chocolate Hill to our front line, four hundred yards in front, across the open in daylight, under a hail of shrapnel and machine gun bullets, their behaviour could not have been excelled.[32]

Allied casualties in the Scimitar Hill action reached some 5,000, many of which were incurred after British artillery shrapnel resulted in surrounding bush catching fire. Turkish losses were put at 2,600.[33]

In spite of the additional soldiers thrown into the battle, and despite their obvious bravery, Hamilton's attacks against Hill 60 and Scimitar Hill in August 1915 came to nought. With Allied casualties running at around 40,000, the troops dug in and trench warfare began. No more major advances were attempted.

In his book *Memories of a Worcestershire Yeomanry Medical Officer*, Captain O. Teichman describes the advance:

> A Brigade of the Tenth Division and part of the Twenty-Ninth Division were to attack Hill 70, aided by our own Second and Fourth Mounted Brigades. A Brigade of the Eleventh Division was to attack Hill 112, aided by our First, Third and Fifth Mounted Brigades, with another Brigade in reserve; while the Divisions holding the trenches in the plain to the south were to rush the Turkish trenches in their front, then turn north-wards and converge on Hill 112 from the south.
>
> Meanwhile the Fifty-third, Fifty-fourth and Eleventh Divisions in the trenches to the north of Hill 70 were also to advance, and in the extreme south the Australians and Ghurkas from Anzac were to advance on Hill 60 and link up their line with our own trenches. The remaining Brigades of the various Divisions were in reserve. At 3.10 p.m. our Division and part of the Tenth formed up behind Lala Baba, and then, crossing the ridge, commenced

to descend to the Salt Lake plain. We were in the following order: Second Brigade (Berks, Bucks and Dorset Yeomanry), Fourth Brigade (three London Yeomanry Regiments), First Brigade (Worcester, Warwick and Gloucester Yeomanry), Third Brigade (Derbyshire and two Notts Yeomanry Regiments), Fifth Brigade (Hertfordshire and Westminster Yeomanry). Each Medical Officer and bearer party followed his own Brigade.

Not a shot was fired until we had gone a quarter of a mile and were well into the plain, when suddenly we seemed to walk into an inferno of shrapnel and H.E. Our first casualty was a Worcester yeoman with a spent bullet in his thigh. After that, men seemed to be dropping like flies. Finding an old Turkish trench, we made it our first Aid Post; this was soon full of wounded, dressed and labelled and fairly safe, as it was deep. I then looked for a Field Ambulance, but ours was at that moment only just starting down the hill behind the last Brigade, and the only Red Cross flag to be seen was 2 miles away across the Salt Lake. So, noting the position of our trench, we moved on. Selecting another Aid Post in a slight depression behind a stunted oak-tree, we were soon busy again bringing in the wounded. It was heartrending work, as so many were past hope of recovery; the proportion of killed was very great and many were quite unrecognisable. Three slightly wounded men were killed in our Aid Post as a shell burst over us.

The H.E. caused ghastly effects, as men were literally blown to pieces. My bearers worked splendidly, and brought the wounded in a perfect inferno of bursting shells. We found that we were now picking up chiefly Notts, Derby's, Inniskillings, Irish Fusiliers, Sherwood Foresters and Hertfordshire Yeomanry, as our Brigade had turned slightly northwards and we, being busy, had not noticed this, and had kept straight on. Our Aid Post now contained about fifty wounded and dying, and I was very relieved to suddenly see a Red Cross flag appear about 200 yards behind our position. This turned out to be our Second Mounted Brigade Field Ambulance, so, after detaching an orderly to inform them of the position of our first Aid Post and the one we were just vacating, we pushed on to form our third. We now entered a piece of land covered with tall rushes, which made the search for wounded difficult. Here I was working with several M.O.'s, but we each had our own zone to draw. On one occasion practically nothing was left of what had been two stretcher-bearers carrying a man. I came upon a group of five yeomen, quite dead in realistic attitudes, without a scratch on them, probably the concussion effect of H.E.

Several men unwounded had completely lost their reason and some were blind. Huge holes seemed to be torn in the squadrons as they advanced, but to quote Ashmead-Bartlett's report, 'they moved as if on parade, and losing many, they never wavered but pressed steadily on.' The Indian Mule Corps advancing with us to bring up ammunition showed the greatest contempt for the enemy's fire. Our men bore their wounds with the greatest courage, and our stretcher-bearers worked in the calm routine fashion, as if they were working at a Field Day on the Berkshire Downs or on the marshes of the East Coast.

One recognized now how important discipline and routine are on these occasions, when one saw each squad of three or four men performing their duties methodically. As we advanced the men of the Signal Companies, R.E., kept on laying their field telephone, and if one man, rolling his wheel over the ground, fell, there was always another behind to take it on. Here and there one came on large holes made by the H.E. shells; they were useful to put men into, as they were safe from rifle fire. We had to work as fast as possible in order to keep ahead of our Third and Fifth Brigades, which were following us, as we knew that if they passed us they would draw more fire on our wounded.

Intelligence reports informed us that the Turks were massing for a counterattack, which might be expected in the early dawn. At midday our ships' guns got to work again, and as we sat on our hill the shells passed directly over us. After lunch a letter was read from our Divisional General congratulating the Division on its magnificent behaviour under fire, and especially the Second Mounted Brigade (Berks, Bucks and Dorset Yeomanry) on the splendid way they had attacked Hill 70. Numerous telephone wires ran from the crest of our hill to Lala Baba and the beach, so that observation officers could inform our ships and Field Artillery of the effect of their fire.[34]

Captain Teichman goes on to describe the ghastly job on 22 August of cleaning up the results of the battle:

Meanwhile, the sections of our field ambulances which had remained under Chocolate Hill, I could see with my glasses, were having a rough time. After a bathe we lunched again in the little ravines by the sea; it was quite peaceful when the guns ceased to fire for a while, but we were not the merry party we had been twenty four hours before – some were missing, some killed and some wounded. At 7 pm we again left Lala Baba and crossed the Salt Lake to Chocolate Hill. Not a shell was dropped on us, only an occasional rifle shot. What a scene of desolation – dead men, mules, rifles, ammunition, helmets and emergency rations lay everywhere. As we marched slowly along, we came across some of our dead and hastily buried them whilst it was still possible. Most of these had not fired off any ammunition as they had been killed by shell fire long before they were within rifle range of the enemy. It was sad work, burying these men, mostly yeomen farmers in the prime of life and of splendid physique – the senseless slaughter of war seemed appalling when viewed calmly after the excitement of battle was over.

Eventually we caught up with our Brigade, who were lying on the ground at the foot of the hill. Whilst sitting on the ground, one man gave a little cough and rolled over against his neighbour quite dead. We could not find the cause of death at first, but it turned out that a dropping spent bullet had entered the left lung just behind the clavicle, leaving hardly any wound. The Division now ascended the hill, each Brigade had a small area allocated to it, and we began to dig in for the night. It was very hard work in the stiff clay, but a certain amount of corrugated iron and balks of timber were obtainable. Extra sandbags were issued to the men, as they used up those which they had carried on the previous day ...[35]

Subsequently, *The Times* wrote of the advance of the yeomanry at Suvla Bay as follows:

They advanced for two miles under a perfect hail of shrapnel. It was the Second Brigade under the Earl of Longford consisting of the Bucks, Berks and Dorsets, which made the final glorious charge, in conjunction with the 87th Brigade, and obtained temporary possession of Hill 70, which had to be subsequently abandoned in the night. The losses of this brigade were very heavy, the Bucks Regiment losing almost all of their officers and men.

The principal journalist embedded with the troops was Ellis Ashmead-Bartlett and his views and reporting has coloured many of our impressions of the whole sad business. He reports a conversation he had with General Peyton as follows:

On Chocolate Hill I met General Peyton, who commands the 2nd Mounted Division of Yeomanry. He gave me some details of the unfortunate experience of his division during the attack on the 21st. All now agree that it was one of the worst managed affairs yet seen on the Peninsula, which is saying a great deal. It seems that many generals resented having de Lisle, a cavalry man, placed over their head. No one knew their orders on the 21st, and some of the Yeomanry regiments had no idea of their objectives. Why on earth they were brought across the Salt Lake in broad daylight under heavy shrapnel fire, instead of being massed behind Chocolate Hill under cover of night, remains a mystery to this day. But this is only on a par with everything else.[36]

The effects would be felt for months and years after that fateful and doomed march. A butcher in Newport Pagnell, William Fleet, recorded many months later the shock of receiving a telegram from the Red Cross informing him that his son John, who was in the Bucks Hussars, had been taken prisoner during the battle for Chocolate Hill and taken to Constantinople where he had died of typhus fever. He had been intending to follow his father into

Bill Cowell (second from right) during his recuperation in the UK. (Bill Cowell)

the family business, but now his was just one more life spent in this all-encompassing conflict.

With both sides dug in, trench warfare became the order of the day, and with no major offensive action by either side, both the Turks and the Allied troops began to suffer badly in the heat of the Turkish summer. The conditions for the troops rapidly deteriorated and, for the British troops in particular, began a period of some three months of truly hellish conditions.

Rations consisted mainly of bully beef, which in this heat rapidly melted into a kind of liquid gooey mess, hard biscuits which were very much like dog biscuits, stale bread, apricot jam, some bacon and cheese and – the British staple – tea. This monotonous diet was rarely, if ever, altered and the troops suffered accordingly.

The chief problem was the flies which infiltrated everything and everywhere. Contemporary accounts refer to this menace as being the primary source of the soldiers' discomfort:

> One of the biggest curses was the flies. There were millions and millions of flies. The whole of the side of the trench used to be one black swarming mass. Anything you opened, a tin of bully, it would be swarming with flies. If you were lucky enough to have a tin of jam and opened it swarms of flies went into it. They were all round your mouth and on any cuts or sores that you'd got, which all turned septic through it. Immediately you bared any part of your body, you were smothered. It was a curse, it really was.[37]

In late September 1915 Bill Cowell fell sick and was evacuated back to the UK out of what had by now become a hellhole. He recuperated in Splott Road Hospital, Cardiff.[38] The conditions in Suvla Bay, with the rudimentary toilet facilities and the thousands of dead bodies inadequately or incompletely buried, led inevitably to disease. Dysentery began to infect the troops and soon the majority of soldiers were suffering from its debilitating effects. Soldiers frequently lacked the strength to reach the hastily dug latrine trenches and just lay helpless in their own filth and many simply died where they lay. There were even reports of soldiers being so weakened by disease that they fell into the overflowing latrine trenches and drowned in excrement.[39]

Officers were not immune and suffered the same atrocious conditions as their men. Writing home, Major Fred Lawson records, 'I am myself inclined to agree with Crocker (John Crocker Bulteel) that we were all of us killed in France and that this is hell!'[40]

In a letter to Lord Burnham dated 15 October 1915, he writes, 'We have lost about 55% of what we brought in.' He then goes on to describe the state of his fellow officers, 'Crocker is still here, Evelyn (de Rothschild), Percy Barker and Young. Evelyn, I am sure will not be with us long, but he is sticking it extraordinarily well, but looks very ill. I am rather moderate with this infernal diarrhoea, but bar the bullets will see a lot out yet.'[41]

Later in the same letter, when his feelings obviously get the better of him, he rails against a fellow officer:

> Have you seen John Grenfell? He went home with diarrhoea, but was not too bad to be smoking a large cigar as the hospital ship sailed out of Mudros Harbour. They had better put him in charge of a munitions factory and I hope someone will see that he doesn't get a war medal. He probably won't have stood it, but he might have had a try. At least gone into hospital in Mudros for a bit and given it a chance instead of thrusting his way onto the homeward bound hospital ship the moment the orders arrived for him to come on. I have heard that heavy shelling is known to precipitate that sort of complaint, but have never known a previous case of it happening at 63 miles range.[42]

His anger at those he believes are out of it is perhaps understandable and even the politicians do not escape when he writes to his wife: 'I should very much like to have Winston tied to the end of the pier here every morning at 9 o'clock when the shelling commences with regularity and watch him from the seclusion of my dugout.'[43]

In the main, the Bucks Hussars seem to have stuck to the unenviable task well and even kept a sense of humour. Fred Lawson describes, in a letter to his wife, how one of his troopers was heard to observe that he had joined up to fight on a horse, but had become 60 per cent navvy and 40 per cent pack mule.

In one letter, Lawson goes as far as to write a pastiche on the old children's song 'Ten Green Bottles' in which the Bucks Hussars take the place of the green bottles:

> Ten little Bucks Hussars sitting in a line
> Zip comes a bullet then there were nine.
> Nine little Bucks Hussars digging on till late.
> One got a septic hand then there were eight.
> Eight little Bucks Hussars looking up to heaven.
> Plop comes a whizz bang then there were seven.
> Seven little Bucks Hussars working with their picks.
> One puts it through his toe then there were six.
> Six little Bucks Hussars trying to contrive
> A new way of throwing bombs then there were five.
> Five little Bucks Hussars thinking of the war.
> One consults a doctor and then there were four.
> Four little Bucks Hussars bathing in the sea.
> Turks looks through a telescope and a shell leaves only three.
> Three little Bucks Hussars eat some bully stew.
> One gets a tummy ache then there were two.
> Two little Bucks Hussars plenty to be done,
> One dies of overwork then there was one.
> One little Bucks Hussar thinks the war poor fun,
> Goes home a specimen then there was none.[44]

Jaundice and paratyphoid (known as enteric fever) were becoming rife and the effect on new arrivals of seeing the state of the troops can only be imagined:

> We walked around after a time like skeletons, finding it difficult even to move at times. If we were out of line on fatigues like water carrying or helping to dig roads and so on it was as much as we could do to lift the tools or whatever we were carrying. There was a time when down on the beach some reinforcements arrived and looking at them it was quite clear the contrast between what would be normal and after life on Gallipoli after a few months. These young fellows had come out from home and we were quite struck with their fresh rosy complexions, we almost thought they were from another world. They too, I suppose, would look at us and see these sallow, lean skeletons and regard us too as from another world.[45]

It is hard to believe that not far from the Dardanelles at Crimea, some sixty to seventy years earlier, the British Army had learnt lessons about how disease could decimate their army. As a result of the publicity and the public horror at what had happened, massive changes had taken place in military medical and supply support. Now, in the twentieth century, it was happening again, and yet again British soldiers were dying from dysentery and gangrenous wounds. It was as if the Crimea had never happened.

With the dismounted yeomanry troops severely depleted in numbers, mainly through sickness but also through battle casualties, the decision was taken at the end of October 1915 to evacuate the remaining troops back to Egypt via Mudros. Of the original 260 men and officers of the Royal Bucks Yeomanry, just sixty were fit for duty by the end of October. Lt Col C.A. Grenfell, Major St John, Captain Cripps, and Lieutenants Rothschild, Fairbairn, Jones, Barker, Grove, Clarke, Bennett and Pearson were all invalided out. General Peyton commanding the 2nd Mounted Division expressed his appreciation to the yeomanry in the following words:

> The GOC 2nd Mounted Division wishes to convey to all ranks his great appreciation of the soldier-like qualities and fortitude which have been so markedly evinced during the last two months in the face of heavy losses sustained in the action of 21st August followed by exposure, often in a cramped and crowded situation. Subject to incessant shell-fire, which caused many casualties, the division has been called upon whilst continually under fire and suffering from the ravages of sickness to carry out abnormal physical and manual exertions to maintain and improve our defences. The time has now arrived that the troops should be withdrawn and rested, and the GOC feels sure that, when reinforcements arrive and the Brigades are reorganised, they will return with the same indomitable determination to face all hardships and difficulties which the service of their King and Country demands.[46]

Despite the best efforts of all of the troops involved in this last offensive on Gallipoli, it was becoming obvious to the authorities in London that throwing more and more troops at Gallipoli was not going to give the Allies any great strategic advantage. Lord Kitchener asked Sir Ian Hamilton to review the options for evacuation and what the possible losses might be. Evacuation was not ordered at that point, but the mere thought of such an action sounded alarm bells with Sir John Maxwell, who was in charge in Egypt. Releasing further Turkish forces from defending the Gallipoli Peninsula was likely to add to the pressure on the Suez Canal. Despite his worries, the Western Front in Northern France and Belgium was still the place where the war would be won or lost, and every soldier was needed to strengthen the Allied forces. To continue to reinforce failure in Gallipoli was simply unacceptable and evacuation of the whole peninsula was the only sensible option. On 14 October 1915 the Dardanelles Committee ordered evacuation. Before doing so, there was the time-honoured job of sacking the generals.

General Sir Ian Hamilton was relieved of his command in October 1915 and replaced by Lt General Sir Charles Monro, who was utterly convinced that the war could only be won in France and Belgium. General Sir Ian Hamilton would never again hold an active service position and retired back to the UK to consider how best to put a good light on the whole operation in his memoirs. One particularly poignant extract from his diaries laments that 'I did not know, to tell you the truth, that they [the Turks] were nearly as good as they turned out to be.'[47]

It is worth mentioning that early pre-war intelligence backed up General Sir Ian Hamilton's initial appraisal of his foe. Early reports had dismissed the Turkish soldier as being inferior, badly led and poorly equipped and, as such, an unworthy foe of the modern, well-equipped British Army. However, events both in Gallipoli, and subsequently in Egypt and Palestine, seemed to rebut this view. Since 1883, the Turkish Army had had German advisers working along-side them and in 1913, following the Second Balkans War, General Otto Liman von Saunders became Inspector General of the Turkish Army together with some seventy other German officers, and by the end of 1914 this had become a cadre of nearly 500 German officers. The problems they encountered were enormous, especially with artillery, motorised transport and general equip-ment. One thing that was not in question was the temperament and steadiness of the average Anatolian Turkish infantryman. Whilst the technical and supply side needed an enormous amount of work, the hardiness of the average soldier was exemplary.

Germany and Austria-Hungary were able to make good many of the equip-ment and technical deficiencies in Palestine and Egypt, which left the basic infantry duties to the Turkish soldier. They proved more than adequate for the job and were renowned for being able to endure extremely harsh conditions in the desert. One of the principle reasons for this was that they seemed to have the ability to survive on very salty water which the British and Anzac troops simply dismissed as undrinkable. They also proved to be impervious to many of the diseases which the Allies succumbed to. When well dug in, they proved to be steady under shellfire and in the main were excellent marksmen. Together with their German military advisers they performed well, albeit mainly in defensive mode. One thing that all the Allied mounted troops were agreed on was the remarkable ability of the Turks to march at high speed in the heat and aridity of the desert. Turkish foot soldiers were often able to outpace the mounted troops over considerable distances in the desert.

Field Marshal Lord Wavell was to comment subsequently in his analysis of the Palestine campaign that it was a mistake to underestimate the Turkish soldier. He pointed out quite correctly that the Turks had succeeded in Gallipoli, Kut, and at the first two battles of Gaza, albeit with German assistance. In short, in the right conditions and led by good officers, they were a worthy foe for any army.

The Royal Bucks Hussars brought into the shore on boats at Suvla Bay. (Mike Holland)

What remained of the yeomanry forces following the attacks at Suvla Bay was evacuated from Gallipoli on a converted warship, HMS *Hannibal*. They were ferried to the ship via a large, flat ferry steamer prior to transferring to the warship in the bay. Initially evacuated to Mudros, they were subsequently moved back to where they had originally sailed from, Alexandria in Egypt.

The Gallipoli debacle ended General Sir Ian Hamilton's military career. He returned to England where he lived on into a long retirement well into his nineties. His account of the campaign called 'Gallipoli Diary' makes it clear that he felt badly let down by those who purported to be his leaders.

Opinion amongst the experts seems to be split as to whether there was ever any chance of success in the Gallipoli campaign. Hamilton was not involved in the initial planning so can be absolved from that particular blame. However, having gone ahead with the landings, he took a very 'hands off' and trusting attitude with his subordinate commanders and for that he has to accept some of the culpability.

The first assault having produced, at best, a stalemate, the final chance for a significant strategic success came with the Suvla Bay landings and the simultaneous breakout from Anzac Cove. Here the planning was clearly Hamilton's responsibility and he has to accept a great deal of blame for the outcome of the August campaign but, at the same time, there is some truth in his published contention that London supported the whole campaign with insufficient enthusiasm. Perhaps with greater resources something positive may have been salvaged from the Dardanelles campaign, but it is unlikely to have had a significant strategic effect on the outcome of the war as a whole.

Among the British company commanders at Suvla Bay was one Clement Attlee, who subsequently rose to be Prime Minister. He was a captain in the South Lancashire Regiment. He wrote the following in his autobiography:

> The Gallipoli Campaign will always remain a very vivid memory. I have always held that the strategic conception was sound. The trouble was that it was never adequately supported. Often I have thought how near we came to victory, and I have tried to work out what the consequences would have been in that event. Unfortunately the military authorities were Western-Front-minded. Reinforcements were always sent too late. For an enterprise such as this the right leaders were not chosen. Elderly and hidebound generals were not the men to push through such an adventure of this kind. Had we had at Suvla generals like Maude, who came out later, we should, I think, have pushed through to victory. Even as it was we came near to success. But for General Baldwin's column losing its way, it would have joined the Ghurkas and the South Lancashires on Sari Bair. But for Mustapha Kemal Pasha being in command of a Turkish division at the crucial point, we might have held that height. It was a tragic failure. I always feel a sympathy with all old Gallipolians; as James Thomson the poet says, I feel the stir of fellowship in all disastrous fights.[48]

With slight changes in place names and regiments, these words could serve as a requiem for so many failed military campaigns. It was a close run affair with so many 'ifs' and 'maybes', but overall was undoubtedly marked, and ultimately condemned to failure, by the high degree of senior military incompetency. What vigorous and virile leadership could have achieved is a matter for conjecture. However, the replacement commander-in-chief, Lieutenant General Sir Charles Monro, pulled off a stunning military coup by extracting all of the troops from the peninsula without loss of life. In a brilliant series of deceptions carried out in pitch darkness, all of the troops were successfully evacuated onto ships without casualties, leaving the peninsula once again to the victorious Turkish Army. If military talent such as this had been available earlier in an offensive rather than an evacuation role, what might have been achieved?

The last word should perhaps remain with the victors. In 1934, Ataturk, the founder of the modern Turkish state and one of its brightest Great War military commanders, had these words carved on a massive stone plinth situated on the Gallipoli Peninsula:

> Those heroes that shed their blood and lost their lives, you are now lying in the soil of a friendly country. Therefore rest in peace. There is no difference between the Johnnies and the Mehmets to us where they lie side by side here in this Country of ours … You, the mothers, who sent their sons from far

away countries, wipe away your tears; your sons are now lying in our bosom and are in peace. After having lost their lives in this land they have become our sons as well.

Bill Cowell would have left Gallipoli having learned several valuable lessons, as would all the members of the Bucks Yeomanry. He had been 'blooded' and had advanced against a well-dug-in enemy, through both heavy artillery and machine gun defences, without losing his discipline and without breaking ranks. He had survived in trenches overlooked by the enemy, seen death on a daily basis and fought off the effects of illness. He was now a proper soldier used to warfare, not the weekend soldier the yeomanry were often portrayed as. He also now knew that however bravely and professionally soldiers fight, if the plans are useless and if the General Staff don't know what they are doing or are not up to the job, then the attacks will fail. Bravery alone cannot make up for incompetent leadership. He was not a great deal older, but he was a great deal wiser, especially in the ways of warfare.

For Bill Cowell, now recuperated in Britain and awaiting a ship to rejoin his regiment in Egypt, his next meeting with the Turkish soldier would eventually see the boot on the other foot.

6

EGYPT

For many people of my age, one of our earliest brushes with poetry was Lord Tennyson's tribute to the Light Brigade and their exploits during the Crimean War. One of the closing stanzas in the poem goes as follows:

> Reel'd from the sabre stroke,
> Shatter'd and sunder'd.
> Then they rode back, but not,
> Not the six hundred.[49]

The yeomanry leaving Gallipoli would have felt something similar for they were much altered in body, in numbers and in knowledge of war. From now on they were soldiers, blooded in battle, but their next theatre of operations was to be very different from that which they had just endured. The men landed at Alexandria and moved to encampments alongside the Suez Canal to rest, recuperate, to be reunited with their horses and to rebuild the muscles necessary for horse riding.

Nor were their Turkish foes unchanged by their experience. They were bolstered by victory in the Gallipoli Peninsula and could now concentrate their forces on the Middle East. They had already made an abortive attempt to cut Britain's link to the Empire – the Suez Canal – and now they could expand their objectives to the Caucasus and Mesopotamia.[50]

By early 1916, General Sir Archibald J. Murray was in charge of a considerable number of troops renamed the Egyptian Expeditionary Force (EEF). Both armies –British and Turkish – were reinforced by veterans withdrawn from Gallipoli.

Sir Archibald Murray (1860–1945) had at the start of the First World War been Chief of Staff to the Commander-in-Chief of the British Expeditionary Force, Sir John French. This combination did not work out that well. French's irresolution was exacerbated by Murray's nervous disposition. He reputedly once fainted upon receiving bad news from the front! Murray's appointment as Chief of Staff had in any case been a compromise solution as the obvious candidate Sir Henry Wilson had rather blotted his copybook with the 'Curragh Mutiny' and was thus considered politically unacceptable. As soon as it became obvious that Murray was not of the calibre required on the Western Front he was moved to the Mediterranean command, which was considered an easier post for his temperament. Soon, two competing positions of command were combined and Murray took command of the EEF.

With the troops evacuated from Gallipoli and other British imperial troops brought in from India and the Antipodes, the Army in Egypt became the largest UK military force outside France and the UK. Some time early in the new year, Bill Cowell rejoined his comrades in A Squadron and, no doubt, soon settled back into the military life in what would have appeared to be a 'cushier number' than Gallipoli. The majority of the men were quartered in the desert close to or east of the banks of the Suez Canal (whence, of course, the main Turkish threat would originate). Many of the newly billeted troops were close to, or could expect leave in, the major Egyptian centres of population together with all the eastern delights that implied. This enabled the remounted yeomanry troops to recover and start to get used to a style of combat that they were better trained for – mobile warfare on horseback where the enemy could be seen and fought on level terms.

Conditions in Egypt, whilst undoubtedly more healthy than those in the recently occupied Gallipoli, were still some way short of five star. A soldier serving in the 53rd Division describes the problems of digging defensive positions in the sandy desert conditions east of Suez:

> Mile upon mile of rolling sand hills, a burning expanse unrelieved by tree or bush – such was our new home, some miles east of the canal. The Brigade was spread over a thirteen mile front, in a series of defended posts, located on commanding sand dunes. Here is spent countless hours of toil, digging and sand bagging – and then destroying the fruits of hard labour and beginning all over again. Never was there such a pointless waste of time, temper and energy. The heat was intense and the flies were a pest.[51]

During early spring the Egyptian desert was swept with scorching winds from the south-west which carried the fine sand into every available crevice. Trenches that had been laboriously dug could be filled within hours and any movement of personnel was almost impossible.

The climate generally was not one that a Buckinghamshire farmer would take to naturally. With a maximum annual rainfall of 1–2in, which usually fell on one or two days during the year, most parts of central and southern Egypt had several years without any significant rainfall. When rain did fall, it was usu-

A Bucks Hussar mounted at a camp in the Sinai Desert. (Bill Cowell)

ally in the form of a brief and sometimes damaging downpour, often causing local floods and washing away tents and defensive trenches etc.

For much of the time, however, the winter weather was warm and sunny with few cold days which occasionally occurred when there were strong northerly winds. So far as the British Army was concerned the most unpleasant weather was caused when very hot winds from the Sahara blew in, often for days at a time. These hot dry *khamsin* winds were dust-laden and raised sand particles from the desert which obscured visibility and irritated eyes, nose and mouth. They were particularly difficult conditions for the horses.

A soldier of the EEF described the experience thus:

Men rushed blindly for their tents and swathed their heads in shirts or blankets in order to keep out as well as might be the flying particles of sand. For three days it raged. Little was possible beyond watering and feeding the horses. The short walk from the horse-lines to the watering troughs was sheer torment, for the hot wind came down the slopes like blasts from a furnace. It did literally turn the stomach. Many a man staggering blindly along with his three or four horses would pause, vomit violently and carry on.[52]

Summer temperatures regularly exceeded 115°F and the ever-present sand flies played havoc with both the troops and the horses.

An officer of the Bucks Hussars. Behind is a typical stable block to shelter horses from the Egyptian sun. (Bill Cowell)

In addition, although leave was granted for the troops to visit Alexandria and Cairo during the time that Bill Cowell served in Egypt, no home leave was granted. Despite the efficiency of the British Forces' postal system, this obviously led to homesickness and a deep-seated longing to see green fields again.

Trooper Arthur Mapley of the Bucks Hussars wrote home to his parents thus to describe his experiences in Egypt:

I am glad to say I am feeling alright. Of course, it is very hot and trying after coming out from England where it was so cold. We are camping near a very large town, and allowed out until 10 o' clock at night, so we are having quite a fine time. We are paid out twelve shillings in piastres – that is 2½d in English money. There is another coin which is half a farthing, so that we can get a hatful of money for about two shillings. I am unable to tell you where we are or what we are doing as our letters are now censored before being sealed down, so it is impossible for us to write about anything important. How are things looking at old Newport? About the same I expect. I wish you would send me a Bucks Standard sometimes, as it would be interesting to get news from old Bucks. That will be the time when we return. We had a narrow squeak on our way out. The boat that followed us from Bristol – the Wayfarer

– was torpedoed by the Germans. I daresay you saw the account of it in the papers. I am unable to write more this time as I have got to get dinner up, for I have gone back to my old job of cooking.[53]

As well as illustrating the conditions as conceived by the eyes of a young man, this letter also helps to explain the allure of warfare. The good times with men of one's own age, travel to foreign countries, comparatively good pay by the standards of the time and the feeling that for once in your life you are doing something important. The letter expresses all of this together with the youth's irrepressible belief that he will be returning to Bucks at some stage in the future.

Whilst General Murray may not have been one of England's finest fighting soldiers, he was an extremely able administrator and he was well suited to dealing with the problems facing him on arrival. Defences and, more importantly, the infrastructure necessary for such defences, needed enormous resources and transport. General Murray set to and increased the capacity on the Cairo-Ismailia railway enormously. To do so took the movement of some 400,000 cubic yards of earth and the transport of over 150,000 tons of material. He organised a camel transport corps of some 50,000 animals. All of this required huge amounts of manpower, both military and civilian. At the same time, he was very conscious of his orders from the Chief of the Imperial General Staff, Field Marshal Sir W. Robertson, sent to him on 29 December 1915:

1. You will realise that the force under your command in Egypt is of the nature of a general strategical reserve for the Empire.

A Bucks Hussar at camp in Egypt. (Bill Cowell)

It is at present quite uncertain what the future action of the enemy in the East and the Near East may be. The Turks may elect to make their main effort in Mesopotamia, while demonstrating against Egypt, or they may make their main effort against the latter country. Again, they may decide to employ their forces in Europe, set free by the vacation of Gallipoli, to assist the Central Powers and Bulgaria in operations in the Balkans or against Rumania.

The War Committee has decided that, for us, France is the main theatre of war. It is therefore important that as soon as the situation in the East is clearer, no more troops should be maintained there than are absolutely necessary, but circumstances may make it necessary to reinforce our troops in Mesopotamia or India or in both. You should therefore be prepared to detach troops from Egypt when and if the situation makes this advisable.

2. Both for the defence of Egypt and for the creation of an effective stra-
tegical reserve, the first requirement is to reorganise the troops in Egypt and to get the depleted and tired divisions from Gallipoli in a condition to take the field ...[54]

This does appear to be of such masterly vagueness and so all-encompassing in its lists of possibilities that it probably brought on a fresh fit of vapours in General Murray. It should also be said in General Murray's defence that, when he received these orders, he was not in charge of all of the British military forces in the area. The authorities in London had cobbled together a command structure which gave command of part of the Egyptian forces to Murray, and the rest to General J. Maxwell. It was not until March 1916 that the situation was sorted out and General Murray given overall command of the whole of the EEF, and General Maxwell dispatched back to the UK.[55]

The EEF was expecting to face the Turks again in battle, but before it could fully concentrate on the Turkish threat another hostile force needed to be dealt with. In the desert and along the coastal strip west of Alexandria (modern day Libya) lived a nomadic people known as the Senussi, named after their leader the 'Grand Senussi'. The Senussi sect was founded by Mohammed Ali el Senussi, who was born in Algeria in 1787 and completed his education in Mecca. His doctrine was a reversion to the original Koranic Law in its simplest form. Mohammed Ali el Senussi settled in the Benghazi district, or Cyrenaica, just beyond the present western frontier of Egypt, and rapidly gained a religious following throughout North Africa from Tunis to the Red Sea. By 1915, the holder of the title 'Grand Senussi' was Sayed Ahmed.

Initially there was no conflict between the Senussi and the British. However, the Turks worked tirelessly to change this state of affairs. The Grand Senussi was a religious rather than a military/political leader, but Sayed Ahmed had taken the tribes to war following the Italian occupation of Libya in 1911. He had not attacked the British based in Egypt as he had considered this to be outside his sphere of influence. In addition the British were well served by their intelligence officer, Lt Col Snow, who had influence with the Senussi hierarchy who admired his approach and fairness.

In a society where religion played such a central part and so intimately affected political decision making, the Grand Senussi was probably ripe for being influenced against the British non-Muslim forces. Turkish money, the perception of the Turks as the winning side, and the leader's wish to cement his rather precarious hold on power were all serving to push the Grand Senussi closer to the German-Turkish side. His hold on power was not certain as he had taken over from his uncle, the previous leader Mohammed el Mahdi, rather than the obvious successor who would have been Mohammed's eldest son. He had been only 14 at the time of his father's death, but by 1915 he was in his mid-twenties and there were mutterings that Sayed Ahmed should stand down and allow him to assume his rightful role. As has so often been the case, Sayed Ahmed could see that a call to unite against a foreign threat would do much to cement his hold on power.

Nuri Bey was the Turk entrusted to treat with the Senussi and he was given generous funding to smooth his way into their confidence. Although General Murray and his political advisers, including Lt Col Snow, did all they could to paper over differences, by November 1915 the Senussi were beginning to act in an extremely provocative, not to say downright hostile, way.

In the first week of November two British steamers, *Tara* and *Moorina*, were torpedoed by German submariners and the captive crews were handed over to the Senussi. Despite strong protests from the British, the Grand Senussi protested his innocence and pretended not to know the prisoners' whereabouts. This represented the breaking point for the British authorities, and Major General Wallace was tasked with forming a Western Frontier Force to deal with what was now regarded as an outright hostile force which threatened the western side of the Suez Canal.

Part of A Squadron of the Royal Bucks Hussars had stayed in Egypt when the rest of the regiment deployed to Gallipoli. Following this new threat, they were required to form part of a composite force under the command of Captain L. Cheape (Kings Dragoon Guards). This force was deployed from Matruh some 180 miles west of the River Nile to fight the Senussi. After the return of B and C Squadrons from Gallipoli and after a suitable period of rest and recuperation and the arrival of reinforcements, the RBH were reunited at Matruh on 14 December 1915. At this point the regiment came under the control of Lieutenant Colonel John Grenfell.

On Christmas morning 1915 the newly reunited Hussars marched out of camp to begin a campaign as part of a column – they were heading towards Jebel Medwa where they anticipated the Senussi were camped. The Hussars rode for some six hours through the desert in a wide half-circle to come upon the Senussi between two *wadis* (valleys or riverbeds), Wadi Senab and Wadi Majid. The action was basically unsuccessful although the Senussi were forced to withdraw. The problem was that the yeomanry troops, employed as forward scouts, were not sufficiently in advance of the main column to provide adequate warning of ambush and, as a result, the right flank of the column came under attack at short range. The yeomanry charged the attackers, which proved ineffectual, and the armoured motor vehicles were forced to intervene. Australian mounted troops were also brought in before the Senussi withdrew. The action finished with sixteen Allied deaths and seventeen wounded, including Lieutenant J.D. Young of the Royal Bucks Hussars. Lieutenant W.B. Bowyer of the Royal Bucks Hussars describes the day as follows:

reveille before two in the morning, our first experience of saddling up in the dark, getting feeds, rations etc. and we form up about two thirty. Our Colonel [Lt Col John Grenfell] wishes us a happy Christmas and we move away into the night, passing other bodies of troops moving off, with artillery rumbling along, irons clanking, and all the familiar sounds of a night march. We ride off to the west of Matruh, the Australian Light Horse riding round in a large circling movement to the east driving the Senussi towards us. We creep along in the dark, all unknown country, and waiting for the sun to shoot up. Immediately after sunrise 'A' squadron are in action on our right. We pull off the road and the guns gallop into action in the open, firing over the Sikhs who had got into position during the night about a mile in front of us. Soon after this, a British gunboat cruising off the coast joins in, shelling the ravines and wadis with H.E. It was all a fine setting for our baptism of fire, more like the Boer War fighting, plenty of rifle fire, and everybody in the open.

As the day wore on curiously enough we seemed to have a cessation midday for our Christmas dinner, bully and biscuits. We keep working round their flanks like a horseshoe, with our artillery and infantry in the curved part. Darkness fell about five o'clock and saved them today from a decisive smashing but they will not again worry Matruh as they retreat towards Shamash leaving about four hundred dead. Our casualties are reported about two hundred and fifty. We start back for Matruh, a fifteen mile ride, about five o'clock. About seven it comes on to rain, a steady downpour, soon all are wet through. The ride seems interminable but eventually we get back to the beach at Matruh, feed, and have some very salt tea given out to us, which with biscuits forms our supper.[56]

Amazingly, for this part of the world, heavy rainfall interfered with further actions against the Senussi until 23 January 1916, when the Bucks Hussars again mounted up as part of a composite column to engage the Senussi at Halazin, some 25 miles south of their camp at Matruh. In the attack that followed, the Hussars found that the ground was so swampy that mounted attacks were simply impossible. They dismounted and operated with some considerable success as infantry, and by 4.00 p.m. the Senussi were in retreat. However, the action was indecisive and allowing the Senussi to withdraw whenever they felt hard-pressed was obviously not going to put down the rebellion – in addition the British troops sustained over 300 casualties. Because of the soft going and the lack of water, the mounted troops were unable to pursue the enemy who were able to withdraw and break off the engagement whenever they felt pushed to do so.

Again Lieutenant Bowyer describes the action:

Towards the middle of January the weather improved, and as our aeroplane reports the Senussi encamped at some wells about ten miles away, we make preparations to get after them. Leaving camp about 21 January our troops did the flank guard to the column and we bivouac down for a few hours before setting off for the scrap early Sunday morning – our favourite fighting day! It was a bitterly cold morning and we got some way from our resting place before running into the enemy. The cavalry open out to let the Sikhs through to the attack. I should say that today the Senussi put up their best fight, as, very fleet of foot, and supported by a few trained Turks, they were continually trying to outflank us. We raced out to the left flank, quite exhilarating, though several come purlers through bullets and also boggy ground. Soon we dismount for action and fighting becomes pretty hot, we lay firing until the enemy are about 400 yards away, when we race for our horses and away, while the artillery opens on the Senussi in the open. Our wounded, poor fellows, have a rough ride, there being a limber full of them with broken limbs, and all laying on top of each other. Crocker Bulteel our Squadron leader, shows his worth, giving his horse to a wounded man, and running some time on foot.

I am a section leader now, and Densfield brings our horses up in a terrible tangle. Croxford's mounts get bowled over, and Dover's little mare won't stand but we get away full cry. Dover, very good company in a scrap, and we blaze away quite enjoying it. Our friendship started in this troop at Matruh in 1915 and was only broken by his death in Palestine in 1917. We form up again to cover the artillery but the Senussi counter-attack clears away and late in the afternoon we are left masters of the field, but far from our transport with the rations and necessities for the wounded. Our loss about 270. Senussi's unknown.[57]

Both engagements demonstrated that the EEF had much to learn about desert fighting and how to move forces about the desert whilst keeping them and the transport animals fit and provisioned in order to fight. Both horses and motorised vehicles needed water and, as a result of these two inconclusive actions against the local tribesmen, the make-up of the composite column was changed. The armoured cars which up until now had been heavy, much-modified Rolls-Royces, were changed for lighter scout cars and a machine gun battery was added. Most tellingly, however, 2,000 camels were added to the force, giving them the ability to penetrate and manoeuvre in the desert for longer periods.

A saddler in the Bucks Hussars, A. Chapman, wrote home to his parents to describe their life in the desert:

> I need not describe the trek across the desert and the two battles we took part in, but I must tell you of my last escapade. We had captured a flock of sheep and lambs. Last Friday we had hungered for the taste of lamb, so some from my tent sallied forth, captured a lamb, slaughtered and dressed it. The feast was fixed for last night and we lit the fire cut the lamb up and commenced to fry parts of it. Some of our fellows found some onions in a very exposed position down at the dock. These we boiled. The meat was nicely done, handed round proportionately, and we commenced to relish it. Remarks were passed on the cooking etc. We had been eating about ten minutes when we were startled by hearing bang! biff! bang!! and bullets came whistling along. One or two tents were hit. We rushed out with our rifles, saddled our horses, and then crawled into positions around the camp. Fortunately it proved to be the work of snipers, and no one was hit. The excitement died down, but in the rush our mutton was knocked into the sand and spoilt. We shall have to try our luck again. It is a bit of a sensation when bullets are flying over you, and I ducked fairly low. The men in action against us are called Sa-lou-chees. They are very cruel, and I trust I shall never fall into their hands. The Berkshire Yeomanry made a charge and rushed down a gulley – all holes – and one poor fellow's horse bolted with him right into the enemy's hands, and they nearly cut him into bits … The enemy must live under very hard conditions as regards food for all their transport is done by camels.[58]

The next action saw B Squadron, RBH being redeployed with the Dorset Yeomanry and sent out to Barrani on 20 February. Almost immediately, they were attacked by a strong force of Senussi tribesmen but managed to beat off the onslaught. At dawn the next morning the column moved out of camp to ride some 14 miles south-east to Agagia where aerial reconnaissance had revealed that the main bulk of the Senussi were entrenched.

The Western Frontier Force which was sent to defeat the Senussi was a multi-disciplinary force which included horse- and camel-mounted troops, motorised armoured vehicles and infantry. As such, it foreshadowed what was to take place later, during the Palestinian campaign. The column caught up with some 1,500 Senussi tribesmen and, with the aid of the Bucks and Dorset

Yeomanry, was able to pin them down such that the infantry could advance against them. There then took place a three-hour fire fight between the South African infantry forces and the Senussi riflemen who were aided by Turkish machine gunners. Eventually the infantry lost touch with the enemy and the armoured cars became bogged down in soft sand.

The Bucks Hussars took off after the Senussi camel force which by now had left the main battle, leaving the Dorset Yeomanry plus odd members of the Bucks Hussars as the only force still in touch with the by now retreating Senussi. Lieutenant-Colonel Souter of the Dorset Yeomanry was the officer commanding but Second Lieutenant J.H. Blaksley describes what happened next:

> The led horses were whistled up, we were ordered to mount and form line. Then and not till then we knew what was coming. Imagine a perfectly flat plain of firm sand without a vestige of cove and 1,200 yards in front of us a slight ridge; behind this and facing us were the four machine guns and at least five hundred men with rifles. You might well think it madness to send 180 Yeomen riding at this. The Senussi, too, are full of pluck and handy with their machine guns and rifles, but they are not what we should call first class shots; otherwise I don't see how we could have done it. We were spread out in two ranks, eight yards roughly between each man of the front rank and four yards in the second. This was how we galloped for well over half a mile straight into their fire. The amazing thing is that when we reached them not one man in ten was down. At first they fired very fast and you saw the bullets knocking up the sand in front of you, as the machine guns pumped them out. But as we kept getting nearer, they began to lose their nerve and (I expect) forgot to lower their sights. Anyhow the bullets began to go over us and we saw them firing wildly and beginning to run; but some of them – I expect the Turkish Officers – kept the machine guns playing on us.[59]

Lieutenant Blaksley's horse was shot from under him, as was a riderless replacement he managed to grab. However, he goes on to describe how, with Lt Col Souter now with him, the Force Commander of the Senussi, Jaafar Pasha, surrendered to them. He goes on to explain the final stages of the battle:

> Meanwhile the rest of the Senussites were running in all directions, shrieking and yelling and throwing away their arms and belongings; the Yeomen after them sticking them through the backs and slashing right and left with their swords … some stood their ground, and by dodging the swords and shooting at two or three yards range first our horses and then our men, accounting for most of our casualties.[60]

Finally, the machine gun section caught up with the action and brought it to a successful conclusion. The British lost four officers and twenty-seven men with two officers and twenty-four men wounded.

The Dorset Yeomanry had charged the retreating Senussi, in order to break up their retreat, with tired horses at the end of a long day across 1,000 yards under heavy fire. Some sixty dead or wounded yeomanry were lost out of the 184 men who took part in the charge. The commanding officer of the Dorsets reported that the Senussi never again stood to await a British attack. It showed that in this particular theatre of war against a less than determined foe, steel and troops on horseback could still play a valuable role in twentieth-century warfare. It was not always to be so.

With the capture of Jaafar Pasha, the Turkish instigator of the uprising, the Senussi army dispersed. Their HQ at Sollum was reoccupied on 14 March and the British could now concentrate on the Turkish threat. The danger posed to the Suez Canal by the Senussi tribesmen was not a really credible military threat, but the campaign did bring up several interesting aspects before they were finally defeated and enabled the EEF to start learning some lessons which would be invaluable later on when the going got tougher. Foremost amongst these was the fact that the war in Sinai and Palestine was to be a war of movement in stark contrast to that being fought by their comrades in France. Movement in the desert required camels, railroads and motorised transport and all of these obviously required water supplies. Whilst fresh water existed in Egypt in great quantities it was all in the Nile and its associated lakes – somehow this would have to be made available across the Sinai Peninsula if a forward defence was to become a possibility.

In the meantime, whilst the planners considered the logistical problems, the distribution of medals took place and Captains Bulteel and Primrose from the Royal Bucks Hussars received the Military Cross for their leadership.

The Senussi leader Sayed Ahmed's leadership was undermined by the military defeat and he was eventually deposed in favour of his nephew Sayyid Mohammed el Idris, who had opposed the uprising from the start and indeed had gone into exile in Constantinople. Idris would soon be recognised by the British and Italians as Emir of Cyrenaica and would eventually become King Idris I of Libya, founding a dynasty that would later be deposed by Colonel Gaddafi. As I write these words, Colonel Gaddafi himself has just been deposed and killed by revolutionary forces as part of the latest coup to shake the Middle East.

7

CROSSING THE SINAI DESERT AND THE BATTLES FOR GAZA

The eradication of the threat to the Canal from the western deserts moved the focus back to the threat from the East. Defensive duties were supplanted by a more aggressive stance against the Turks and there began a move back across the Sinai Desert. The 6th Mounted Brigade, which included the Bucks Hussars, came under the command of Major General H.V. Hodgson as part of the Imperial Mounted Division. Also included were two brigades of Australian light horse soldiers. Direct command of the 6th Mounted Brigade was passed to Brigadier General T.M.S. Pitt.[61]

From a military point of view, it was unsatisfactory to conduct the defence of the Suez Canal from a fixed line immediately to the east of the Canal itself. Even a more advanced defence was difficult as it would leave outposts of soldiers out in the desert needing a resupply of water etc. which would be logistically difficult.

Ideally, what was needed was a more aggressive stance which would prevent any potential Turkish threat of the oases and, even better, drive them out of Egypt. Lord Kitchener had originally made this clear to the EEF when he referred to the necessity of maintaining as active a defence as possible and, most importantly, of keeping Turkish forces from establishing themselves within artillery range of the canal. Initially this resulted in Murray constructing a defensive line some 11,000 yards to the east of the canal. Fixed defensive lines, however, were extremely difficult to both dig and maintain in the desert and the typical trench, if not constantly maintained, would refill with sand within twenty-four hours.

General Murray recognised this and as early as 15 February 1916 set out his ideas in an assessment of the situation sent to Field Marshal Robertson:

> It is clear that the security of Egypt against an attack from the east is not best assured by the construction of a great defensive position in proximity to the Suez Canal – amongst other reasons because such a position is wasteful

in men and material. In order to effect the object aimed at, it would be far preferable to push out across the Sinai Peninsula towards the Egyptian frontier, making dispositions for an active defence. Less troops will actually be required for an active defence than for a passive or semi-passive defence of the Canal Zone.

In the Sinai Peninsula itself there are four chief points of importance, El Arish, El Hassana, Nekhl and El Kossaima. The three latter are important road centres – the course of the roads in Sinai being determined by water supply – which any hostile invading force, except one marching by the northern coast road and El Arish, must pass on its way to Egypt. Of the three El Kossaima is of greater importance than either of the others for enemy forces, moving down from Syria and Palestine must pass El Kossaima or between El Kossaima and the northern Sinai coast, whether the subsequent line of march is via Nekhl or El Kossaima.

Strategically, therefore, the true base of the defensive zone of Egypt against invasion from the east is not the 80 or 90 miles of the Canal zone but the 45 miles between El Arish and El Kossaima.[62]

A further consideration for Murray was morale. Following the defeat of the Senussi, and with the absence of a concerted threat from the Turkish forces, the EEF descended into a lax and easy-going way of life. The lures of Cairo and Alexandria made it all too easy for officers, in particular, to lead a fairly sybaritic existence. Shepheard's Hotel in Cairo was regularly inundated with British, Australian and New Zealand officers all enjoying the delights the hotel had to offer. An officer from the Imperial Camel Corps described it thus:

> The highest possible standard of living throughout the entire war, and it would be an understatement to say that we made the most of it … There were at least three bars, one of which was presided over by a gentleman called Hannibal, and was alleged to be the second largest in the world … there were also two enormous dining-rooms and the food was absolutely superb in its own right, and not simply by what we had been consuming during the last few months.[63]

If the officers partook of the luxurious delights of the better hotels, the soldiers were not far behind and frequented the many bars and brothels the cities had to offer. Some, of course, also took the opportunity of sightseeing. Egypt was rich in history for those prepared to move out of the cities. All in all it was not a good environment for an army and General Murray recognised that if he was to keep the troops fit for action then he needed to organise discipline and targets for the men to stay on a war footing. General Murray's Chief of Staff, Major General Sir Arthur Lynden-Bell, told the authorities back in

London that when they had arrived in Egypt their greatest difficulty had been to convince everybody of the need to be ready for war, to inculcate a warlike spirit. Up until their arrival in Egypt, he complained the officers there had been totally preoccupied with having a good time and amusing themselves. He stated that Cairo and Alexandria were a positive scandal with thousands of officers hanging around the hotels. Despite ordering all officers back to their units, it was obviously difficult to keep up a martial spirit unless they actually located the enemy and got to grips with them.

Having identified the line he felt needed to be defended (El Arish to El Khossaima), General Murray set about the considerable task of crossing some 120 miles of almost waterless desert, driving the pockets of Turkish troops out of the oases and, most importantly, putting into place the infrastructure to support troops and their horses, camels and mules. It was not just necessary to support them as they marched across the desert, but also to resupply them in their semi-permanent defensive positions which would deny Turkish forces watering holes etc. should they attempt to re-enter Egypt. It was a formidable task and required great logistical skills to accomplish. It probably displayed General Murray's greatest strengths and it is to his credit that he put in place an infrastructure and an organisation which served subsequent military leaders in the Middle Eastern theatre so well.

The Royal Bucks Hussars were allocated to the 6th Mounted Division which consisted of the Berks, Bucks and Dorset Yeomanry mounted troops, three battalions of West Indian infantry, a squadron of Royal Flying Corps aircraft, two batteries of artillery and several ancillary units, signallers, medics etc. They were initially allocated to the Western Frontier Force under the overall command of Major General W.E. Peyton. The mounted troops themselves came under the command of Brigadier General (Temp) Viscount Hampden. Their job was to prevent any threat to the Canal Zone coming from the western approach (Libya). As such, they were spared the long slog across the Sinai Peninsula.

Tens of thousands of camels were purchased and organised together with a local Egyptian Labour Corps and camel drivers. Supplies of railway sleepers, engines, rail lines and, most importantly, a huge number of water pipes were brought from the USA and the UK gradually running from the western terminus at Kantara along the coast into Palestine.

Although the British Army made extensive use of local Egyptian labour, it was, for anyone, backbreaking and soul-destroying work. Sgt William Barron described a typical day's routine:

> The Camp was roused at 03.45am and started work at 04.00am, carry on until half past five then we used to knock off for half an hour for gun fire which meant a cup of tea and some bully beef stew, and in that half hour we had to clean our tents and lay our blankets out in the sun to air. At 06.00am

we started work again and carried on until 08.00am when it was too hot to be outside one's tent let alone working, then we had our breakfast, just fancy finishing a day's work before breakfast, at least finished until 4.00 in the afternoon when we went and done another hours work, but in between nine in the morning and four in the afternoon it was almost too hot to breathe and we used to strip naked and lay in the tent, trying to keep cool, but even then we simply poured with sweat and our skin blistered, yes it was hot, enough for fowls to lay hard boiled eggs all day long.[64]

The answer was to make as much use of the local labour as possible, 'gyppos' as the troops referred to them. Unfortunately, it has to be said that they were not treated that well and there were several recorded instances of brutality and ill-treatment. A young officer from the Essex Yeomanry probably expressed commonly held views when writing home to his sister:

I now look upon Arabs as no longer picturesque, but as loathsome scum. There is a certain amount to admire in the sunsets which are very fine but otherwise this is a land of filth, garbage, flies and dust.[65]

Sadly, this was not an atypical view and obviously it was a short step from such views to treating Egyptian labour in a cruel and unthinking manner.

The first task was to build the railway out to Qatiya, an oasis some 25 miles east of the canal. It was to be followed all the way by a 12ft water pipe which took water from the Sweet Water Canal to wherever the railway reached. It must be remembered that not only did troops, camels and horses rely on water, it was also essential fuel for steam locomotives. Existing railway lines within Egypt were ripped up to supply the military and as the line grew so Kantara itself grew from its 1914 status as a small Arab village with a few mud huts and a mosque to a thriving town by 1918, with tarmac roads, electric lighting and a massive railway yard with workshops, cinemas, theatres and even a golf course. Even in 1917, it was reputedly the largest British military base in any theatre of war.

The 5th Mounted Brigade, consisting of the Warks, Worcs and Gloucs Yeomanry under the command of General E.A. Wiggin, were detailed to act as a defensive screen to protect the labourers building the track. As they approached Romani, which is only some 25 miles from the canal, the German-led Turkish forces raided them with a force of some 3,500 men. The raid was a complete success, catching the 5th Mounted Brigade in the oasis at Qatiya and, outnumbering and outgunning the yeomanry forces, they wiped out almost three and a half squadrons. It was a significant setback for the yeomanry and the view taken amongst the senior EEF commanders was that the disaster was due to inadequate leadership amongst the yeomanry cavalry. The 5th Mounted

Brigade had failed to send out a forward observation force and was caught in ill-prepared defensive positions with no cleared fields of fire. The result was a disaster for the yeomanry forces which went a long way to counter-balance, if not overwhelm, the credit they had gained for the successful action against the Senussi tribesmen. The reputation of amateurs fighting in a professional war was to dog them for a considerable time.

As a result of their losses, the 5th Mounted Brigade were withdrawn back westwards to the canal to be reorganised and their place was taken by the Anzac Mounted Division. Despite the success of the Turkish raid, the British pushed on with construction.

The German Commander Kress von Kressenstein now needed to wait for supplies and technical support, which gave the British time to push on with construction and reach Romani by May 1916. At this point the British dug in with a defensive shield which ran from Mahamdiyah on the Mediterranean coast along the highest sand dunes in a fish hook shape around the Romani railhead. By now temperatures at midday approached 123°F and no work on the railway could take place after about 10.00 a.m. The Turkish forces were also quiet, but aircraft based at El Arish were active and several bombing raids on the canal were attempted.

The difficulties of operating in the desert at this time of the year were amply illustrated by an expedition carried out by the 6th Australian Light Horse Brigade which, on a reconnaissance from the Qatiya Oasis out to Bir Bayud – a distance of some 19 miles, nearly ended in disaster from lack of water. Soldiers lay prostrated from heatstroke in the oasis for hours after they arrived back at base.

A more effective patrol was carried out by the Middlesex Yeomanry, who advanced to Moiya Harab where, over three days, they blew up the ancient stone water cisterns and effectively got rid of over 5 million gallons of water and thus denied any potential Turkish army the benefit of the central Sinai route to the canal.

By July the British began to note increased activity in the air. The German aircraft had always been superior to those of the British and anti-aircraft defence was rudimentary at this stage of the war, which enabled them to operate in a reconnaissance role with relative impunity. However, it was a British aircraft with Brigadier General Chaytor on board that got the first sight of what looked to be a build-up of Turkish forces heading towards Romani. Mounted patrols confirmed the position and by 28 July the Turkish were occupying positions 5 miles from the British dug in at Romani. There they waited for heavy artillery to be brought forward but, at the time, the British were unaware of this and there were worries that the Turks themselves were going to dig in defensively and just provide a block to the British railway.

On 4 August the Turkish forces attacked the British defensive positions and a full-scale battle developed. The British had prepared their defensive positions well and, with the advantage of water and mounted troops, the Turkish Army was well beaten. However, they withdrew in good order and the British were in no position to pursue the defeated troops. The British troops again witnessed the Turkish soldier's ability to travel overland through the most hostile desert environment at a very quick pace, surviving on the most brackish of water.

Whilst this was going on, the Royal Bucks Hussars remained in the Western Defence Force which remained at the Canal Zone. General Murray was always conscious of the need to guard against any possible threat from the west and the need not to commit all of his troops to offensive action as he may be required to send troops to the Western Front at any stage.

The Western Defence Force was by now rather larger than the threat warranted. The time was rapidly approaching for General Murray to reorganise his command. With the battle of Romani over and the Turkish troops pulling back to El Arish and Gaza, Murray continued to push the railhead forward, broadly following the Mediterranean coast at a rate of some 15 miles per month. By November, Murray's railway engineers were roughly halfway across the Sinai Peninsula. In Murray's own words:

> The desert, until then almost destitute of human habitation, showed the successive marks of our advance in the shape of strong positions firmly entrenched and protected by hundreds of miles of barbed wire, of standing camps where troops could shelter in comfortable huts, of tanks and reservoirs, of railway stations and sidings, of aerodromes and of signal stations and wireless installations, by all of which the desert was subdued and made habitable, and adequate lines of communication established between the advancing troops and their ever-receding base ...[66]

The hubris inherent in this statement was shortly to be rewarded by the gods of war but, at the time when Murray carried out his assessment, it represented the pinnacle of his achievements in Egypt. He undoubtedly deserved to take pride in what had been accomplished, especially when looked at in the context of the lukewarm support he had received from London and the contradictory and vague nature of much of his correspondence with the Chief of the Imperial General Staff.

El Arish was taken without a fight and Magdhaba fell after a short but fierce fight. On 22 December, the Turkish forces withdrew from Sinai to the Gaza-Beersheba line and General Murray became the de facto military commander of the entire desert peninsula.

During January 1917 Murray reorganised his forces, leaving the canal defended by what could be described as a skeleton force. By late March he had completed both the infrastructure and the necessary transfer of troops to a jumping-off position whereby he could threaten the Turkish lines from Gaza to Beersheba. It was a reasonable position to take to make Egypt and the Suez Canal completely secure as Beersheba represented the end of the Turkish railway and had plentiful water supplies, whilst Gaza was, as the ancient name suggests (derived from the Hebrew verb 'azaz' – meaning to be strong – hence Gaza roughly translates as 'stronghold'), a fortress providing a stronghold at the seaward end of the Turkish line.

By 20 March the Bucks Hussars, with their other yeomanry regiments, which together formed the 6th Mounted Brigade, were stationed just outside Rafah, some 18 miles short of Gaza. From here the mounted troops were moved mainly at night to their final battle positions for an attack designed to break the Turkish defensive line. On 25 March the brigade moved forward to Wadi el Ghazze, a riverbed some 3–4 miles south of Gaza. Their role was to move round to the eastern and north-eastern side of Gaza, thus preventing Turkish troops from bringing reinforcements from the Beersheba Road whilst at the same time cutting off the line of retreat should Gaza be taken.

Around dawn on 26 March, an extremely thick fog rolled inland from the Mediterranean which cut visibility down to some 20 yards in places. By then the mounted troops had already set out towards the target areas. By 8.00 a.m. much of the fog had lifted and, with the help of some excellent navigation, most of the mounted troops were on course. The yeomanry troops had been slightly delayed in the rough ground just out of the Wadi el Ghazze, maybe because navigation is a less instinctive skill to soldiers coming from the heavily populated UK compared to the Australian troops, many of whom came from the outback where signposts were at a premium.

By 10.00 a.m. all mounted troops were in position and in contact with the enemy. Indeed, the Australian Light Horse brigade furthest to the north of Gaza intercepted and took prisoner the commander of one of the Turkish divisions, so complete had been the surprise. Telegraph lines were cut as the cavalry crossed the Gaza-Beersheba Road and, as the yeomanry established contact with the southern end of the Australian Light Horse Brigades, scouting patrols were sent out further eastwards and north-eastwards towards Huj and Khe er Reseim.

The infantry were faring less well, although by mid-afternoon Gaza was essentially surrounded. Infantry troops making the frontal assault on Gaza were meeting stiff resistance. It was a vital part of the planning process that Gaza would be taken in the day. Both ammunition stocks and water were critical and by midday this was looking unlikely. General Chetwode, who was commanding the mounted troops encircling Gaza, requested and received permission to attack the city from the north. The communications, however, took time and it took General Chetwode further time to reorganise the cavalry before making his assault on the northern side of the city.

It was about 4.00 p.m. when he finally made his attack on Gaza. Although they met with some success, the British were further slowed by the Turkish use of large cactus hedges which had to be hacked through by hand before horses could breach them whilst, at the same time, coming under rifle fire from the Turkish troops concealed behind the hedges.

While all this was going on, the Royal Bucks Hussars and the Berkshire Yeomanry were continuing to cover the northern and eastern approaches to Gaza. By now the Turks had begun to counter-attack and the Bucks Hussars were under pressure, attacked by the Turks around a hill to the north-east of Gaza known to the British as Hill 405. The Bucks Hussars were in the process of watering their horses when they received their orders to attack the hill, and the delay enabled the Turks to occupy the hill. Further Australian mounted troops assisted the Bucks in fighting off the Turks to hold this vital position. The Turkish reinforcements were by now pressing the mounted troops strongly as they moved forwards from the direction of Huj.

Lieutenant Bowyer recounts his part in the battle:

The division at this time all massed together, halts just across the Beersheba road, the New Zealand Mounted Rifles are in touch with the enemy from Beersheba and about a mile away a battery of our guns is firing steadily in that direction. A few odd high explosives come our way but we seem to be unnoticed, and everybody is talking of being right through on the Jerusalem Rd by the morrow. A good deal of rifle fire is going on back towards Gaza but we understand the day is going well. About 2 o' clock we push on and go forwards about six miles, Gaza now well behind us, and we are just unsaddling to rest our horses for night work when some news comes in. Saddle up immediately and away! Still forward – it is reinforcements marching on Gaza from Hebron and Megdel. The Division lines a long range of heights, and rifle, machine gun and artillery fire becomes common all along the line.

The head of the column is annihilated. This is the position when dark comes upon us. Unfortunately, Gaza has not fallen: however, we start to dig in, knowing on the next day the position will be at least difficult. We dig away in the darkness; every now and then the machine gun rips out and we imagine we can hear the Turks shouting; anyhow, one could hear them moving at times.

We have just got our trench dug for my section and were thinking of an hour's sleep when the order comes up – get back to your horses quietly. 'C' Squadron lays out in the open while the remainder get all together and get mounted. I fancy I slept for a bit: then off into the dark and dust at a steady trot – apparently the Turks have got round us. We ride to where a signal lamp flashes, and then on, wondering what daybreak will disclose. The Bucks Yeomanry are rearguard, 'C' Squadron the last squadron. The sun rose fine and red on our left so we were riding due south. Just at daybreak, about

5:30, our flank guard rides right into the midst of a body of about 60 Turkish infantry, rifle fire immediately breaks out along our left flank. Crocker Bulteel leads us straight up a valley towards the firing. At the end we dismount for action and scramble up the right bank opening fire on the Turks whom we could plainly see. After perhaps about five minutes blazing away word is sent up from the valley that some cavalry are approaching on the other bank. We leave the Hotchkiss guns to deal with these Turks and run back through our horses and up the other slope. Half way up the slope I feel a tingling sensation in my left hand and a bullet kicks up dirt at my feet. No 1 troop following behind saw the incident with ease and tell me I used awful language for a minute or so – I don't think so.

However, as it did not feel very bad I thought I would have a look over the top of the ridge. I was just in time to see the Turks dismounting for action and as my two fingers now seemed to be useless and I could not hold my rifle I thought 'this is no place for me' and retired on the horses. Here Mr Deverell kindly did my hand up and I was able to watch the scrap. Frank Clark is soon hit and brought down, ditto Slim Jim (Mr Stewart) coming back supported by Venner and Thatcher. The firing now seemed to be all round us: horses are getting hit, and it is an anxious period till all come back to the horses: we mount and strike up the valley.

I have a vision of Sambrooke's horse leading the way riderless and one or two coming purlers. Claude Vize going past hanging grimly to his pack-mule with its Hotchkiss gun. Palmer is shot through the back and all is dust. We pull up behind a hill about a quarter of a mile away, and get together and allow the unfortunates to catch up. Both Sobey and Jack Abbott have their horses shot and come panting up over the hill. We hear Sambrooke is hit and left behind, but nobody knows very definitely then. Actually he was left for dead but was taken badly hit by the Turks and is alive in England today although a cripple. While here Captain Bulteel, who was as cool as ever all through … sent us wounded on to find a field ambulance and so taking Palmer with us, Williams and I set off for what we imagine are our lines, passing Frank Clark with Marks. The Squadron eventually got away from its position, although under considerable difficulty, and two Military Medals were won.[67]

The disjointed nature of the attack and the lack of clear communications hinted at in Lieutenant Boywer's short cameo are typical of the larger picture. Darkness comes early in Palestine and by 6.30 p.m. on the first day of the action it was too dark for the Turks to press home further attacks. The situation to the troops on the ground seemed positive as they had Gaza surrounded and the vast majority of the enemy had withdrawn into the city. In some areas British troops had actually entered the city itself. If they stayed overnight in position and renewed their attacks in the morning, it looked like there was an excellent chance that Gaza would fall and that the Turkish defensive line from Gaza to Beersheba would start to crack.

This was not to be, as the General Staff at HQ were worried about the condition of the mounted troops or, more precisely, the condition of their horses. There was no reliable source of water and it was not possible to ferry water supplies to them as they were spread out over many square miles of territory. General Chetwode felt he had to order the withdrawal of the mounted troops to the only guaranteed supplies of water which was at the Wadi el Ghazze to the south of the city.

In making this decision he was all too aware that this would allow the Turkish forces to reinforce Gaza from the north and east and thus effectively end the first battle of Gaza. As the mounted troops pulled back, the decision was taken to withdraw the infantry from the advanced positions south of the city.

The attack was renewed the next morning by the infantry, but by now the Turkish troops had reinforced Gaza and artillery was being used to shell Wadi el Ghazze. Without the mounted troops to shield the right flank, there was no real possibility of success; nevertheless, it took all afternoon to consult the relevant HQ staff and to finalise the decision. By nightfall on day two it was decided and the British troops withdrew to their pre-battle positions.

The British had initially described this battle as a *coup de main,* which the dictionary defines as 'an offensive operation that capitalizes on surprise and simultaneous execution of supporting operations to achieve success in one swift stroke.' The Turkish forces, however, were cock-a-hoop, convinced that they had defeated a major British attack. Whatever the truth, there was no doubt that the Turks were now in a stronger position than previously had been the case and the British had failed to achieve their objective.

Basil Liddell Hart summed up the First Battle of Gaza as follows:

> Murray attacked Gaza on March 26th, but the attempt fell short when on the brink of success. By nightfall Gaza was practically surrounded, but the victorious position was given up bit by bit, not under enemy pressure, but on the orders of the executive British Commanders, through faulty information, misunderstandings, and over-anxiety. Nor did the harm end there, for Murray reported the action to the government in terms of a victory, and without a hint of the subsequent withdrawal, so that he was encouraged to attempt, without adequate reconnaissance or fire support, a further attack on April 17–19th which proved a costlier failure against defences now strengthened.[68]

What the Turkish forces had failed to achieve was a significant defeat of the British Army. Both the British and the Turks knew that this was not an end to the matter. The armies were too close for there not to be another British attempt. In the intervening period, whilst the British planned for a full-scale assault on Gaza and Murray composed his telegrams to report back to the Chief of the Imperial General Staff, the Turks dug in. They reinforced Gaza and prepared effective defensive strongholds along the Gaza-Beersheba lines. They were not continuous trenches such as existed in France, but interlinked and mutually supportive strongholds.

Murray and his HQ planning staff did not feel able to outflank the Turkish lines by attacking the much weaker point at Beersheba. Lack of water supplies meant that mounted troops could not operate that far east without extensive infrastructure and/or preparations being made.

Murray was, in modern parlance, economical with the truth in his report of the First Battle of Gaza. In fact, he had not mentioned Gaza in his report to Field Marshal Robertson, merely reporting on the advance to Wadi el Ghazze: 'On the 26th and 27th we were heavily engaged east of the Ghazze with a force of about 20,000 of the enemy, we inflicted very heavy losses on him; I estimate his casualties at between 6,000 and 7,000 men, and we have in addition taken 900 prisoners including General Commanding and the whole Division Staff of 53rd Turkish Division.'[69]

On the strength of this report, British newspapers proclaimed a great victory and the defeat of a 20,000-strong Turkish army! There is great skill in putting a positive spin on what might otherwise be described as a total cock up, and to get away with such presentation Murray urgently needed to take Gaza, otherwise the advance into Palestine and the liberation of Jerusalem was a non-starter.

Although the second attack on Gaza was to take place a mere four weeks after the first, it was to be a much larger affair. A great deal was done by both sides in the intervening period and certainly the Turkish defenders did not waste the respite granted to them.

In addition to the strongholds referred to above, Gaza itself was made into a modern fortress, proof against all but the most determined of assaults and artillery barrages. Extensive wiring together with trenches, sandbagged strong-holds and fixed artillery which had been calibrated in on the likely lines of attack, meant that the British were facing a reinvigorated foe. It should not be forgotten that the Turkish defenders were led by a German commander who not only had their confidence but was a product of possibly the most advanced and scientific military training establishment in the world. German military officers were second to none and in Colonel Kress von Kressenstein the Turks were blessed with an extremely intelligent and able military leader. He was of German aristocratic background and by the start the spring of 1917 he had gained considerable experience and skill in fighting in this region. The one possible weakness was that it was, of course, a Turkish army and therefore nominally was commanded by a Turk, Jamal Pasha. Col von Kressenstein and Jamal Pasha were by no means friends. Indeed, looking at contemporary photographs of the rather austere-looking German officer, one might doubt whether he had any friends at all, not least Turkish ones. The defences, however, were well thought out and robust and the Turks (boosted by Austrian artillery) were rugged and determined soldiers, especially when well dug in.

Meanwhile, the British pulled up reinforcements, particularly in artillery. This second attempt to take Gaza was to be a more measured affair far more reminiscent of the Western Front than the first battle. The intention was to subject the defences to a preliminary artillery bombardment, move infantry forward to dug-in positions immediately in front of Gaza and then assault the city. The cavalry were to play a far smaller role in this attack, but were again to hold the right flank and thereby prevent the Turks from potentially bringing in reinforcements from their left flank.

When allied to Royal Flying Corps reconnaissance, naval artillery support and the use of tanks, this truly was an integrated, all-arms attack and was reminiscent of tactics used in northern France. There was at least one crucial difference from the tactics employed on the Western Front, and this difference was probably one of the principal reasons for the failure. The weight of the preliminary artillery bombardment was simply insufficient for the task. Bombardments on the Western Front were often several days long, numbing defenders into comatose zombies who could, in extremis, be rendered almost helpless by the weight and intensity of the bombardment. General Murray simply did not have the resources for such tactics. Nor could the British offer any degree of surprise.

Thanks to extending the railway still further so that it now ended just 5 miles south of the Wadi el Ghazze, General Murray was able to bring up artillery ammunition and, for the first time in the Middle East, supplement high explosives with gas shells. Eight tanks were also to be employed in the assault. One significant drawback was that, although the Royal Flying Corps outnumbered their enemies' aircraft, the RFC machines were markedly inferior to the German aircraft, which were still able to fly with relative impunity over British lines, acting as artillery spotters and intelligence gatherers.

The British outnumbered the Turkish forces by approximately two-to-one on 17 April. However, the Turks had learnt from the first encounter and whilst they had a healthy respect for the mounted forces, they now knew that well dug-in troops, so long as they kept their discipline, were not really vulnerable to cavalry. The situation was to be markedly different once they were forced out of the Gaza citadel, but in the heavily defended redoubts, cavalry was not a viable weapon.

The initial artillery bombardment lasted approximately an hour and included both gas shells and fire from a French warship anchored off Gaza. The bombardment was not really effective, and left the defences essentially unmarked. Even the gas shells were ineffective as the liquid evaporated too quickly in the heat and dispersed before inconveniencing the defenders.

The first of the tanks to move forward with the infantry was rapidly knocked out of commission by the Turkish guns. However, the infantry troops were moved successfully to their forward jumping-off positions, and spent the rest of the day digging in, preparatory to the main assault which was scheduled for the second day.

Meanwhile, Bill Cowell and his colleagues moved forward from the *wadi* towards two heavily fortified redoubts which the Turks had dug on the slightly raised ground running along the main Gaza to Beersheba road. They halted as planned about 2 miles short of the redoubts as they were intended merely to threaten the Turkish position rather than actually attack it. The idea was to fix the defenders to prevent them moving westwards to reinforce the Gaza garrison.

The Worcester Yeomanry moved forward to the road to cut the telegraph lines and succeeded in doing so without coming into contact with the enemy.

The frontal infantry assaults were unsuccessful, as the lessons from France should have made clear they would be. Troops advancing in open countryside against well dug-in and determined defenders need both an enormous artillery barrage and an overwhelming numerical advantage in order to succeed. General Murray had neither and was therefore doomed to fail yet again. The yeomanry were to play a peripheral part in the overall battle. Nevertheless, they did, for the first time, come into contact with Turkish cavalry under the command of a Venezuelan officer, Rafael de Nogales. He led a fairly disparate group of Turkish regular cavalry and Bedouins. He was himself an interesting character who initially offered his services to the Belgian military and, having been refused by them and five other Allied countries, eventually joined the Turkish side. He was obviously determined to join in the fight and not particularly worried about which side he fought on.

By 19 April it was obvious that the Allies had failed again. As the casualty figures came in and the British infantry withdrew to their trenches, it became clear that this had been a heavy defeat. The final figures showed over 6,500 British soldiers killed, wounded or missing against comparable Turkish figures of some 2,000. The battle had almost wiped out the Allies' numerical superiority. The cavalry withdrew back to the water supplies at the *wadi* and by 20 April the battle was over. The official British military historian summarises the engagement thus:

> A dogged advance against imperfectly located entrenchments and in the face of fire from hidden artillery, without adequate cover from that arm on the side of the attackers … There were wide gaps in the Turkish position, but the redoubts were well sited for mutual support and permitted the retention of reserves for counter-attack outside the danger zone. Since the Turkish infantry did not flinch from counter-attack, the result was never in doubt.[70]

The situation could have been infinitely worse as Colonel von Kressenstein planned to counter-attack across the whole front. Luckily for the British, the order was never given thanks to disagreements between the German military command and the Turkish leaders.

Bill Cowell and the majority of the yeomanry were used mostly as infantry during the battle, albeit being transported to the battlefield on horseback. The redoubts at Atawineh and Hareira were assaulted repeatedly but with no success. Losses taken by the yeomanry were light when compared to their infantry colleagues. One significant gain, however, was made by all of the yeomanry divisions as gradually, and probably grudgingly, they were gaining the respect of their Australian cavalry counterparts. I have earlier explained that the yeomanry officers were in the main members of the British aristocracy and it is therefore not surprising that initially the more down-to-earth Australians took a while to take them seriously. There were enormous cultural differences to overcome before mutual respect could begin to grow. It is important to recognise that in this early part of the twentieth century few people had travelled abroad and there was little migration. If there was, it was all one way: the mother country to the dominions. The age of regular Aussie backpackers turning up in London was still a long way off in the future and people were far more insular than may be the case today. To fight alongside someone and to know that your life may well depend on them is a great leveller and, after Gaza, this respect and belief in each other's abilities began to grow. It was perhaps helped by a growing mutual distrust in the leadership.

Whilst any individual soldier only ever sees a tiny part of the overall picture, they could not be fooled forever. It was becoming increasingly obvious that General Murray was losing the support of his army. For one thing he was never seen by the troops in any of the advanced positions and, following the First Battle of Gaza, it was also becoming obvious that among the critical factors in the unsuccessful attacks were weak communications and the fact that those directing the battle were too far to the rear to know what was going on.

8

GENERAL ALLENBY AND THE THIRD BATTLE FOR GAZA

The failure to take Gaza left the Bucks Yeomanry to settle into a routine of regular aggressive patrols against the Turks in a line between Gaza and Beersheba. Their greatest risk when out on patrol, or watering the horses, was falling victim to attack from the air. Germany had supplied Turkey with several modern aircraft which proved adept at sudden sorties against moving patrols. In an extract from his war memoirs, Capt Teichman writes:

> We heard on arrival that Fritz at his usual visit had inflicted very heavy losses on the Bucks Yeomanry while watering at Shellal. It was a very unfortunate thing that when regiments were watering at the troughs in the Wadi they were absolutely at the mercy of enemy aircraft, and the latter knew from observation exactly when and where the various Brigades watered.[71]

The regimental diaries are, in the main, a fairly repetitive tale of patrols and occasional contact with the enemy interspersed with periods of training back at the camp established at Marakeb.

It was during this period that not only did the troops start to lose confidence in General Murray but, more importantly, the War Cabinet and the Army hierarchy also started to have doubts. On 7 December 1916 there had also been a major change in the make-up of the War Cabinet. For over two years of the war, Asquith had been in charge as Prime Minister, initially with a Liberal cabinet and subsequently with a three party coalition cabinet. By late 1916, Lloyd George, in co-operation with the Conservatives, was able to exploit setbacks in the war effort to oust him and form a new coalition. For an arch conspirator such as Lloyd George, disposal of a general in faraway Egypt would be easy.

From vague disquiet it was but a short step to the thinking that the general who had been unsuccessful in battle should be replaced and, as early as 23 April 1917, the War Cabinet had discussed the subject. It was not an easy decision as the military advice would obviously err on the side of keeping the best military

Royal Bucks Hussars relaxing during the Palestine campaign. (Bill Cowell)

talent where they felt it would do most good, in other words on the Western Front, whereas Lloyd George wanted a victory. From the perspective of public morale and therefore the continuation of Lloyd George's administration, he could really do with some good news to counter-balance the increasingly long casualty lists.

At first, and somewhat against orthodox military thinking, Lloyd George wished to offer the post to General Jan Christian Smuts who, as a former South African guerrilla leader, had led troops against the British Army. He was now a wily politician and a devout Christian, attributes which no doubt endeared him to Lloyd George, but not necessarily to the British Military High Command. Smuts was offered the post on 1 May and took a month to consider it, during which time he went to consult with Field Marshal Robertson. Robertson made it abundantly clear to Smuts that he was against the appointment and that it was, in any case, a very secondary appointment with little possibility of additional resources, as France would always take precedence. On this basis Smuts, not unnaturally, refused the post. It has to be said that Lloyd George and Robertson did not always work as smoothly together as perhaps they should have. Indeed, Robertson confided to military colleagues that he thought Lloyd George an out-and-out liar. Given that strict adherence to the truth is not the commonest of virtues in politics, this was probably not the worst epithet thrown at Lloyd George during his long career.

The choice of who to replace Murray was becoming increasingly constrained; however, there was one possibility Robertson and Haig were willing to go along with: General Sir Edmund Allenby. He had never got on that well with Field Marshal Haig ever since they attended staff-college together. Following a failed British offensive at Arras on the Western Front, General Allenby seemed to be the ideal compromise choice and consequently he was chosen to replace General Murray. At first, Allenby was reluctant to take up the posting as he had interpreted it as an implicit criticism of his conduct of the Arras offensive and, like so many others on the Western Front, he perceived Palestine as being very much a sideshow to the 'real war'. However, Lloyd George was nothing if not persuasive. He also easily outwitted Robertson, promising Allenby additional resources and impressing on him the need to supply the British people with a Christmas present by liberating Jerusalem. Allenby, as a regular serving officer in the British Army, was in no position to refuse, but after listening to Lloyd George he went to the post with a somewhat more positive outlook than may have previously been the case. Allenby already knew the strain that war was placing on British society and would have known for himself that a victory as stunning as liberating the holy city of Jerusalem, with all its overtones of a Christian crusade, would have a positive effect on morale.

Allenby arrived in Egypt on 28 June. He was 6ft 4in tall, well-built and well deserving of his nickname 'The Bull'. He was known not to suffer fools gladly and to lose his temper with those he felt were not pulling their weight. Nevertheless, he was to make an immediate impact on the soldiers' thinking and outlook as he immediately set out to revolutionise the EEF HQ. He was very keen on delegation and knew how important it was for troop morale to know that there was not a multitude of time-servers back at HQ. One of his first acts was to move EEF HQ from Cairo to Umm-el-Kelab near Rafa, which must have made a great impact on all of the front line soldiers. This placed the GHQ some 20 miles away from Gaza and the front line rather than in the far distance (and comfort) of Cairo. He obviously understood that first impressions count and his priority was to stress that generals needed to know intimately what sort of country his troops would fight over.[72]

Major General Money, a staff officer who served under him in Palestine, describes Allenby thus:

> There were two things that always infuriated Allenby: if he thought a man was not straight, and did not give him a direct answer to a direct question, and if he found that a man did not know the job with which he was entrusted. I have seen at Corps conferences the knuckles of his fist grow white with strain, when he asked the Australian Corps Commander a question as to what his Corps was to do, which the latter as usual could not answer. When once he had given an officer his complete confidence, he was a delightful fellow to serve under, as I found out; and a refreshing contrast to Maude.[73]

An unnamed Bucks Yeoman in the desert outside Gaza. (Bill Cowell)

Bill Cowell outside Gaza. (Bill Cowell)

Much of what he did was essentially showy, almost theatrical in nature, but it had the effect he wanted on the troops. They began to see that in Allenby they had a man determined not just to fight the enemy but to defeat them. He was not going to allow staff officers to wallow in the fleshpots of Cairo; from now on everything was subordinated to defeating the Turkish Army and liberating Jerusalem. General Allenby had a massive advantage over his predecessor as he had come to Egypt with the Prime Minister's support and, most importantly, a promise that he would get the resources he needed to complete the job. This was a luxury that General Murray never had and it was to be critical in the days to come. He was also fortunate in having General Chetwode as his immediate subordinate. They were old colleagues and trusted each other. They had fought together in South Africa and since then their paths had crossed several times, thus the necessary trust so vital to the success of their mission was easily rekindled.

The Bucks Hussars initially welcomed the introduction of General Allenby, as did the rest of the Allied Army. One of the members of Allenby's HQ staff was Lord Dalmeny, the elder brother of one of the Bucks Hussars officers, Major Neil Primrose. It was ironic, therefore, that one of the early problems that Allenby had to deal with was directly caused by the officers of the Bucks Hussars.

The Royal Bucks Hussars' commanding officer, Lieutenant Colonel J.P. Grenfell, had written a letter to the honorary colonel of the regiment, Lord Burnham (proprietor of the *Daily Telegraph*) and copied it to his uncle, a field marshal. In the letter, which was opened by the censor, Lieutenant Col Grenfell revealed that the main initial target of the forthcoming attack was Beersheba. He compounded the offence by going on to criticise his senior officer Brigadier Pitt, who failed to meet the standards expected by Grenfell. In one particular incident, when the Royal Bucks Hussars were part of the Brigade HQ reserve, they had travelled out into the desert on a reconnaissance which revealed no sight of enemy forces but, as they unsaddled and tied the horses to the picket line, Turkish artillery suddenly opened fire and shells began to land amongst the troops and the horses.

Contemporary reports indicate that Brigadier Pitt and his HQ staff subsequently left the troops to take cover. Grenfell, however, stayed. Displaying great calmness and reassuring the troops he then managed to extricate them from the exposed position. It was this behaviour by Pitt that Grenfell complained of in his letter to Lord Burnham and Field Marshal Lord Grenfell. In truth, there seems to be evidence that things were not happy or as they should be amongst the officers of the Bucks Hussars. Both in Palestine and earlier in Egypt some of the officers had been writing back to their old colonel (Lord Burnham) on a regular basis.

Copies of the letters sent back to Colonel Lawson from an officer who called himself 'elephant' show that Grenfell was not the only officer who could have been court-martialled. A letter sent on 16 January 1916 reads as follows:

> Well I daresay you know where we are, or can guess. If not I'll risk the Censor, and I don't suppose he would mind much! And tell you the place is Mersa Matrus about midway between Alexandria and Salume on the Tripoli border.[74]

Whoever the officer was behind the pseudonym 'elephant', he would have been required to discipline any of his troops had he been aware that they were revealing place names and locations in their letters home. It is difficult to know why he felt he should be exempt. However, worse was to follow as he then went on to explicitly criticise his fellow officers. Further on in the same letter he writes:

> The C.O. did the usual thing. We went out on the right flank, and when we were fired on he departed. I don't know where he went to, but I was told he was sitting near the hospital wagons about 2,000 yards in the rear. Anyway he might have told me, as his second in command, that he was going.[75]

In a letter written to Colonel Lawson on 26 January 1916 the same correspondent writes:

> I haven't seen JB for ages. He of course was not present at the fight. I am very
> sorry for him, but he is so silly, and is so absurdly dissatisfied with any and
> every job he gets. He is like a child … one might be really quite – or almost
> quite – happy here if fate would only move to some other sphere of activity
> or usefulness our Saturn and his ring of satellites.[76]

Such letters speak eloquently of a perhaps less than happy spirit amongst some
of the officers. Perhaps one of the downsides of recruiting the vast majority of
the officers from such a closely knit and narrow section of county society is that
one automatically imports all of the petty jealousies that exist in peacetime. Of
course, there are also difficulties in bringing in outsiders from different back-
grounds which might have perhaps lessened the claustrophobic atmosphere.

Lt Colonel Grenfell's letter is therefore not an isolated example of unhappy
officers using their colonel back in the UK as a sounding board for their dis-
satisfaction; when the contents of Grenfell's letter were brought to Allenby's
attention, he was forced to take action, whatever the undoubted merits of
Grenfell as a military commander. A general court martial was convened under
Major General Hodgson on 14 September 1917 and by 17 September they
were able to promulgate their decision, which was a 'severe reprimand'. The
affair was handled quickly and by 20 September Lt Col Grenfell is reported
as travelling to Alexandria to catch a ship back to England. Major Fred Cripps
was temporarily promoted to Lieutenant Colonel and took control of the regiment. He recalls the event in his autobiography:

> Now came an unexpected and startling event. In August I was given leave
> to go home to England, just before the Russian Revolution. I went to
> Alexandria to join the steamer, but as we were about to leave, a staff officer
> came aboard, sent for me, and I was ordered ashore. He told me he knew
> nothing about the reason for this order, but instructed me to return to my
> regiment immediately. I could not imagine what had happened, but when
> I rejoined my regiment, after a long and arduous journey, our Adjutant told
> me that Colonel John Grenfell was under arrest. Astonished and very dis-
> tressed, I rushed to find him. He said: 'I'm terribly sorry that you should have
> been recalled. It will be quite all right; you will be able to get your leave in
> a few days' time. I am under arrest simply because I wrote a rather injudi-
> cious letter home. Unfortunately it was opened by the censor. But,' he added,
> reassuringly, 'There was nothing of any real importance in it.' Grenfell asked
> me to be his prisoner's friend at the court-martial. He handed me a copy of
> a long communication addressed to our old Colonel – Lord Burnham – at

A British tank destroyed outside Gaza. (Bill Cowell)

that time owner of the Daily Telegraph – and also to his uncle, Field-Marshal Lord Grenfell. I read the letter carefully, but, despite Grenfell's assurance, found there was scarcely a line in it that was not, in my opinion, actionable. At the court-martial I did my best in his defence, making an earnest plea on his behalf. Grenfell was reprimanded and sent home, while I was appointed to command the regiment. Much later he congratulated me on my acquittal at the Old Bailey, when I told him I had then 'the great advantage of a first-class lawyer to defend me. About this time Brigadier-General Pitt also left for home. General Godwin, a fine cavalry soldier, succeeded him.[77]

Captain C.W. Battine, military correspondent on the *Daily Telegraph* and one of Lord Burnham's editorial staff, tried to intercede on behalf of Grenfell but was given short thrift by Allenby, as can be seen from the following letter:

General Headquarters
Egyptian Expeditionary Force
20th November 1917

I have your letters of 22nd and 25th October. You take a wrong view of Grenfell. The destination of the letter mattered nothing. I have absolute confidence in Lord Burnham, and I would trust him with my secret; there-fore, I was quite sure that he would make no use of the letter. The letter was brought officially to my notice, and I had no course open to me but to take the necessary disciplinary action. I know Grenfell, and I like him; but, whatever my personal feelings might be, I could not retain as command-ing a Regiment in my Army an officer who could write such a letter. The whole letter was improper; but I could have condoned all of it except for the writer's criticism of his Brigadier, and his reference to future operations in the Beersheba area. I have no ill will towards Grenfell. He has had his lesson; and I should have no hesitation in recommending him for further employment. As to what people think of my action; I care nothing. I must maintain disci-pline; and I shall always take whatever measures I think necessary.[78]

Before the battle started, Allenby had to endure one more trial. On his return from one of his morale-raising tours at the front, he received the news of his only son's death. His son had been a young officer in the Royal Horse Artillery and had been killed by shrapnel. Allenby's letter to his wife shows a different side to his character:

My darling sweetheart, I wish I could be with you; but I know how brave you are; and you will be strong to bear this awful blow. You and Michael fill my thoughts, and I feel very near to you both. Every remembrance of him is a joy. From his birth to his death there is not a day that you or I would have wished changed or to have been lived otherwise than he lived it … Whenever he came to stay with me, he was always the same; a friend, on equal terms; and yet, unaffectedly, he always kissed me when we met and parted – as he did when a child.[79]

The emotion and tenderness expressed in this letter, but rarely seen in his day-to-day contacts with his subordinates, show a different, more human, man and may perhaps help to explain how he won the trust of both his HQ staff and the frontline soldiers.

However, it was Allenby's qualities as a strategist that were about to be tested rather than his qualities as a human being. In his study of Napoleon, Georges Lefebvre records the latter's approach to managing the large set piece battles which deservedly made his name as a master strategist:

Victory was contingent upon the speed and daring of Napoleon's decisions, followed by a precipitate execution of troop movements. Surprise was an important element, and demanded the utmost secrecy. Always covered by cavalry, the army used rivers and mountains as natural screen for its marches, whenever possible.[80]

Bill Cowell tries camel riding. (Bill Cowell)

This describes Allenby's approach to the battle for Gaza to a T and it is quite believable that Allenby could have studied Napoleon's strategies during his earlier soldiering career.

By 12 July, Allenby was in a position to make his bid to the Chief of the Imperial General Staff for the resources he would need to defeat the Turks. As he probably expected, the War Cabinet agreed to some, but not all, of his demands. Robertson, who was nothing if not canny, sent reinforcements which included what he thought would be a spy in the camp, the young officer Lt Col Archibald Wavell. His mission was to keep an eye on Allenby and to report back personally to London.

It is difficult to believe that Allenby did not know exactly what was going on. Indeed, he made a determined effort to charm Wavell and get him on his side. When Wavell arrived, Allenby was able to quote the whole of one of Rupert Brook's sonnets to him. He had obviously done his homework and knew that Wavell had a lifelong love of poetry. He further won the young officer's admiration by his stoic bravery following the death of his son.

The Bucks Hussars mounted up in the desert, with horses' bridles equipped with ropes to deter flies. (Bill Cowell)

A Royal Bucks Hussars camp in the Sinai Desert. (Bill Cowell)

Meanwhile, as the EEF waited for the reinforcements, Allenby made sure that the troops on the front line in the trenches running south of the Gaza-Beersheba defensive line were continually rotated so that they all spent as much time as possible having rest, recuperation and, most importantly, training for the task ahead. He allowed the troops time by the sea at Deir el-Belah, where swimming and proper sleep were the order of the day.

He also ensured that both the troops and their horses gradually built up the stamina and ability to go without water. Allenby was in no doubt that as soon as the British broke through the Gaza-Beersheba line, if they did not manage to cut off the lines of retreat, they would need to chase the Turkish hard in the retreat north to ensure that they could not dig in again in new defensive lines. The ability to 'keep going' when times and the going got hard was to be critical in the forthcoming battles.

Whilst Allenby waited for reinforcements, the situation was made more difficult by the attitude of his military masters back in London. When he transmitted his plans to London on how he would break the Turkish lines, the War Cabinet backed Allenby completely and asked Robertson to reply requesting that he liberate Jerusalem and hit the Turks hard. Robertson dutifully transmitted this back to Allenby, but also sent him a private message requesting that he not fight too big a battle, asked him not to commit too many resources to the battle and not to take territory which would require large numbers of troops to defend. As ever, the Western Front must come first.

Allenby, however, had his official sanction from the War Cabinet and was determined to press on. His hand was further strengthened when he received new Bristol fighters, which gave him, for the first time, the opportunity to establish air superiority and thus prevent the German aircraft from conducting aerial reconnaissance and from harassing his troops. The other news on his reinforcements in infantry and artillery was not so positive as he had to wait until September to fully build up his strength and thus the attack had to be delayed until October, taking it into the rainy season.

In the intervening period, Allenby set out to deceive the Turkish and German forces as to where his attack would hit. He wished them to believe that the main and first thrust would be against Gaza and that, at the same time, there would be amphibious landings north of Gaza. He wished at all costs to dissuade the Turks from reinforcing Beersheba as the early capture of that point was vital to his plans. Once the capture of Beersheba, together with its guaranteed water supplies, was accomplished, he was more flexible as to the exact order of the following assaults.

With this in mind, he set up dummy camps in Cyprus to try to convince Turkish spies that a naval assault north of Gaza was part of his plans. He ensured that the Beersheba defences became used to cavalry movements in their area and finally, in a move which foreshadowed the Second World War, he devised

The Royal Bucks Hussars in desert camp. (Bill Cowell)

an elaborate series of false plans. These papers were stained with blood and given to an officer who was to put himself in a position whereby he would be chased by a Turkish scouting party and would pretend to drop the documents whilst in flight.

Finally, by late October, Allenby had everything in place for what he hoped would be the defining battle of the campaign. His deception regarding the point of initial attack appeared to have been bought by the Turks; he had some sort of air supremacy and his troops had moved under cover of darkness to their jumping-off points. The opening salvo of the campaign came at Gaza on 27 October when all of the available British artillery, including Royal Navy vessels anchored off the Palestine shore, opened up with the largest artillery bombardment of the campaign. By the standards of the Western Front it could be dismissed as a pretty small show, but by the current standards of the Middle East it was more than sufficient to convince the Turks and their German military commanders that, yet again, the British intended the main thrust to be against Gaza.[81]

The objective was not just to confuse the enemy; Allenby knew that Gaza had to fall to defeat the Turks and he wanted to do all he could to make the retreat northwards as difficult as possible. He had the Royal Navy to assist the barrage with a monitor vessel (basically a large floating gun emplacement). HMS *Raglan* had huge 14ft guns and was able, from its position offshore, to shell Deir Sneid, one of the Turks' key rail junctions, plus bridges and ammunition dumps to the north. The bombardment continued for five days and nights.

With all of this going on, distracting the Turks from keeping their eye on the bigger picture, Allenby moved his Desert Mounted Corps and the XX Corps from their camps south of Gaza eastwards towards Beersheba and it was here, to the south and to the east of Beersheba, where Allenby had amassed his initial attack force. It was essential that Beersheba fell on the opening day. Just as important was that the Turks did not get the chance to destroy the water and wells before the British moved in. Water supplies from Beersheba were essential to Allenby's plans, as he intended his forces to move rapidly north-west from this most easterly point of the Turkish defensive line to cut off the main Turkish army in Gaza, effectively destroying the Turkish presence in Palestine.

It was absolutely essential that he keep the Turkish defenders 'honest' and not allow them to move forces to Beersheba. The longer the defenders remained in Gaza, the better it would be for Allenby's forces as he planned to roll up the defensive line from the east and from the north, thus enveloping the Turkish army and cutting off the lines of retreat to the north.

Like all great commanders, Allenby sought to keep his plans as flexible as possible; the key was the early capture of Beersheba and its water supplies. With this in his hands, Allenby would hit the Turkish defensive lines with a series of flanking moves enabling enfilading fire and attacks at points where the defences were weakest. The fixed sequence of these attacks was not critical – only the capture of Beersheba. The interdiction of the lines enabling Turkish troops to move west to east was in the hands of the central parts of Allenby's forces and it was in the centre that he was most thinly stretched. Allenby gambled on the Turks not mounting a counter-attack against his centre, which was to prove a worthwhile bet.

By the night of 30 October 1917, the fourth night of the Gaza bombardment, the British had amassed their forces both to the south and south-west of Beersheba and were ready to commence the real battle. The first attacks went in at 4.00 a.m. on 31 October. The initial target was a hill half a mile in front of the Turkish lines and by mid-morning the hill was taken, which enabled the infantry to move in on the main Turkish trenches. By mid-afternoon these trenches were taken. However, the number of prisoners taken indicated that the Turks were withdrawing into the city rather than defending the lines to the last man. Not unreasonably, the Turks believed that time was on their side, as previous battles had indicated that by nightfall the British and Allied troops would need to withdraw in order to water the horses.

Whilst the infantry were assaulting what could be termed the front door of Beersheba, from the south and south-west, mounted troops in the form of the New Zealand Mounted Brigade were moving round to attack from the north-east. By mid-afternoon the city was effectively surrounded on three sides. By 4 p.m. the Turkish local commander, Colonel Ismet Bey, knew that he would have to withdraw from Beersheba and retreat if anything was to be saved from the battle. All of this, however, was not necessarily clear to General Chauvel, in charge of the surrounding Allied forces. Infantry forces had previously been

The ruins of Gaza following the British bombardment during the Third Battle of Gaza. (Bill Cowell)

ordered not to take the town: their job was to take the trenches situated outside. It was believed that the slower approach of infantry would allow the Turks to destroy the precious wells and water supplies and the actual taking of the town was planned as a job for the cavalry.[82]

General Chauvel's performance at the first two battles of Gaza gave cause for concern as his excessive care for the horses had arguably led to the loss of position in both of the first two battles. At this critical stage in the third battle he hesitated again and referred the decision back to Allenby. The crucial difference between Allenby and previous HQ staff now became obvious. Allenby's HQ was up with the battle – it had been moved forward to the Divisional HQ at Bir el Esani, Allenby knew the ground and had not wasted his first months in command.

When Chauvel requested permission to withdraw to water the horses, Allenby issued an order which, in hindsight, may well have been the most decisive intervention of the battle. He ordered Chauvel to take Beersheba to secure the water and prisoners. The order was peremptory and allowed no ambiguity, and Chauvel took the correct decision and put the Australian 4th Light Horse Brigade in to take the city. There was less than half an hour between Allenby's order to take the city and the Light Horse Brigade starting their advance. The Australians went in at the charge, overran the remaining defenders and by 9 p.m. were camped in the city having taken it intact. An Australian sergeant, H. Langtip, describes the day:

> We rode all night to get right around Beersheba, 32 miles in all. It is 9:30am and we are all standing to. Our horses ready to go into the line to attack within the next few minutes. It was a heavy ride in terrible dust all the way. The horses have still got their saddles on and I don't know when they will get them off to. The attack started at 4:30pm and within half an hour the first trenches were cleared and then they never stopped until they got to Beersheba. Our casualties were fairly light considering the ground was as flat as a table. Nine o'clock we are camped in the town with outposts out. The Turks blew up the station and the engine, set fire to the ammunition and the stores.[83]

The damage done to the wells by the German and Turkish engineers turned out to be reparable and in the circumstances was fairly light. By the evening of the first day of the battle proper, Allenby had achieved one of his main objectives and had placed his own personal mark on the campaign. The final occupation of Beersheba had to be undertaken carefully as the retreating troops had done all they could to booby trap the city and had tried to destroy the wells and pumping equipment. Because it was critical to Allenby's plans to have a guaranteed source of water at Beersheba, there was a lull in the battle lasting several days as the engineers got the water running again.

Meanwhile, Bill Cowell and his fellow Royal Bucks Hussars had been moved up to Shellal where the headquarters of the Yeomanry Mounted Division was situated. As part of a mobile reserve their job would be to reinforce whichever of Allenby's strikes needed them next. Shellal was the ideal point for a reserve force as it enabled Allenby and his commanders to move troops from this central point to Tel es Sheria (a critical point in the Turkish defence) or to either Gaza or Beersheba – all of which were within range of mounted troops.

The Bucks Yeomanry spent the opening day of the battle in bivouac at Shellal but by day two (1 November), with Beersheba taken and safely in Allied hands, Allenby began to bring in all of his troops to ensure that they were exploited to the full. The next stages of the battle saw Allenby hit the Turks at Gaza, where he made a full-blooded assault on their defences between the city and the coast, opening the way for the Indian cavalry to get behind the city and exploit the breakthrough. However, this was not intended to be the final blow. In the manner of a boxer who attacks the body in order to bring his opponent's guard down before moving up to the head for the knock-out blow, Allenby intended to pound Gaza in order to keep the defenders in situ. The knock-out blow would occur nearer Beersheba, at Tel es Sheria.

The key to the Turkish defensive effort was hinged on Tel es Sheria, the central point which, if taken by the Allies, would enable them to roll up both sides of the Turkish defence. Allenby had by no means won the battle at this stage. He had achieved his initial objectives, but the Turks were far from out of the game. Indeed, von Kressenstein, the German commander of the Turkish forces, described the Allies' attacks as having been 'repulsed'. Whilst this was probably overstating the case, there was still scope for optimism on the Turkish side.

For the next two days (2 and 3 November), the Bucks Yeomanry ranged in patrols out from Shellal into the Wadi Imleih and Wadi es Sheria where they scouted, occasionally reporting contact with enemy patrols but rarely getting into a fire fight. By this stage, the weather had changed for the worse as the dreaded *khamsin* wind was blowing, charged with sand, making conditions difficult for both man and horse. Allenby was utilising this lull in the fighting to ensure water supplies in Beersheba were delivered at maximum capacity and that troops, horses and camels were watered and refreshed for what was to come.

Allenby then unleashed a series of hammer blows on the Turkish line; the Bucks Hussars supported the 74th and 53rd Divisions. These divisions consisted of infantry troops – the 74th Division consisting mainly of dismounted yeomanry regiments and the 53rd Division mainly drawn from the Royal Welch Fusiliers, The Welch Regiment and Cheshire Regiment, plus other county regiments and supported by field artillery. Collectively, they were under the command of Lieutenant General Sir Philip Chetwode and, together with the Desert Mounted Corps, were designated the XX Corps.

Their job was to capture Tel el Khuweilfeh and Tel es Sheria. In driving through the middle towards high ground where the Turks defended their critical administrative and communications points in some depth, Allenby still hoped to push north-westward towards the coast and cut off the main Turkish forces from their retreat north up the coast. At one point, the Bucks Hussars' war diary reports, they captured a Turkish ambulance, fifty camels and

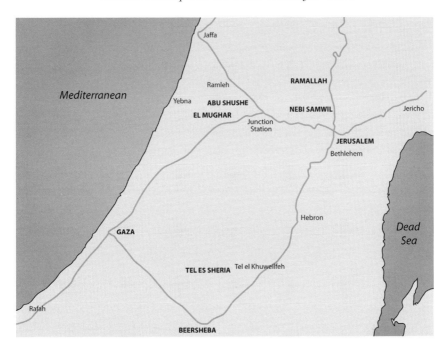

thirty wounded soldiers. The yeomanry and the Australian Mounted Division were sent round Gaza and the Anzac Division farther north to patrol the gap between the two infantry corps. The weather was getting worse, but on this coastal strip the heaviest rain drained through the sand immediately. Half an hour of sunshine was enough to dry the surface. For the first time in many weeks the horses had clean, dry standing, and the effect of this was soon evident in the improved condition of their legs and coats.

There were signs that the Turks were breaking, but their defence was sufficiently robust to allow much of their army to escape Allenby's encirclement of Gaza and what had been a rolling up of the enemy lines became a pursuit northwards. The war diary of the Royal Bucks Hussars reports little of the fighting that took place over these few days. There were obviously some hard days, as the Adjutant reports watering the horses at Beersheba on 7 November not having had any previous opportunity to water the horses for forty-eight hours.

In conjunction with the other mounted yeomanry regiments (6th, 8th and 22nd Mounted Brigades), the Royal Bucks Hussars advanced on Tel el Khuweilfeh, mainly guarding the flanks and providing cover for the 74th and 53rd Divisions. However, there are reports of casualties in the Bucks war diaries so the fighting was not totally passing them by.

The infantry and their artillery support successfully took both Tel el Khuweilfeh and Tel es Sheria, and the way was now open to take the rest of the defensive line without the need for expensive 'face-on' attacks. The fixed defensive points built by the Turks were obviously constructed on the under-standing that attacks would be launched directly from the south. With the allies now through the main line and attacking from the north and west, there was no further prolonged resistance from the Turkish troops. Allenby had emerged from his first major battle in the Middle East as the undoubted victor. However, he had failed to take significant numbers of prisoners as, crucially for his plans, a large proportion of the Turkish forces had successfully withdrawn northwards and were setting up new defensive lines based at Wadi el Hesi.

9

TURKISH RETREAT AND THE CAPTURE OF JERUSALEM

Following his success in breaking the Turkish line between Beersheba and Gaza, General Allenby was determined to keep the Turks on the run and deny them the chance to dig in and fortify further positions within Palestine. Good generals always have an eye for the bigger picture, not just the immediate battle, and Allenby was a good general. He knew well that, though it was a substantial battle in itself, breaking the Gaza-Beersheba defensive line was just a start. If there was to be a chance, however remote, of knocking the Turks out of the alliance with the Central Powers and thus making a real contribution to winning the war, they had to be completely defeated in the Middle East.

Even the liberation of Jerusalem was presentational rather than an overriding strategic objective, but, nevertheless, Allenby was under no illusion that it was expected of him. Lloyd George and his beleaguered administration made it quite clear that they needed some good news in order to raise morale back in Britain. For well over two years the British public had been subject to horrific casualty lists with few commensurate gains in territory in France, and the Prime Minister needed a clear-cut victory to celebrate. It was, however, not as clear cut as a direct order from the War Cabinet; military leaders throughout time will recognise the telegrams which flowed between the War Cabinet, via the Chief of the Imperial War Staff, to General Allenby. They certainly wished him to liberate Jerusalem, but, at the same time, they did not want further major casualty lists, nor did they want Allenby to tie up large numbers of troops holding territory which had little strategic value. It was the classic politician's trick of 'I take the credit if you succeed and you get sacked if you fail.'

However, Allenby was nothing if not determined. One look at the photographs of him shows this quite clearly, both in his face and the way that he seems to be pushing out of pictures as if eager to get on with things rather than wait for photographs to be taken. The high-quality cavalry troops he now had, with the yeomanry, the Australian and New Zealand light horse brigades, gave him a useful weapon to push home his advantage, though it had to be weighed against the difficulties of resupply and the topography of the country the troops were expected to fight over.

The area of Palestine which was fought over was some 50 miles wide from west to east. Looking at it from west to east, there is, firstly, a coastal plain which is approximately 10 miles wide and rises from sea level to approximately 300ft above sea level. The limestone hills which rise from the eastern edge of the plain rise to some 3,000ft above sea level and then, on the eastern side, drop down into a rift valley which is a deep trench well below sea level and includes the Dead Sea. To the east, the Judean Hills rise again to the plateau of Moab, which at the highest point is some 5,000ft above the Dead Sea. The hills are in the main rocky, sometimes terraced, but not heavily cultivated as they are too stony and devoid of any topsoil to produce crops. Agriculture is mainly located on the coastal plain and along the *wadis*.

From the Gaza-Beersheba line Allenby's forces pushed northwards up the coastal plain and north-easterly towards the gap between the Turkish Seventh and Eighth Armies. Allenby knew he had to keep the Turks rolling back to stop them creating another defensive line. The problem, as always, was resupply as the Turkish rail lines were a different gauge to those the British had built up to Gaza and therefore were not immediately available. Equally, resupply from the sea was hampered because of the lack of suitable harbours on the coastline north of Gaza. Allenby had to deal with the age-old problem to which successful generals have always had to find an answer. As he conquered new territory and moved forward, and as his enemies retreated, he was constantly moving away from his supplies whilst the enemy's lines of communication were shortening. It was now that the value of the training which had taken place prior to the Third Battle of Gaza was proven. Allenby was asking for one last great effort from the troops, the supply officers and, not least, from the animals, to drive the Turks out of Palestine and not succumb to fatigue. In the end it was to be a close-run race, but not the least of Allenby's gifts as a military commander was his ability to judge when and how much he could push the troops and when recuperation periods were essential.

During the initial stages of the Battle of Gaza the Bucks Hussars, together with the remaining elements of the Yeomanry Mounted Division, were moving north-west from their position midway between Gaza and Beersheba at Shellal towards the left wing of the Allied attack, and joined the Australians and New Zealanders in rolling up the line before beginning the move northwards. Their first objective was Junction Station, which was where the Haifa-Jerusalem and the Beersheba line met. Not only was it important from the point of view of being a major rail transport point, it also enabled Allenby to dominate the road system, such as it was. Junction Station was also level with Jerusalem and would thus enable the army to push eastwards into the city. There was also rolling stock stored at Junction Station, which the British could use on the captured Turkish rail track to assist their resupply.

On 11 November, the day after the Allies burst through the Gaza-Beersheba line, Allenby received a telegram from the Chief of the Imperial General Staff pointing out that his activities should be limited as he may well be required to release troops at any time if the situation on the Western Front demanded it. He was reminded that, whilst he should do all he could to weaken the enemy's offensive power, he should not take on difficult positions which may be subsequently expensive to defend. There is a very old joke which concerns a person walking down Whitehall looking for the War Office: on seeing a soldier he asks him which side the War Office is on and receives the reply 'Ours, I hope'. There must have been times when Allenby appreciated the ironic nature of this joke.

Nevertheless, on receiving assurances from the Chief of the Imperial General Staff that he should not take the telegram as forbidding the capture of Jerusalem, he pushed on. The rainy season was about to begin, which was bound to make campaigning more difficult as the coastal plain rapidly turned into a morass under the hooves of countless horses, camels and pack mules. On 10 November, as the Bucks Hussars started the move northwards, the weather was beautiful. With the enemy already out of contact to the north, the Hussars rode along the coastal strip in ideal conditions before swinging north-eastwards in a wide arc north of Junction Station to a village in the hills called El Mughar.

The Turkish troops were building a defensive line along the ridge which joined the two villages of El Mughar and Qatra. The ridge was not particularly high, but was steep-sided and, as was typical for the region, the villages made excellent strong points as they were surrounded by stone walls and prickly pear hedges which were impenetrable for troops on horseback.

At 10.30 on the morning of 13 November, the Bucks Hussars were assisting the County of London Yeomanry in clearing the large village of Yibna of a Turkish machine gun crew. Having achieved their objective, the Bucks Hussars moved on to Wadi Jamus and, together with the artillery from the Berks Yeomanry, began to bombard El Mughar. The Royal Bucks Hussars were in a *wadi* waiting for infantry to take a line of hills, but the infantry got bogged down thanks to heavy machine gun fire and Lieutenant Perkins is reported afterwards as quoting Brig-Gen Godwin, saying 'We'll gallop it.' Lieutenant Perkins was then ordered to fetch A Squadron under Major Lawson who had been detached from the main body of Hussars for reconnaissance purposes.

Before this, however, Lt Col Cripps sent forward Perkins to reconnoitre the ground ahead. Lieutenant Perkins trotted around in full view of the Turkish machine gunners which was described by an eyewitness thus: 'He cantered up and down under a hail of machine gun fire which followed him as the spotlight follows a dancer on stage.'[84]

He evidently lived a charmed life as he returned to report back without a scratch and, following his report, Brigadier General Godwin took the decision to attack the ridge on horseback. The enemy were dug in on the ridge on two

The Action of EL MAGHAR.

13th November. 1917.

Charge of 6th Mounted Brigade.

(Falls, *Official History of the Great War Egypt and Palestine*) prominent spurs and, following consultation, the Bucks Hussars were to attack the right-hand spur and the Dorset Yeomanry the left-hand spur, with the Berkshire Yeomanry held in reserve. On the flat ground between the brigade and the Turks ran the narrow Wadi Jamus, wide enough only to take horsemen in single file. Two squadrons of Bucks Yeomanry were already in the *wadi* and the Dorset Yeomanry were ordered to join them. The brigade's three machine gun sections, the 17th Machine Gun Squadron and the Berkshire Royal Horse Artillery, were ordered to take up positions to support the attack.

At 3 p.m. the Bucks Yeomanry emerged from the *wadi* to cross some 3,000 yards of open ground covered by Turkish machine gunners to reach their objective. The mounted troops had already learnt the lesson from previous engagements that it is better to cross fire zones at a brisk canter than on foot. The simple lesson was that the less time spent in the killing zone, the fewer the casualties. The Dorset Yeomanry also emerged on their left to cover some 4,000 yards of similarly open ground. A Squadron was ordered to gallop the spur and then attack dismounted. B and C Squadrons followed and dismounted where A Squadron's horse holders were seeking to make use of the limited cover available. Here they too formed up and advanced up the hill.

During Perkins' ride back to the *wadi* he saw a pool of water in a *wadi* and, as they were so water conscious, he rather foolishly let his horse drink. On getting back he was just in time to find Troop Sergeant Durrant bringing B Squadron out of the *wadi* to charge. He took over from Durrant and soon found his squadron commanding officer, Major Bulteel, trotting in front.

It was about 2 miles to the summit of the ridge and hard uphill going for most of the way. Major Bulteel intended to keep to a trot, but inevitably everyone got excited and keyed up and it became more a reined-in canter. Major Bulteel drew his sword, so Perkins drew his, as did the rest of the men.

It had, by then, became more difficult for the officers to set a controlled gallop in order to hit the Turks more or less in line – Lieutenant Perkins describes the sensation as they breasted the ridge as like being knocked in the face by a pillow as he rode along. It was the blast from fire directed at them. He clearly remembers thinking about the need to follow the Tidworth training, especially about how not to be pulled out of the saddle after striking a man with the sword. He thinks that he may have killed at least one, but may have hit several others. Having reached the top of the hill, his horse stopped dead and he slapped it hard with a sword, but she would not move – she was probably blown from the water drunk earlier. He, along with other Hussars, dismounted and hopped into a slit trench. The Dorsets had been slower to reach the Turks as they had started further back and, for a short time, until they arrived, the Turks were able to enfilade the Bucks Hussars.

Lieutenant Perkins walked over the top of the ridge when fire had died down and found a quarry in which a corporal had several hundred Turks whom he

At camp in the desert. (Bill Cowell)

had apparently apprehended. Major Bulteel had by then already spotted the problem as, looking out from the ridge, he could see a mass of Turks at the foot of the ridge trying to reform, but out of range, and the yeomanry could do nothing to stop them moving off.

One Turkish officer, being marched along as a prisoner, came over and tried to say, in French, that he wanted an officer's escort instead of being compelled to march along with the rabble. Bulteel got Pte Cox, an amateur boxer, to come over and take charge of the officer. Cox, seeing the Turk's epaulettes, whipped out his clasp knife and, to the shock of the Turk, cut them off.

The Turks could have only seen B Squadron and the lead squadron of Dorset Yeomanry originally, and yet, despite being in trenches, they panicked when the cavalry got close. The mounted troops could not have got to them if they had stayed in their slit trenches as they would not have been able to reach them with their swords. The Turks committed the fatal mistake of running, which was exactly what they should not have done. The pre-war training undertaken at Tidworth Training Camp had stressed that no cavalry charges should be more than 600 yards, yet the yeomanry went over 2 miles at a canter and then a gallop. The famous painting by James Beadle of this charge depicts the Buckinghamshire Yeomanry's part in the action, led by the left-handed Major Bulteel.

The Royal Bucks Hussars' losses were comparatively light, with six ORs and one officer killed. Two Distinguished Service Orders, one Military Cross, three Distinguished Conduct Medals and seven Military Medals were awarded for actions on this day to yeomanry soldiers. Sadly, Major Bulteel reported that he had only two married men in his troop – Cpl Shaw and Sgt Durrant – and they were the only two killed, both shot through the forehead in almost identical fashion

The charge, which is officially regarded as the last major cavalry charge carried out by the British Army, was subsequently described by Lieutenant Cyrus H. Perkins as follows:

> General Godwin our much admired Brigadier, ex Indian cavalry, who had recently taken over the command of our 6th Mounted Brigade, was up among us looking over the situation with my Colonel Fred Cripps and when a request for assistance was received it was offered at once. The Colonel then asked me to recce the ground between us and the ridge about two miles away. Having learned in my days with the 7th Reserve Cavalry at Tidworth that cavalry charges should not exceed 300 yards, I had in mind looking for cover for led horses, whence a short dismounted attack could be made and although the map indicated what seemed a depression about a mile away between us and the ridge, it wasn't obvious whether it would serve as sufficient cover for the led horses after dismounting.[85]

He subsequently goes on to describe the charge:

> My troop was on the left and away to my right I could see Crocker Bulteel, my squadron leader, out in front keeping us at a trot to save the horses for the two miles to the ridge. As the enemy's fire hotted up it became harder to hold the horses to the trot, so gradually the pace quickened while we tried to keep the galloping squadron in line. As we neared the ridge swords were drawn and very soon we were breasting the rise with their guns blasts feeling like pillows hitting one's face. Then in seconds they were all around us, some shooting, some scrambling out of slit trenches and some sensibly falling flat on their faces. It had taken us, I suppose, a bit over five minutes.
>
> Blown and galloping horses are hard to handle one handed while you have a sword in the other – so hindered by the clutter of rifle butt and other equipment troopers found it nearly impossible to get at a low dodging Turk. One missed and missed again until the odd Turk wasn't quite quick enough. In just such a case, the hours spent in arms drill paid off for one instinctively leaned well forward and remained so to offset the jerk as the sword comes out – in fact precisely as one has so often been told.
>
> By then, those of us who had got there still mounted were among a seething mob – literally like mounted policemen in a football crowd – shouting at them to surrender in the only words we were supposed to know, sounding like '*Tesleem Olinuz*'. Years later in Cyprus I learned the proper translation – said to be Hands Up the lot of you.

All this shouting however didn't seem much good – probably because on our bit of the front only about nine blokes had arrived on the ridge until the next squadron reached us. The Turks were milling about and heading down the far side of the ridge where a few hundred got into what I found later to be a quarry.[86]

Lieutenant Bowyer, whom I have already quoted at some length on the attacks on the Senussi, was also present at El Mughar, and I will allow him again to take up the story:

The Hon Neil Primrose, our squadron leader, comes up to our troop which was doing the advanced work. From the hill we are on we can see bodies of Turks moving from Katra to El Mughar, and continually entering the cactus gardens that abound there, while from direct in front the Turks are shelling the brigade on our left from Yerbna. Captain Primrose sends Dodger back with a report: also Lieutenant Alston takes Hedges and his section out to a village on our right, finding it practically unoccupied, but capturing half a dozen Turks. Meanwhile Mr Primrose goes on himself to a higher hill in front, taking my section and self as escort.

We can now overlook all of the plain to Mughar village and ridge, on which there is a great deal of enemy activity. Luckily he leaves us there as a look-out, so we make ourselves snug behind some boulders, and have an excellent view of the morning's attack. A Scotch brigade of infantry is going to attack across the plain to el Mughar, right round to the far side of Katra. We can see their supporting batteries coming up and about twelve o'clock they start the attack, the infantry starting in waves covered by their artillery. They reach a wadi about half way across the plain, but after that they cannot push home the attack, the ground being open and swept by fire of all sorts from the top of the ridge. They make about four attempts, and returning wounded infantry say it is hell in the valley.

It is now about midday, and our post is called into the main body. We are going to gallop out to the wadi for an attack. We spread out and go a troop at a time: most of us get across safely. Keigwen, in my section, gets a bullet through the neck, luckily too as he was feeling the strain of continuous operations. The mounted machine gun corps follow us across, and we know the Berks and Dorsets are somewhere on the flanks. Meanwhile 'A' squadron have attacked Yebna, galloping straight at the village, capturing it and its defenders at a comparatively slight loss. Dodger, about all that is left of my original section, comes along with the news that we are going to gallop the position. This suits us better than a long tiring advance dismounted, but it seems rather an awkward finish. Anyhow we have dinner together, finishing a whole tin of jam in great style.

A typical mountain pass in Palestine.
(Bill Cowell)

Soon we get our definite orders, up on top at three o'clock sharp, spread out, and go for the position in lines, a squadron at a time, with 'B' squadron leading, Crocker Bulteel at their head. 'C' follow immediately. At three o'clock we scramble out all along the valley and start galloping. Johns, now in my section, is my next door neighbour and we strike over the first troop. Immediately a great clatter of fire starts all along the top of the ridge. Old 'Owen' one of the original Bucks horses and well known before the war with Leopold de Rothschild's staghounds, is struck full in the chest, and blood is pumping out, but he galloped the whole mile and three quarters and then dropped dead at the foot of the position. Gallant old fellow. For a moment the shellfire is heavy, as Johnny has the range of the gulleys, and a H.E. drops just between a machine gun pack horse and its fellow. A few yards in front I have a momentary vision of two horses, a man, and a lot of smoke, flying outwards as I flashed past.

Half a mile from our starting point we come on another slight wadi. He also has this ranged for our guns. We cannot get down and through all along so several casualties occur here. Johns and I get through straightaway, and, after this, are up in the middle of 'B' squadron. I can see Captain Bulteel just in front so know we have a good 'un to follow. I believe the rifle and machine gun fire got heavier as we neared the slope. Anyhow, several horses and riders turned over in quite the approved battle picture style, and the ground was zipping and spluttering as the bullets hit it.

We seemed now to be an extraordinary few to be charging a position, but we drew our swords and 'forward on!' We had come through a line of infantry lying flat on the plain and not enjoying life a lot. On seeing swords come out, not flash out as a saddle with two feeds and extra bivvy sheets will not allow of this, the Turks began to crawl back over their trench. This put fresh cheer into us and our shouts redoubled but the last hundred yards up a steep slope, horses blown and almost in a walk, with heavy enfilade fire, were trying moments.

However, now we are on top we jump the Turkish trench and sweep over the hill, down the far side, right through a mob of Turks, and swinging round and driving them into a very convenient ravine on the far side. I think there were about eight of us under Captain Bulteel, and about 90 Turks, all shouting and gesticulating, but quite willing to lay down arms. Immediately we are through the line, the Turks sweep the top of the hill with shrapnel, and we are glad of our shelter, several of the Turks being hit with their own fire. The trouble is that we are isolated – we do not know where the rest of the attackers have got to. I have never seen Captain Bulteel so excited, and we have some rare shooting at bodies of the Turks running back out of the cactus gardens. Soon the firing dies down a bit and we get in touch with the remainder, who, under Captain Primrose, had driven a wedge in, about a quarter of a mile to our right. Here, Major Evelyn Rothschild is mortally wounded at the foot of the hill, and the fire is even hotter than where we went over.

The Dorsets and the Berks almost simultaneously have attacked further along the slope, and the position by dusk is finally won. This was imagined to be the Turks' next big position behind Gaza and it was a great feat of cavalry to have taken it. I have never known our boys in such high spirits as we were that night although our losses had been grievous. We had had what every cavalryman longs for – and had been successful against an almost impossible position. To turn to our own squadron losses, Joey Harland was wounded, also Stroud, Spink, and Sgt Revel of our immediate troop. In all, I think, we lost about sixty percent of our horses hit and about forty men killed or wounded in our two squadrons.[87]

The following extract is taken from *Memoirs of a Worcestershire Yeomanry Officer* by Capt O. Teichman and is dated 1 December 1917:

We heard details of the brilliant charge by the Berks, Bucks, and Dorset Yeomanry at El Mughar some weeks ago, when they galloped across from Yebna over 3 miles of open plain, and eventually routed some thousands of Turks with numerous machine guns and some artillery on the opposite hill. After exchanging our experiences with one another, the two Brigades parted, and we received orders to take over the line from Suffa to Tahta, with an advanced dressing station south of Beit Sira. We rode through the native vil-

The Royal Bucks Hussars with Turkish guns captured at El Mughar. (Bill Cowell)

lages of Barriye and El Kubab, and, descending the serpentine road from the latter, halted on the Wadi Neda orders were then changed, regiments being sent back via Annabeh, Berfilya, and Burj to approach the line from the west, while the guns and the bearer section of the Field Ambulance proceeded up the Amwas track to Beit Sira. As I would not be of much use in rough country with my arm strapped to my side, I was given charge of the remainder of the Field Ambulance, with all transport, horses and camels. Accordingly, together with the rest of the Brigade transport and the horses of the three regiments, we proceeded back to El Kubab in order to bivouac for the night. This place was on a considerable hill on the main road from Jaffa to Jerusalem, and it was interesting to examine the trenches, now two and a half years old, which had been dug by the Turks in 1915, when they feared the possibility of an Allied landing at Jaffa and consequent march on Jerusalem.

At the end of the first fortnight, which was a period of rest for the men as well as the horses, there was an all round improvement. Forage was plentiful again and of fair quality. After the first fortnight, training recommenced, gradually at first, so as not to check the recovery of the horses. By the end of the month however, brigade and divisional schemes were in full swing.[88]

One other section involved in the charge at El Mughar was the 22nd Mounted Brigade. Their view is contained in the following account by Col J.F.M. Robinson, who was at the time a captain (acting major) in the East Riding Yeomanry:

I commanded one of the leading squadrons (A Squadron East Riding Yeomanry) in this action, and in my opinion the enveloping movement and charge on the Turks' extreme right and rear considerably helped the success of the day. As it was the only occasion in the war that two brigades of cavalry actually charged with swords in the same action, I therefore add a description of the action as seen by me, whether it is worth keeping as a record is, or for your consideration. Probably there are plenty of eye witnesses who could describe it better. The Yeomanry mounted division was moving round to, the Turkish right, the 22nd mounted brigade being on the left of the 6th mounted brigade had further to go. We were halted behind a ridge when General Fryer our Brigadier sent for his commanding officers, after which Major Moore our C.O. called our squadron leaders up the ridge. When we got there we were shown our objective on the Mughar ridge by the Brigadier himself, and also saw the Bucks patrols coming in and then the 6th Mounted Brigade deploy and set off.

We should be half an hour at the most behind them. We charged in the same open order, one squadron of Staffords and one of East Riding Yeomanry in front, the other following Lincolns behind deployed over the width of the preceding regiments. Just before dropping into the Wadi Janus [sic] I look round, the 6th Mounted Brigade was spread out galloping in after line on my right front in open order. I then looked back and my own brigade was cantering down the slope behind in similar lines, every bit and button shining and swords drawn, all horses in hand and beginning to lather, shells dropping, and the men cheerful and ready to go all out. After a breather for the horses

Turkish troops fighting in the desert. (Wikimedia Commons)

we got well away and came under machine gun fire as well as shell fire, but it was too high as a rule as the Turks' could not shorten range quick enough. As we came up the ridge I saw what we had previously suspected that the point we were to attack was a false crest and there was a machine gun emplacement covering it. Although the men were by then going all out I managed to control half the squadron and lead them to the real crest, killing what Turks we could on the way, captured the machine guns, and went into action dismounted, doing good execution with our rifles and Hotchkiss guns that had kept up well.

A wonderful sight was the far side of the ridge, it is very much steeper, and there were two to three thousand Turks retiring and running down it and across the valley to Old Aqir one thousand yards off. I must say that at no time was the 22nd Mounted Brigade held up in this fighting. Our orders were – 'under no circumstances whatever were we to go beyond the Mughar Ridge' – it was not until reading an account of the fighting in some book that I knew that the railway was our objective, had the Regimental officers in the Brigade known this then, the leading regiments, there is no doubt, could have galloped on, leaving Akir on our right, and cut the Railway before dark as there was little opposition in that direction at the time. I base this on the following narrative. On reaching the crest and dismounting under cover I very soon had a strong defensive position among the rocks. Two other squadrons joined me, one under Captain Sidebottom of the Staffords and B squadron my own regiment under Captain Sykes. No commanding officer was present. The two squadron leaders came to me for instruction as the senior. We could see Old Aqir below, half a mile away, and the Turks streaming into it from all directions, and we could also see the red roofs of a civilised European village which I, for one, had never heard of. Our maps from which we fought showed only one village of Aqir, the new village was the first of the new places (Jewish colonies) we had come across.

I decided that now was the chance to both kill Turks and capture Old Aqir and the ridge beyond, which obviously was the jumping off ground to capture New Aqir. I remember pointing out to Captains Sidebottom and Sykes that it was against our orders, but we must go after putting up all our Hotchkiss Guns and sufficient men to hold the present position, and leaving somebody in charge (as per Chapter 5 F.S.R) to report to the C.O. when he came up. I only had half a squadron, the half having stopped on the false crest and no officer available I therefore left a corporal Appleton in charge, and told him to report to Major Moore O.C. East Riding Yeomanry. Captain Sidebottom went off to the North and Captain Sykes towards a prominent knoll North East, and I went straight for Aqir. By that time I could see C. Squadron East Riding Yeomanry under Major Lyon on the Mughar ridge on my right. He afterwards came down and got into the village at the southern end.

I collected about fifteen men and we slid in single file down a water course, spread out when the going was better and raced amongst the Turks, killing some, and so through the cemetery into Old Aqir, a village with only donkey paths where we went in single file, shouting and I using a revolver when I could, driving the Turks out before us we went across the square, out the other side and dismounted behind a ridge. Here the men were able to use their rifles with wonderful effect as there was a solid column of Turks retiring across our front at under a thousand yards, and we could see them falling. I had four signallers and a Helio with me, this was set up in the cemetery but we could get no answers, and no one came to support us so I withdrew after watering ourselves and the horses at the well there, and reported to my C.O. before dark on the Mughar ridge. I was ordered to dig in an outpost line at once for the night. I put in for recognition for gallantry for one or two of my men, but nothing came of it. My casualties were, one killed, and two or three slightly wounded. I found that the other squadrons had returned before me, after doing some damage also. From what I have written, which can be confirmed by others present and alive to-day, I think you will agree that the 22nd Mounted Brigade should be given credit to a certain extent, as well as the 6th Mounted Brigade for the finest cavalry action of the war. Had the staff of the 22nd Mounted Brigade, realised the position, and informed us before starting that our objective was the railway, we should have got it that night.[89]

The loss of Major Evelyn de Rothschild, mortally wounded at El Mughar, was another of the terrible coincidences which seems to plague this most terrible of all wars. His father had been the moving force behind the British Zionist movement which had lobbied the British Government to press for a Jewish home state. The Bucks Hussars were moving against the villages where the Turkish troops made their rear guard defences, many of which had been built by Rothschild money.

A few days prior to the action at El Mughar, there had been another cavalry action at Huj carried out by the Warks and Worcs Yeomanry. Whilst successful in driving off the Turks, the charge had resulted in seventy wounded and killed out of the 120 troops who took part in the charge. At El Mughar the results were much more in favour of the British as a result of ensuring adequate machine gun and artillery support for the shock troops. However, Lieutenant Perkins also offered the following thoughts:

One may ask why Johnny Turk, acknowledged to be a tough customer, was overcome in perhaps 10 to 15 minutes by galloping cavalry? Imagine, however his reactions, a line of horsemen appear out of a wadi two miles away, but too far to shoot at. Soon they are in range, but by then another line of horsemen

Turkish artillery hidden behind one of the feared prickly pear hedges. (Wikimedia Commons)

emerge and apparently your rifle fire and the machine gun show no dramatic result. In your growing anxiety your aim is dodgy to say the least, and again a third line of horsemen appear. It is all very quick and even in those days when most men were used to horses the galloping onrush is frightening – so do you stand pat, or run? Foolishly, in their indecision many of them got out of their slit trenches – shooting or running. Had they sat tight they would have been an almost impossible target for troopers' swords on galloping horses, and our success could not have been so sudden.[90]

The capture of the El Mughar ridge was just a start for the Berks and Bucks Yeomanry and other members of the 6th Mounted Brigade. Their next task was to advance and capture the ridge from Sidun to Abu Shushe, and by early morning of 15 November the troops were in place and ready to attack. The fortified Turkish were positioned on a formidable ridge even steeper than El Mughar. It constituted one of the last points at which the Turkish forces could reasonably expect to make a stand to hold a continuous front line and thus protect Jerusalem from Allenby's forces. Advancing into the Judean Hills negated any advantage that cavalry had given Allenby on the plains. General Barrow described the countryside as resembling:

On a small scale, the Himalayas that compose the northwest frontier of India. It is a waterless wilderness of tumultuous hills broken by small ravines and stony valleys and marked by the built up terraces and decayed wine presses of a bygone system of agriculture. Stones are everywhere, ranging in size from pebbles to boulders a couple of feet high. There are no paths or tracks between villages as are usually found in mountainous regions that are inhabited.[91]

Horses now became a liability rather than a useful means of transport. The troopers were mainly leading them, which naturally led to increased tiredness as well as adding to the burden of needing to be fed and watered at regular intervals. Nevertheless, Allenby was determined to push the troops on. The Turkish rear guard had formed their defensive line on high ground above the village of Abu Shushe, thus blocking the Vale of Ajalon which was the principle point of entry to the Judean Hills. The positions had to be occupied in order to be able to overlook and thus safely capture Jerusalem and, even more importantly, dividing the two Turkish armies.

Again, as at El Mughar, the 6th Mounted Brigade were sent in. This time they approached in a far more measured fashion. The troops moved forward against the Turks from three different directions, taking advantage of any shelter afforded by the rocky approach and expertly covered all of the way by machine gun and field gun fire. Only the last few hundred yards were covered at the charge and by then the Turks had had enough and retired to fight another day. Major Neil Primrose was killed in the charge on the top of the ridge. He was the younger son of Lord Rosebery, who had been Liberal Prime Minister. Neil Primrose was himself an MP and had, prior to the war, been carving out a career for himself as a Liberal politician. One more death of many hundreds of young men who would have undoubtedly been leaders of the new inter-war generation, had the war spared them.

The battle, which had commenced at 6.00 a.m., saw the Bucks and Berks Yeomanry attack the ridge while the Queen's Own Dorset Yeomanry were ordered to capture the village of Sidun. Two squadrons charged the village from the south, while B Squadron worked its way around the back and charged from the north, capturing over a hundred prisoners, one Krupp gun and two machine guns. The Krupp gun is today on display at Sherborne Castle in Dorset. Major Wingfield-Digby of the Dorset Yeomanry commanding B Squadron was awarded the DSO for his courage and for the way he had handled his squadron.

The attack, though successful, highlighted yet again that attacking the enemy on horseback at the charge left the horses blown, unable to follow up the retreating Turks and take significant numbers of prisoners. The Turkish troops deserve much credit for their discipline and fighting qualities. To be constantly retreating over 70 miles and being driven out of their defensive positions by an enemy that considerably outnumbered them was, to say the least, dispiriting. Yet the Turkish soldiery remained phlegmatic and never gave in. They sold each position hard and maintained a disciplined retreat when it could have so easily become a disorderly rout.

The Age, an Australian newspaper, reported the battle:

> Our eye-witness gives the following interesting details of the charge in Palestine in which Captain Primrose, MP, youngest son of Lord Rosebery, was killed.
>
> Captain Neil Primrose charged at the head of his men over two miles of perfectly flat plain swept by shells and machine guns. Three thousand Turks held an almost impregnable position at the top of a steep ridge, 200 feet high. Our men and horses, mad with excitement, went straight to the top, and, charging the Turks, captured all their guns and twelve hundred prisoners. They ne'er stopped to count the dead, as a second charge was essential. Another ridge had to be taken at all costs. We dismounted and led our horses for a time, then charged again, notwithstanding that the enemy outnumbered us six to one. But the Turks hated the sight of our swords and they ran as we reached the height. Captain Primrose was killed in the last charge and Major Evelyn Rothschild, Captain Neil Primrose's second cousin, was mortally wounded.[92]

The rather breathless and 'heroic' style aside, what is interesting about this report is the similarities with the situation faced by the Bucks Hussars at Suvla Bay in Gallipoli. In both battles, the Bucks soldiers faced a well-dug-in, well-prepared enemy who held the high ground and had them in their artillery sights for some 2 miles before the defenders could be attacked. What made Abu Shushe successful and differentiated it from Suvla Bay was the fact that the troops were now mounted and not acting as infantrymen. Crossing the 'killing zone' on horseback dramatically shortened the time the soldiers were exposed to enemy fire and thus lessened the numbers killed or wounded before coming to grips with the Turks. Even with the invention of the internal combustion engine, horse soldiers still had a part to play in the First World War, albeit in certain types of warfare which suited them. Facing soldiers approaching at over 20 miles an hour on horseback and armed with swords was a discipline which armies had lost since the days of the French revolutionary wars and there would be no time to re-learn the skills and mindset required.

On 16 November, the regimental diary records the sad duty of burying Major Neil Primrose at Ramleh. Unfortunately, Lord Dalmeny (Primrose's elder brother) from the General Staff, had chosen to visit his brother. He arrived in time to attend his brother's funeral. General Barrow, commanding the Yeomanry Mounted Division, and Brigadier General Godwin, commanding the 6th Mounted Brigade, also attended the funeral.

Captain Cyrus Perkins wrote a letter home in which he described the recent actions:

For the first time since my last letter we've pulled up – it's been just wonderful – everything has gone perfectly and my greatest ambition has been fulfilled! I'm sure you wouldn't know me – today is the first time I've taken my clothes off and they are in ribbons. Of course I may not tell you where I am but we've covered about 350 miles – it's much nicer country and I find German comes in very handy with the Jews. We've had two actions which we are pleased about – one perhaps you will hear about – it was a charge – it was a great success. Two Regiments of us got 1000 prisoners 2 field guns & 15 M.Gs. It was 3000 yards to the high ridge they were on – I only had two killed and 5 wounded in my troop. I tell you, it's the most exhilarating thing in the world – we went mad. Damn funny, I was wounded but you can scarcely see it – just a piece out of my bridle hand. After getting through them I had to leave my mare – she was stone cold, so I've lost all the kit I ever did have!!! I'm glad to say I wetted the old sword a bit. Old Abdul doesn't wait for British cavalry any longer. Oh! Thomson was wounded in the thigh and my other servant took in his place yesterday. We buried poor Neil Primrose in the churchyard here this morning – he was killed yesterday. He was one of our squadron leaders. Stewart has not been with us – he had a septic hand before we started. Don't worry any more, all will be well now – I will write again when I've time. Please would you look up Mrs Shaw, 18 Nelson Road, St. Albans – her husband was killed – a corporal in my troop – a better or braver man never breathed I'm witness – shot in the forehead early in the charge.[93]

In order to fulfil his promise to the Prime Minister and capture Jerusalem before Christmas 1917, Allenby knew he must secure the roadway that ran from Nablus to Jerusalem at the point where it ran through the village of Ramallah. At this point the road runs along the main north–south plateau and is over 2,000ft above sea level. It was a critical line of communication for the Turks linking back to the north. Without control of this road, holding Jerusalem was unsustainable. It was therefore heavily defended by the Turks. The 6th Mounted Brigade advanced into the Judean Hills on 18 November. By now the weather had taken a turn for the worse and there was almost continuous rainfall. The yeomanry were still dressed in their desert gear and were not equipped for the wet and cold conditions in which they found themselves. In addition, they were advancing quicker than the supplies could keep up with and both men and horses were existing on meagre fare.

The rain turned the tracks along which the yeomanry marched into quagmires. Although marked on the general staff maps as 'roads', they were nothing of the sort and were totally unsuitable to take the punishment meted out by thousands of soldiers' boots, metal horseshoes, camels and heavy artillery. They simply disintegrated and, for the majority of the time, the soldiers were lead-

The charge of the Royal Buckinghamshire Hussars at El Mughar. (T.C. Dugdale, reproduced courtesy of the Bucks Military Museum)

ing their horses rather than riding them. On top of the awful conditions, the soldiers were experiencing the constant threat of ambush from Turkish rear guards. The country they marched through was perfect for defensive actions and guerrilla type tactics. Whilst none of the actions were 'battles' in themselves, they all added to the strain the army was now feeling.

By 20 November, the yeomanry, by now dismounted, were in a position some 4 miles short of their target but were meeting very strong resistance around Beitunia. On that day the yeomanry were operating as infantry and were holding a thinly manned front line which consisted of pockets of men, some with machine guns, manning points in a straggling line. The Turkish forces were determined to drive them off as this really was their last throw of the dice. They attacked over and over again and at this point they undoubtedly had considerable superiority in numbers. Eventually, the yeomanry were driven off and retreated to the line from where they had started, in the valley between the settlements of Beit el-Foqa and Beit Ur el-Tahta.

The Royal Bucks Hussars charge at El Mughar. (J.P. Beadle, reproduced courtesy of the Bucks Military Museum)

The Turks had prepared their positions carefully, with all the approaches targeted by their artillery and machine gun positions, and they simply were too strong for the tired Allied troops. General Allenby knew the strength of the men under his command and, after a couple of days rest, the 6th Mounted Brigade was sent back into the Judean Hills to begin the process yet again of driving the Turkish forces north from Jerusalem.

The Bucks Hussars were under no illusion that what was expected of them in this particular action was far more difficult than either El Mughar or Abu Shushe. This was to be their ultimate test in Palestine and they needed to call on all of their reserves of courage and endurance to continue the fight.

The village of Beitunia was overlooked by a kind of small terraced mountain. Lieutenant Perkins was again ordered forward to undertake a reconnaissance on foot. As he went up accompanied by Captain Bulteel, he came under enfilading fire and stopped behind one of the derelict stone-built terraces. Captain Bulteel had come up to see for himself what was happening. Any man who moved out into the open was sure to be hit as the Turks were able to target all of the paths leading up to their positions. Next, Lt Col Cripps came up and as he did so they called to him to be careful. He ignored this advice and was hit on his field glasses in front of his chest, which sent him to ground quicker than any shouted warning. They stayed there until they were ordered to attack at 3 p.m. with fixed bayonets. Captain Bulteel and Lieutenant Perkins, not unnaturally, did not like the sound of this and freely admitted afterwards that as they sat in the shelter of the terrace they smoked many a cigarette.

Around about 3 p.m. they suddenly saw the Dorset Yeomanry running back followed by large numbers of Turkish soldiers. A Turkish deserter had previously warned them of the presence of thousands of Turks in this area, but no one had believed him. The Turks then attacked the Bucks Hussars with what was apparently a fresh division, not the rabble expected. The Bucks Hussars retired in a hurry. As they did so, one of the troopers went down, shot through the thigh, which was broken. Four men put a rifle under his knees and one under his armpits and jumped him down the hill. Amazingly he survived that and a camel ride to the railhead. It had been raining the night before; they had had no breakfast and were now under a severe attack. Lieutenant Perkins, who by the nature of his duties was farthest forward and therefore the most exposed, eventually got down, albeit somewhat discomfited by his experience. On his return to the Brigade HQ, Lt Col F. Cripps told his batman, Lawrence, to give Perkins some biscuits as he had not had anything to eat. The batman could only give him crumbs as that was all that was left. The horses had been left in the village without water and food, and had eaten bark off the trees as they were so hungry. Not unnaturally, given the paucity of their diet, the horses were all in bad condition. Subsequently, the position was shelled by the Turkish artillery and many horses were massacred, which created an awful smell for the troops billeted there.

The yeomanry troops were by now severely depleted, with some 800 troops holding a 3-mile front. It was a sketchy front line to say the least and was under desperate pressure from the Turks. Far from splitting the two Turkish armies and then picking them off one by one, the Allies were in danger of being split themselves by this determined counter-attack. Fighting continued for several days in what was surely the hardest fighting the yeomanry had been faced with since Gallipoli. They gave ground but the Turkish forces could not advance into the gaps without exposing their troops to exactly the same enfilading fire from strongpoints to which they had been exposing the Allies. The front line was not really a line at all, but a succession of groups of men with machine guns and rifles grimly determined to hang on. They were freezing cold, dressed in desert gear, now fighting in the mountains with torrential rain and very cold. Many of them wore boots that were falling apart. As cavalry men they were wearing riding boots which were simply not made for slogging over rocky terrain and most of the movements were now on foot as the going was simply too tough and too slippery for horses.

Allenby and his commanders were eventually able to reinforce and thus strengthen the line with the addition of the Australian Light Horse Brigade and then subsequently with infantry troops. By 28 November it was becoming obvious to the Turks that they had failed to make the breakthrough into the British rear lines. With this knowledge, the Turkish resolve began to crumble and by 1 December Allenby was in the position to plan the liberation of

Jerusalem as the Turks began to stream northwards to regroup at a point well to the north of the Holy City.

Allenby had the great advantage of being able to pull forward fresh troops who had not been immediately exposed to the fierce fighting of the last two weeks and thus relieve the worn out, malnourished troops which included the Bucks Yeomanry.

By 29 November, the regiment was relieved by infantry and withdrew to Katrah. They were emaciated, most of their boots were in tatters and most, unable to shave for two weeks, had beards. It was going to take some time in the rear lines to recover and build up the strength of the regiment before they would be fit for duties in the front line. Ten days later the regiment returned to camp at El Medjel, where it spent Christmas 1917 and New Year. The regiment received Allenby's personal thanks.[94]

In the meantime, fresh troops were brought up by Allenby and although the Turkish troops counter-attacked bravely, they were inexorably pushed eastwards and northwards so that the pressure on Jerusalem grew and, by the first week of December, Allenby had circled Jerusalem and cut off the Turkish occupiers' line of retreat by straddling the Jerusalem-Nablus road. As neither side wished to destroy the Holy City, the end was inevitable. Allenby fixed the date for the final attack for 8 December.

He now had Welsh troops, with a cavalry regiment on the south side of the city as they had advanced from their positions north of Beersheba up the Hebron-Jerusalem road on 4 December. They had come across none of the Turkish Army during their advance, so they were still relatively fresh and situated just to the south of Bethlehem by the evening of 6 December. Allenby ordered them to push further north so that by the morning of 8 December they would cut off the city, though they had strict orders not to enter it.

On the 7th the weather broke, and for three days atrocious conditions held up the troops. The hills in which they were operating were covered in fog and observation from the air and visual signalling became impossible. The rain also severely hampered the supply operations. Despite the weather, Allenby's troops were now threatening Jerusalem from north, south and west, and the end of the Turkish occupation of the Holy City was inevitable.

During 8 December over 300 Turkish prisoners were taken and many killed whilst the British casualties were light. On 9 December Allenby continued to tighten his stranglehold and as the troops to the north of the city pushed further eastwards to finally cut off the Nablus–Jerusalem road, they found the Turkish forces had withdrawn from their defensive positions the previous night. By midday the Turkish occupation forces accepted the situation and they sent out a parlementaire and surrendered the city.

In the operations from 31 October to 9 December, over 12,000 prisoners were taken and about 100 guns of various calibres, many machine guns, more than 20 million rounds of rifle ammunition, 250,000 rounds of gun ammunition, and more than twenty airplanes were destroyed.

Allenby officially entered Jerusalem at midday on 11 December. In deference to the importance of the city to three Abrahamic religions, he entered the city on foot via the Jaffa Gate. He placed guards over the holy places and appointed a military governor who in turn ensured that a British officer was appointed to supervise them. Certain areas, such as the Mosque of Omar and the area around it, were placed under Muslim control, and a military cordon of Muslim officers and soldiers was established around the mosque. Orders were issued that no non-Muslim was to pass within the cordon without permission of the military governor and the Muslim officer in charge.

Thanks to the sensitive way in which Allenby took control of the city, the population, in the main, welcomed him and his army. As the situation in Jerusalem settled down, the Allied troops continued their advance to establish a defensive line sufficiently far north of Jaffa and Jerusalem to secure those two places from all but long-range enemy gunfire. Allenby's proclamation on taking control of Jerusalem, fulfilling his earlier promise to Lloyd George, was as follows:

> To the inhabitants of Jerusalem the Blessed and the people dwelling in its vicinity:

> The defeat inflicted upon the Turks by the troops under my command has resulted in the occupation of your City by my forces. I therefore here and now proclaim it to be under martial law, under which form of administration it will remain as long as military considerations make it necessary.

> However, lest any of you should be alarmed by reason of your experiences at the hands of the enemy who has retired, I hereby inform you that it is my desire that every person should pursue his lawful business without fear of interruption.

> Furthermore, since your City is regarded with affection by the adherents of three of the great religions of mankind, and its soil has been consecrated by the prayers and pilgrimages of multitudes of devout people of those three religions for many centuries, therefore do I make it known to you that every sacred building, monument, holy spot, shrine, traditional site, endowment, pious bequest, or customary place of prayer, of whatsoever form of the three religions, will be maintained and protected according to the existing customs and beliefs of those to whose faiths they are sacred.[95]

A period of trench warfare now set in, which, excluding minor operations, lasted until the autumn of 1918. German advisers to the Turkish forces subsequently summarised the effects of Allenby's campaign resulting in the capture of Jerusalem as follows:

The new commander-in-chief, General Allenby, began the operations on October 31st, 1917, by capturing the strategically highly important point, Beersheba, the former chief halting-place of the Turks on their advance to Egypt, and now the chief station for the protection of Palestine.

The position at Gaza, in consequence of this victory, now became untenable. An immediate attack with his left wing and centre brought Allenby in possession of the entire Turkish line extending from the coast to Beersheba by way of Gaza.

The latter city was entered by the British on November 7th. The energetic pursuit which followed soon led to the capture of Ascalon, on the coast and to a nearer approach to the railroad between Jaffa and Jerusalem.

The British general finally succeeded in surrounding Jerusalem, and on December 9th, 1917, the city was captured with the cooperation of French and Italian contingents. The moral significance of this event was even greater than its military importance.

For the first part of this period, the Desert Mounted Corps remained in the neighbourhood of Gaza to rest and train, camped on deep sand among the coastal dunes. Their horses were in a poor state. Owing to the shipping shortage, there was no prospect of any fresh remounts arriving in the foreseeable future and the remount depots were empty save for a few animals which had been returned from the veterinary hospital after treatment for wounds or other injury. All horses therefore had to be nursed back to condition before the cavalry could take part in any further serious work.

Whilst Allenby was basking in the success of his Palestine campaign things were not going so well on the Western Front. He was always aware that when push came to shove the Western Front would take precedent and, in late March 1918, the circumstances on the Western Front were such that the British Army was going to need every soldier it could lay its hands on. The old preconception that Territorial Forces were not good enough for the Western Front was history. The yeomanry had proved themselves and, with the Western Front forces pushed to the limit by a new offensive set in place by the German Army, the chief of the Imperial General Staff ordered Allenby to give up some of his forces to reinforce France.

The Western Front did not require cavalry, machine gunners were what was needed, and so the Berks and Bucks Yeomanry reluctantly gave up their beloved mounts, which they handed over to the Remounts Service on 3 April 1918 together with all of the transport animals, the equipment and saddles. The soldiers themselves began the process of amalgamating the Berks and Bucks Yeomanry into a Machine Gun Battalion.

On 4 April at 11.30 a.m., the commander of the Desert Mounted Corps, Lieutenant General Sir H. Chauval, together with the general officer commanding the 6th Mounted Brigade, Brigadier General Godwin, visited the Bucks Hussars in their camp, said their goodbyes at a special parade and expressed their thanks for a job well done. The rest of the day was spent reorganising the regiment into machine gun companies.

At 9.15 a.m. on 23 May 1918, the Royal Bucks Hussars paraded at Sidi Bisr Camp for the last time and marched to the railway station (not entirely coincidentally called Victoria Station), and there they were placed in rail trucks which left at 11.00 a.m. with 543 other ranks of the Warwickshire & South Nottinghamshire Yeomanry MG Battalion. The transfer to the Machine Gun Corps was no sinecure. They had seen action in virtually all the main theatres of war. In France, Belgium, Palestine, Mesopotamia, Egypt, Salonika, East Africa and Italy the Machine Gun Corps, despite their comparatively short history, had gained an enviable record for heroism as a front line fighting force. Indeed, in the latter part of the war, as tactics changed to defence in depth, it commonly served well in advance of the front line. This need to position the machine guns in advance of the main line in many cases led to a pretty horrific casualty rate. In total, some 170,500 officers and men served in the Corps and by the end of the war 62,049 had become casualties, including 12,498 killed. This astonishing 36 per cent casualty rate earned it the nickname 'the Suicide Club'.

However, before the Bucks Hussars could begin their training in France, fate had a further card to play. The journey across the relatively narrow stretch of the Mediterranean between Alexandria and Italy had still to be negotiated.

10

THE SINKING OF
HMT *LEASOWE CASTLE*

Nobody would call His Majesty's Troopship *Leasowe Castle* a lucky ship. Sailing through the eastern Mediterranean during spring 1918 required a modicum of luck because they were definitely hostile waters. The U-boat was Germany's most effective weapon and had probably come closest to driving the British out of the war.

The shipping losses to German submarines had peaked during 1917 when nearly 4,000 Allied vessels were sunk, but in 1918 unrestricted warfare was still the order of the day. From an average of over 300 ships per month in 1917, sinkings had reduced during 1918 to approximately 160 per month. It was still a formidable threat, especially in the Mediterranean. The Berks and Bucks Yeomanry, now combined into the 101st Machine Gun Battalion, were set to embark on the ship in Alexandria to cross the Mediterranean to disembark in southern Italy, where the plan was to complete the journey to northern France by train.

I know from my own days in the Merchant Navy that sailors have always believed ships are either lucky or unlucky, and that everything that happens to a particular vessel is utilised to reinforce this particular belief. In the case of HMT *Leasowe Castle*, it is not difficult to guess which side of the divide the ship fell on. The *Leasowe Castle* was built by Cammell Laird in their Birkenhead ship-yards. Her keel was laid in 1915 for the National Steam Navigation Company of Greece and was originally called the *Vasilissa Sophia*. On completion, work was suspended on her for some time and she was transferred to the Byron Steamship Company. During this period the War Office requisitioned the ship for trooping duties and she was then launched in 1917, renamed the *Leasowe Castle* and placed under the management of Union Castle, who never actually owned her but were responsible for crewing and operating her on behalf of the British Government.

The ship was 9,737 grt, some 488ft long with a 58ft beam and, with twin screws, was capable of some 17 knots. In an age when the average cargo vessel

The *Leasowe Castle* in her delivery colours.

was capable of 10–12 knots at maximum speed, this was a respectable rate of progress. She had eight decks for the accommodation of troops and was fitted with forty-two lifeboats.

On 20 April 1917, during one of her first voyages under the command of Captain H.B. Harvey, the ship was attacked just off Gibraltar by German submarine *U-35* commanded by the rather exotically named Lothar von Arnauld de la Perière. The attack damaged the ship quite severely, including smashing the rudder. However, the engines and propellers remained intact, and the ship was able to limp into the Port of Gibraltar.

Thus, on 23 May 1917, when the troop train arrived at the docks at about midday, and embarked on HMT *Leasowe Castle*, they were, unbeknown to them, embarking on a ship which had already been through an eventful, albeit short life. It was by any definition an 'unlucky ship'. The embarkation of the Warwickshire, South Nottinghamshire, Berks and Bucks Yeomanry via a single gangway took some three and a half hours, and baggage stowage took a further hour. On completion, the ship left the quay and anchored out in the middle of the harbour.

The ship was by now under the command of Captain Holl. Luckily for all on board, he was strict in his insistence on practising lifeboat drills and did not skimp on his organisation of both the soldiers and the crew. While the ship lay at anchor he used the time to lower a number of his boats and train the men in rowing, sailing, the use of sea anchors and, of course, in the clearing away and launching of boats. Before leaving port he also trained a portion of the troops under his charge in the handling of boats, and he saw to it that complete arrangements were made for the falling in of the men at emergency stations.

The ship left the harbour at 5.00 p.m. on 26 May and set sail northwards for Taranto in southern Italy. She sailed as part of a convoy of five other transport vessels, a destroyer escort and other vessels such as trawlers and even a captive kite balloon for observation. Several sea-planes accompanied the convoy for some distance. The balloon was towed aloft until dark when it was hauled down. The convoy steamed in line ahead until it came to the end of the swept channel and then came into a 'T' formation, with the *Leasowe Castle* third in the leading line. Every precaution was taken to prevent light showing after dark, and as many men as possible were ordered to sleep on deck at their emergency station. Given the lack of air-conditioning and the number of soldiers crammed into the vessel, this was probably not the hardship it sounds.

The *Leasowe Castle* was carrying 2,900 soldiers plus the crew. The weather conditions were considered good, with the sea calm and a full moon in a clear sky. Some 104 miles north of Alexandria, at 1.30 a.m., the *Leasowe Castle* was struck on the starboard side by a torpedo fired from German submarine *U-51* commanded by Captain Ernst Krafft. She was hit a little forward of amidships under the after funnel. The engines were stopped almost immediately following the explosion, but initially she remained on an even keel, albeit settling slightly by the stern. The troops were paraded on deck and mustered at their emergency stations immediately and without panic; roll calls were then made to ensure that all were present and it rapidly became apparent that Captain Holl's briefing and training drills were beginning to pay dividends.

The task was undoubtedly made easier because all the men berthed in the lower decks were sleeping on deck and as near as possible to their emergency stations, and well over half the soldiers were therefore already on deck. The amount of movement was thus reduced and there was no confusion.

It was soon apparent that the ship was badly damaged and that she would have to be abandoned. The order was given by Captain Holl for the crew, helped by the troops, to lower the boats and life rafts. Meanwhile, the remainder of the convoy had disappeared, leaving the Japanese destroyer *Katsura* and HMS *Lily* to rescue those taking to the lifeboats. As soon as the first batch of boats was on the water they were ordered to be filled, even as the remaining lifeboats were still being lowered. Troops went over the ship's rails down ropes and ladders in order to take up places in the boats. They were ordered by the master to pull over to the sloop and destroyer, discharge troops and pull back to the ship.

When the order to take to the lifeboats is given on any ship there is bound to be a certain amount of panic. Young men from rural areas of England born at the end of the nineteenth century were unlikely to be able to swim and indeed in many cases the only time they would have been to sea would have been on their journeys from Britain to Egypt and to and from Gallipoli. There would, then, have been ample reason for them to feel apprehension. Captain Holl's example, and the calmness and professionalism of the crew, would have been of enormous comfort and this, coupled with the military discipline of the passengers, ensured that the ship's evacuation went as smoothly as could be expected.

About forty boats and rafts were lowered into the water over a forty-five-minute period. The ship remained fairly steady at this point, though still sinking slightly by the stern and now beginning to develop a slight list to port. One of the Royal Navy vessels, HMS *Lily*, separated from the convoy about fifteen minutes after the torpedo had struck, returned to assist the sinking ship. The captain of this small vessel bravely ran her bows up right alongside the starboard side of the *Leasowe Castle* and made fast so that troops were able to pass directly from the sinking ship to the rescue vessel without using lifeboats. Meanwhile, the *Katsura* put up a smoke screen for protection. About an hour and a half after the torpedo first struck, a bulkhead in the after part of the ship gave way and the ship sank suddenly by the stern.

The *Leasowe Castle* sank quickly and there was barely time to cut the ropes tying HMS *Lily* to the larger ship. Had it not been for some quick work with axes by the crew to sever the ropes, she would undoubtedly have been dragged under. The remainder of the boats and rafts in the water remained guarded by a smoke screen put up by two destroyers and were picked up towards noon the next day and brought back into the port of Alexandria.

During the ninety minutes it took the *Leasowe Castle* to sink, some 2,000 of the 2,900 officers and men originally on board had left on lifeboats. The remainder were mostly troops stationed in the forecastle on the starboard side where some of the boats hanging outboard had been smashed by columns of water from the explosion. They were taken off partly by the boats which came back after discharging, partly by the sloop *Lily*. Many men jumped into the sea during the last few moments and were picked up from rafts, amongst them the battalion commander Major Sir St J. Gore Bt. Prior to the CO leaving the ship, the battalion adjutant Captain C.H. Bennett MC had reported to him on the ship's bridge that all the battalion were, as far as could be seen, off the ship. The CO then ordered Bennett to go, but although Bennett left the bridge he was never seen again. Of nearly 3,000 lives on board, ninety-two troops and nine of the crew, including Captain Holl, were lost. No attempt was ever made to recover their bodies.

Captain Holl had been last heard giving the order, 'Every man for himself,' but only after ensuring that all the boats were away safely from the sinking ship. In his report, the chief officer wrote of the captain that, 'in his consideration for the safety of all those under his care, he never for one instant thought of his own safety, and went down with his ship.' During those ninety minutes that the

The Royal Bucks Hussars famous 'Dizzie', a mobile kitchen devised by Coningsby Disraeli which went down with the *Leasowe Castle*. (Mike Holland)

ship remained afloat, whenever the chief officer reported to him, Captain Holl said, 'Do your utmost; they must be saved.' It was reported that several times he came down on to the boat deck, encouraging and exhorting the men to further efforts, always cheerful and hopeful.

There can be no doubt that Captain Holl was a hero in every sense of the word, a comparatively unknown British mariner who deserves to be mentioned whenever people talk about the bravery and professionalism of British sailors. Owing to his insistence on practising lifeboat drills properly, and due to his unselfish and heroic behaviour during the sinking of his ship, he ensured that what could have been a wholesale tragedy was managed in the best traditions of British naval history and that many of the yeomanry soldiers owed him their lives. He is now remembered on the Commonwealth War Graves Memorial for Merchant Navy personnel at Tower Hill in London. He richly deserves his nation's recognition. The following morning, on arrival back at Alexandria, it was found that the battalion was nearly complete, with the exception of one officer, Captain C.H. Bennett Adjutant, and three privates, Private Poole (both of the Royal Bucks Hussars) and Privates Stead and Andrews (both Berks Yeomanry). Four officers (Major Young MC, Lieutenant Senior MC, Second Lieutenant Sauvage and Second Lieutenant Blackman) and fourteen men were admitted to hospital with trivial injuries such as cuts and bruises. Such light casualties from an original complement of 2,900 men, in an incident in the middle of the night and in hostile waters, is a fantastic tribute to the bravery and discipline of the *Leasowe Castle*'s crew and in particular to their captain.

There are two contemporary accounts of that frightening night, one from an officer, Captain Sutton, the other, which follows here, from Private Marshall of the Berkshire Yeomanry:

We had got about 9 hours out. Nearly all of us were asleep in bed. I was sub-consciously aware of a sudden jar, but what I do remember was sitting on my berth and asking what happened, and was told if I didn't get out pretty quickly I should pretty soon know what it was. I pulled on a pair of shoes and tying on my lifebelt scuttled along the corridor, and slipped up at the foot of the stairs. I went straight to our emergency station and found the other men arriving. They were awfully good on the ship, and there was no panic. The yeoman is a downright good fellow and I take off my hat to him. The ship soon stopped. There was a very slight list. The boats were got off and the rafts too and when all the men were off the ship and I said to about half a dozen still there 'Well we'll go now.' The water was then awash in the after well deck. So clad in pyjamas, canvas shoes and a wrist watch, I climbed down about six feet of ladder, held my breath, looked at the black water, and dropped quietly in. I had a swim of about 30 to 50 yards. I had a life belt on, a splendid thing. When we got the life raft (a collapsible canvas sided boat), we rowed and rowed round in circles till a motor launch came and took us in tow, and then we arrived in an auxiliary ship of war. While we were getting on board the auxiliary had 2 tor-pedoes launched at her but both were misses thank God. A few minutes after, the ship went down with a rush. We made off back towards Alexandria with over 1,100 survivors on board. The night was wonderfully warm and I never felt cold, even in wet pyjamas. However some kind naval officer fitted me out in a naval tunic and a pair of trousers, and of course I was the butt of many jests. All were fitted up with blankets or something to keep the warm and some food. About ten hours afterwards we arrived back in Alex. On the quay we were give clothes, army issue, and the red cross gave us tea and biscuit.[96]

We were on transports going to France, actually to Marseilles. Six transports and about 2 cruisers 7 destroyers and a couple of sloops named The Lily and The Ladybird. When we got 150 miles from Alexandria which would have put us somewhere opposite Cyprus, we were torpedoed, it was just midnight. I think we had left Alexandria about teatime, 4 o'clock. The officer in charge of us on board, Lawson, came round to ask for volunteers to lower the rafts and all that sort of thing after the crew had got the lifeboats down. Then once finished he stepped up to me and my mate 'Come on boys the decks are awash, every man for himself. So we scrambled over the side and the ship stood up. The deck was above water. We had life jackets on which was just as

The *Leasowe Castle* in wartime 'dazzle' camouflage. (Bucks Military Museum)

well since I couldn't swim very well. Once in the water I kicked myself off the side of the ship and got my legs tangled round a piece of rope. So I pulled myself back, kicked myself clear and out I went into the blue. Sixteen minutes past one when my watch stopped, course they wouldn't go in those days, they weren't waterproof. I swam about out there, and we were anxious that we couldn't get as far as we would want because of the suction of the ship (when it went down.) The crew consisted of a load of Lascars, took the life boats to the rescue ships, the Lily and Ladybird and all those others. When they got there, they got onto the ships themselves and they let the lifeboats go. And it was one of these which I swam out to. Well as we were being trained as Hotchkiss machine gunners and our horses taken away, we'd lost our breeches and putties and all that sort of thing. We just wore shorts. The sergeants and the sergeant majors they kept their breeches as did the officers. So through the movement of this boat up came somebody in the dark beside of me, my Sergeant Major Legg. We went to clamber up in to the boat together, and he said to me 'let go of me you bloody fool, I can't get up there with you hanging on to my breeches.' So when we eventually rolled in to the boat, I was free minus one sock and one shoe. He had his breeches full of 2 or 3 gallons of water which had held him down from getting in the boat. That made me laugh did that. Having got into the boat there was only one oar left. About 5 or 6 other fellows gathered together and got into the boat, and we tried to get away with only one oar. The Leasowe Castle with 3000 of us on board, big ship she was. As she was going down we tried to get the boat 50 yards from her so she wouldn't suck us down. Anyway eventually round came this motor-boat with 2 sailors in and chucked us a line and towed us round to where we got on the Ladybird. I think there was two more ships in attendance while the rest of the convoy had gone on, otherwise they'd be in danger too. I think it was the lady bird I got on, and luck for us they stayed. There was so many of us on this little sloop that the Captain of the ship asked us to get more equally spread all over the ship to keep her balanced. The sloop lily having about 1100 survivors on board started back to Alexandria immediately. The Destroyer R with about 400 on board remained in the vicinity of the ship's boats which numbered about 34 and carried the remainder of the survivors. At about 1200 H.M. torpedo boat Chelmer (34), H.M. monitor LADYBIRD and H.M. auxiliary Lychnis arrived and took over the survivors from the Katsura and the ships boats. The officers and men of the Royal Navy and the Imperial Japanese Navy did everything in their power to assist the survivors many of whom were almost without clothes. The rescuing vessels arrived at Alexandria at times between 1400 and 1830. There all arrangements had been made for their reception: men of the Battalion were sent straight to Sidi Bishr transit camp and officers to various hotels for the night.[97]

On 17 June the troops re-embarked on the HMT *Caledonia*, again bound for Taranto, and this time they made it successfully across those dangerous waters to the Italian port, there to be put on trains for the long journey the length of Italy, through the south-west of France all the way up to Etaples in northern France, where they arrived on 28 June 1918.

11

FRANCE

The Royal Bucks Hussars finally arrived at the British training camp of Etaples, in northern France, on 28 June 1918. Many of the soldiers were sick after the long and fatiguing journey, which they had made without proper halts. The regimental war diary reports that the 101st Battalion had taken three weeks to cover the distance from Alexandria. There was much sickness due to overcrowding on the ship HMT *Caledonia* and the long train journey through Italy and France. Although the weather was good, it also gave the enemy clear conditions for bombing raids and the first two days in camp were interrupted by enemy air attacks.

At this point the health of the regiment was not good. Second Lieutenant Macfarlane and fifty men were sent to hospital after leaving the train, and within a few days there were over 100 men and some fifty officers in hospital with a fever possibly caused by the cramped and dirty quarters in troopship and on the train. During the train journey there was no break and, as the train ran sometimes six to eight hours behind schedule, arrangements for hot tea and sanitary and washing facilities were often quite inadequate. The cumulative effect of these conditions was evident in the general health of the troops. Many others were sick but did not go to hospital. The daily sick parade on arrival was typically 120 to 130 of the total strength of just over 850. The single blessing was that the weather on arrival in France was fine and warm, thus easing the transition from Egypt's warmer climate.

The arrival of the machine gun battalion in the summer of 1918 was to reinforce the Allies' big push against the Central Powers. With the huge benefit of hindsight we now know that the end was in sight, but this was far from obvious to the Allied forces who were there on the Western Front at the start of 1918. In a war which has come down to us redolent with massacre on a vast scale, with Passchendaele, Ypres and the Somme part of our national consciousness, it is easy to forget that 1918 was probably the bloodiest and hardest-fought year of the whole war. By then the Allies were being reinforced with US troops and the Central Powers had brought all of their forces to bear on the Western Front as Russia had by now left the war and there was no significant threat to the Central Powers from the East. Quartermaster General Ludendorff summed up the situation with the following appraisal made at the start of 1918:

> Owing to the breakdown of Russia the military situation was more favour-able to us at New Year 1918 than anyone could have expected. As in 1914 and 1915 we could think of deciding the war by an attack on land. Numerically we had never been so strong in comparison with our enemies.[98]

Although the German Army may have agreed with the above statement, the reality was that they needed a dramatic turnaround in their fortunes as the situation back in Germany, with both public morale and the economy suffer-ing, was undoubtedly taking a turn for the worse. The year 1918 represented an opportunity for one last throw of the dice and Hindenberg and Ludendorff were determined that they would 'go for broke'.

At twenty minutes to five on the morning of 21 March 1918 the full force of the German Army was thrown at the British forces just to the north of St Quentin. It was a foggy morning and in places the fog was so thick that British Army defensive posts had only approximately 10 yards of visibility. In the first five hours in this one sector the German artillery fired some 1.2 million shells, which effectively obliterated the British defensive artillery. Under cover of creep-ing barrages, the German infantry overran the British forward positions, and by 11.00 a.m. that morning had already made deep inroads into the British defences.

This first German offensive was codenamed 'Michael' and over the next few weeks the Germans followed up with renewed offensives, 'Georgette' against the British forces south of Ypres, and 'Blucher' and 'Gneisenau' against the French armies on the Marne.

By 26 March the Allies were fighting for their lives and the alliance between the French and British was stretched almost to breaking point. Sir Henry Wilson, the Chief of the Imperial General Staff and Field Marshal Haig met the French Premier Georges Clemenceau, the French President Raymond Poincaré and the French Chief of the General Staff, Field Marshal Ferdinand Foch, to agree the way forward. Field Marshal Haig summed up the outcome from his viewpoint:

> It was decided that Amiens must be covered at all costs. French troops are being hurried up as rapidly as possible and Gough has been told to hold on to his left at Bray. It was proposed by Clemenceau that Foch should be appointed to co-ordinate the operations of an Allied force to cover Amiens and ensure that the French and British flanks remain united. This proposal seemed to me to be quite worthless, as Foch would be in a subordinate position to Pétain and myself. In my opinion it was essential that Foch should control Pétain, so

I at once recommended that Foch should control the actions of all the Allied Armies on the Western Front. Foch seemed sound and sensible, but Pétain had a terrible look. He had the appearance of a commander who was in a funk and had lost his nerve.

Whoever came up with the idea, whether Haig was manipulated by the wily politician Clemenceau into making the suggestion that Clemenceau himself wanted, we do not know. However, a unified command and an agreed strategic supremo was plainly what the situation demanded and Haig's assessment of Pétain's character would be proved right by subsequent events.

By 30 March the massive German offensive was beginning to tire and Ludendorff called a halt to allow the army to resupply and draw breath. On 9 April, however, another massive offensive hit the British Army on the River Lys just south of Ypres.

As with the previous offensive, the Germans made big inroads into the British positions on day one. This time the situation was even more serious in that there were definite strategic targets for the German Army to aim for if they could break the British line. In the huge battlefields of northern France, territory captured had little effect unless there was a strategic goal to be gained. In this case, there was a vital rail interchange at Hazebrouck, which was the intersection of a rail network linking the channel ports to all of the key military sites in northern France. To lose this would be a serious blow for the British and would threaten the whole supply chain. In addition, the German troops thrust towards Mont Kemmel and threatened the whole Ypres salient.

On 11 April the situation was sufficiently grave for Field Marshal Haig to issue what was probably his most famous battle order of the whole war:

> Many amongst us are now tired. To those I would say that victory will belong to the side which holds out the longest. The French army is moving rapidly and in great force to our support. There is no other course open to us but to fight it out. Every position must be held to the last man: there must be no retirement. With our backs to the wall and believing in the justice of our cause each one of us must fight on to the end. The safety of our homes and the freedom of mankind alike depend upon the conduct of each one of us at this critical moment.[99]

By 29 April it became obvious that, although severely stretched, the British were going to hang on and Ypres and Hazebrouck were saved.

The 'Michael' and 'Georgette' offensives of March and April had carved out huge new salients jutting into the British lines, but crucially the latter held, and just as importantly, the links between the British and French armies held and indeed their co-operation strengthened. Now the emphasis switched to the

French sectors and the Germans attacked at the Aisne sector, trying to drive for Paris. Again, as in the British sectors, the French buckled but did not break and gradually, as spring turned to summer, the Allies held and began to consider how to hit back at the Germans. Both the Allies and the Central Powers had suffered badly during the fighting but, crucially, the Allies were making good their losses by bringing in more troops from Egypt, from the Dominions and, of course, the United States, who were beginning to arrive in large numbers.

Bill Cowell and the Royal Bucks Hussars' arrival in France was part of a massive injection of manpower designed to allow the Allies to move onto the attack. Although they were replacing some 270,000 British casualties lost during early 1918, the situation was now becoming far worse for Germany, who had burned up all of the additional troops released from the Eastern Front without any possibility of making good their losses. In addition, they had three huge salients jutting into the Allied lines which were inadequately defended and ripe for being chopped off by the next Allied offensives. In fairness to all concerned, this had been realised by some of the German staff officers. Colonel Wetzell of the General Headquarters of the Imperial German Army had been quoted saying as much back in November 1917:

> It must not be forgotten that in a successful offensive, the attacker will be forced to cross a difficult and shot-to-pieces battle area and will get gradually further away from his railheads and depots, and that, having to bring forward masses of artillery and ammunition columns, he will be compelled to make pauses which will give time to the defender to organise resistance. Too optimistic hopes should not be conceived, therefore, as regards the rapidity of the breakthrough attack on the Western Front. If our foes act only in a more or less planned and rapid manner, as we have done so far in spite of the most desperate situations, they will also succeed in bringing our offensive to a stop after a certain time.[100]

Field Marshal Haig was determined that 1918 was to be the year when the Central Powers were to be defeated. To this end he was building up his forces and, together with the rapidly expanding US Army, he began to think that he could realistically begin the push which would finally break the spirit of the German Army. Haig's determination to finish off the Central Powers in 1918 was not universally shared by the politicians back in London. In an interview he had with the then Minister for Munitions, Winston Churchill MP, a man not renowned for his pessimism, he bemused Haig with his views on finishing the war during 1919, as Haig reported:

> He is most anxious to help in every way, and is hurrying up the supply of '10 calibre head shells', gas, tanks etc. His schemes are all timed for completion in

next June! I told him we ought to do our utmost to get a decision this autumn. We are engaged in a 'wearing out battle' and are outlasting the enemy. If we have a period of quiet, he will recover, and the 'wearing out' process must be recommenced. In reply I was told that the General Staff in London calculate that the decisive period of the war cannot arrive until next July.[101]

It must have been galling for Haig to be second-guessed by the so-called experts back in London and it is greatly to his credit that he recognised the golden opportunity, that he was able to sense the feeling within the German army and that he was prepared to take the chance. It was immeasurably to the credit of the British Army that they were able to find the strength for this last great effort and outlast the enemy and begin the last great push.

By the middle of July the Berks and Bucks Yeomanry were training hard in Cucq just outside Etaples, getting used to being infantry and, more specifically, to using the Vickers Machine gun, which was one of the vital cogs in what came to be known as the 'all-arms battle'. This was the concept of linking infantry, machine gunners, aerial reconnaissance, artillery and tanks into one cohesive force which maximised the effect and ensured that all parts of the war effort co-operated.

The Vickers machine gun was a sustained fire weapon. It could hammer out twenty-five round bursts for hours and days. By today's standards, however, it is a real nineteenth-century design and unbelievably complicated, requiring a great deal of training, maintenance and spares. Its major defects were the slow rate of fire, the muzzle flash and blast, and clouds of smoke and steam. The gun was 3ft 8in in length, and its weight could vary, according to the type of barrel casing and whether 'lightening' had been carried out, but was approximately 42.5lb plus 7.5 pints of cooling water to prevent overheating. The actual mounting weight was 48lb. Not only did they have to carry the gun and tripod, the poor soldiers also had to carry the belt boxes, which weighed 22lb, with 250 rounds of ammunition in each belt. Therefore, while one member of the eight-man gun team carried the gun, another would carry the tripod and the other six would have laden themselves down with belt boxes to be sure their action would be effective once the gun was set up.

Centralisation of machine guns and the appointment of divisional and corps machine gun officers eventually led to the development of sophisticated machine gun tactics in which the Vickers machine gun was used for indirect fire to the limit of their considerable range, 3,000 yards and beyond. The job of the Machine Gun Corps was to provide barrages, the neutralisation of enemy rear areas with harassing fire, 'fixed line' shoots and numerous other tasks previously thought to be beyond their capabilities. By 1918 the Vickers was understood to be a gun that needed to be fought more as an artillery piece than an infantry weapon.

Having completed their training at Etaples by late August, the combined Bucks and Berks Yeomanry, now redesignated as the 101st Machine Gun

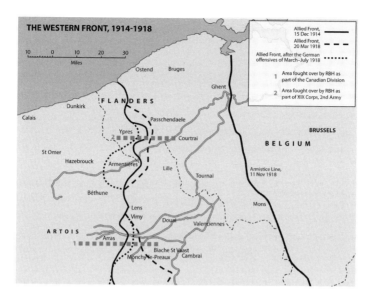

THE WESTERN FRONT, 1914-1918

Battalion, were considered fit to join the front line troops now being mustered by Haig. They were designated as A and B (Bucks) Companies and C and D (Berks) Companies, thus retaining their original regimental loyalties.

They were now ready for the push that Field Marshal Haig was determined would finally break the German Army's morale. The 101st Machine Gun Battalion was attached to the 51st Division of the First Army commanded by General Sir Henry Horne. They were amalgamated into the Canadian Corps and formed part of the Canadian Composite Brigade. Pushed into the Arras area of the front, their objective was to push the German Army back across a 4-mile front towards Monchy-le-Preux.

The area was just south of the River Scarpe, which runs broadly west to east at this point, and was considered difficult to advance over as it is split by a number of small valleys which were overlooked by a ridge of higher land running round in a broad arc from Thilloy-lès-Mofflaines to Monchy-le-Preux. The British and Canadian troops engaged in the attack were to advance under Lt Col Cripps, whose orders were to capture the German trenches on high ground between Pelves and Biache-Saint-Vaast. The attack was preceded by a heavy artillery barrage.

The battalion first saw action in support of the 51st Highland Division at the Battle of Scarpe. The fighting was in complete contrast to that in Palestine; the dash across the desert on horseback was now replaced by deliberate assault across muddy fields and shell holes. The Bucks Hussars moved forward at night from Saint-Laurent-Blangy, a suburb of Arras, towards the river to take over the front line from the Canadians, which they did by 4.00 a.m. on the night of 24 August 1918. The attack took place the next day and all the objectives were achieved – many prisoners and several machine guns were captured. The front lines moved forward over a mile on a line some 1,500 yards long. This was the Bucks Hussars' first experience of Western Front trench warfare and they acquitted themselves admirably; their experience of fighting in the Middle East, albeit in a very different environment, served them well. It came at a cost, however, for two officers were wounded and thirty other ranks killed or wounded.[102]

They were to remain in the front line at Arras, just south of the River Scarpe, until the middle of September, when they were transferred to the XIX Corps within the 2nd Army at Cassel. The battalion moved to the infamous Ypres salient in Belgium on 16 September in preparation for the attack on the Wytschaete Ridge to the south of Ypres. This attack began on 28 September and the battalion's task was to support the 35th and 14th Divisions in the assault on the Comines Canal. In contrast to many of the Great War attacks, there was no preliminary artillery bombardment and the machine gunners went forward with the leading waves of infantry.[103] The attack was successful and the battalion remained with the 35th Division for their last action of the war, that at Tieghem on 31 October 1918, which resulted in the capture of the western bank of the River Schelde.

Late October found the Bucks Hussars operating with the XIX Corps, pushing out from what had been the Ypres salient. However, by late October the Second Army, in co-ordination with the whole of the line, was on the move and had shifted the line of battle into what was, by First World War standards, fairly open territory. This did not mean, however, that there was a battle of movement. The corps were under the command of Major General S.T.B. Lawford and their job was to push on eastwards towards the Schelde. The German machine gunners were still determined to hold every defensible position and there were still plenty of those. The land was still low lying and constantly pierced by the rivers and canals which had made so many of the previous battles so difficult. Every canal and every river which crossed the path of the advancing Allied armies represented another opportunity for the German machine gunners to mount a defensive line.

A further difficulty for the advancing troops was that this land was now new territory – it was relatively unmapped and the artillery had not been able to calculate their ranges and targets as had been the case whilst still back in the 1914–17 battle lines. It was difficult for the artillery to stay up with such rapid advances. Nevertheless, despite all the problems, there was to be only one winner and the German Army knew this as well as the Allies. The Bucks Hussars' war diary still records deaths and wounded troops, but increasingly these numbers were decreasing as the German resistance lessened and morale fell.

Plans to cross the river on 11 November were brought forward after the Germans withdrew on the 8th. The 101st Battalion was no longer required for the assault and was back in Courtrai when the Armistice was announced, and there it remained until demobilisation.

12

PEACE

At around 10.00 a.m. on 11 November 1918, Private George Ellison of the 5th Irish Lancers was shot dead in Mons. With the terrible symmetry and coincidence which marked so much of the Great War, Mons was where the British Expeditionary Force had first come into contact with German forces at the start of the war. It was here that the first British casualty, Private Parr, was buried. Now the first and last British casualties of the Great War lie just a few yards apart in the same Commonwealth War Graves Cemetery just outside Mons. It was the 1,559th day of war for the British Army and, during the four terrible years from 1914 to 1918, over 16 million had died only for the armies to get back to the positions they had held at the outbreak of hostilities. The Armistice had been signed at 5.00 a.m., but hostilities would not end until 11.00 a.m. and on the last day some 11,000 casualties were sustained – more casualties than the Allies sustained on D-Day some twenty-five years later.

It is a sobering thought that for every twenty young men aged between 18 and 32 when the war broke out, by the end of the war three were dead and six wounded. If the British dead were to rise up from their graves and march past a given point four abreast at British Army regulation marching pace it would take more than two and a half days and nights for them to pass. Bill Cowell survived this carnage, thus allowing me to tell this story. The official figures showed some 750,000 British dead plus another 200,000 from the British Empire. Added to this were a further 1.5 million men wounded or gassed, out of some 5 million men who served in our armed forces. Neither were casualties evenly spread as they were proportionally heavier amongst junior officers than any other class of soldier.

Young men were buried from south-west Africa through Saharan Africa, the Middle East, Eastern Europe and in uncountable numbers through a broad swathe of Europe from the Swiss border all the way up through France to Belgium. Even more tragically, many were not properly buried as their bodies were never discovered or had simply been atomised by the effects of high explosive.

The programme from the Royal Bucks Hussars' own entertainment concert whilst acting as part of the Army of Occupation. (Berkshire Yeomanry Museum)

The British names of those with no known grave are commemorated on the Menin Gate in Ypres, some 55,000 names in all. But the dead are dead; they cannot suffer any more. For many, the signing of the Armistice did not end their suffering; they were irrevocably mentally scarred by the whole experience, as indeed were many grieving parents. The famous soldier/poet Siegfried Sassoon expressed this loss of innocence eloquently in the following lines:

> You smug-faced crowds with kindling eye
> Who cheer when soldier lads march by,
> Sneak home and pray you'll never know
> The hell where youth and laughter go.

The official diary kept by the adjutant of the Bucks Yeomanry states, in what surely must be the most laconic record of that day, 'training, recreation, Armistice news received'. For the Royal Bucks Hussars that was it – the end of the Great War. It was not to be a quick demobilisation, however, as the Bucks Hussars were selected to be in the army of occupation.[104]

Bill Cowell was demobbed and returned to England on 18 February 1919. His journey ended in a country that was irrevocably changed by the war. In his famous History of England, A.J. Taylor states that, prior to the First World War,

a sensible law abiding Englishman could pass through life and never notice the existence of the State beyond the Post Office and the policeman. He could live where he liked and as he liked. He had no official number or identity card. He could travel abroad or leave his country for ever without a passport or any sort of official permission. He could exchange his money for any other currency without restriction or limit. He could buy goods from any country in the world on the same terms as he could buy goods at home … All of this was changed by the impact of the Great War. The mass of the people became, for the first time, active citizens. Their lives were shaped by orders from above; they were required to serve the State instead of pursuing exclusively their own affairs.[105]

By the time the soldiers returned, the modern interfering state had started, telling them when they could drink, imposing the necessity for travel documents; time itself changed with the introduction of daylight saving time. Many of the measures brought in ostensibly as wartime measures, such as licensing laws, stayed in place and became part of our national life.

The collapse of morale in both the German Army and back in the German homeland, and the influx of American manpower, made the end of the war inevitable. Whilst the end was undisputed, with the utter collapse of German military might, the outcome and the worth of all that loss of life was more problematic. For my grandfather and millions like him, the experience of this first mechanised war was utterly traumatic. They had been told many things by the government and its propaganda machine: 'the war to end all wars', 'a fight to protect little Belgium against Prussian militarism', 'all over by Christmas 1914'. So many lies, and then to top it all, it must have been hard to stomach returning, having left peaceful Edwardian England, to find everything they loved had changed. There were precious few homes for heroes and the society they returned to must have seemed totally different from the image that was in the mind of the soldiers far from home.

It was lucky for British society that these soldiers belonged to a tough generation and not one familiar with the concepts of post-traumatic stress disorder. There would not have been sufficient psychiatrists to treat the psychoses and neuroses caused by the war, even if they could have diagnosed them. Men and women were left to get on with life and to manage the nightmares on their own, as best they could.

Soldiers returning from war have always had difficulties in adjusting to peace, and none more so than those in 1918. If nothing had changed it

Bill Cowell returned from the war with his family: Dorothy his wife and George, Molly and Joan (the author's mother). (Bill Cowell)

Dick Turner of Radnage. A member of C Squadron, badly wounded at Gallipoli on 21 August 1915. (Mike Holland)

would still have been extremely difficult to re-integrate, but it was surely impossible when the England they had dreamed of so many times during the four years of war had disappeared whilst their gaze was averted. British society was scarred for many years after by the neuroses, the physical scars and the loss of so many of the male population – crippled men begged on street corners, wives put up with husbands who couldn't sleep with the lights out and frequently awoke during the night screaming with horror – and all this set against a society which had no free universal healthcare to look after it.

Bill Cowell returned to North Buckinghamshire a changed man. A 19-year-old farm boy had left in the spring of 1915, but now he was a hardened 23-year-old soldier – he had walked nearly 3 miles under intense artillery and machine gun fire towards an enemy he could not see, all too aware of his mates around him dying, being maimed, burnt alive and of not being able to help them. He had charged on horseback armed with a sword and rifle against an enemy armed with machine guns and artillery. He had been torpedoed and rescued from a sinking ship and finally delivered to the mud and gore of the

Western Front. No man could be unchanged by such experiences. Exposed to different cultures by the soldiers he fought with and against, and having travelled and fought in countries he would only have heard of from school text books, the Bill Cowell of 1919 was a very different person from the one just five years before. His triumph was that war did not brutalise him as it had many soldiers returning from the terrible conflict. It is true that Bill Cowell did not endure the worst horrors that were suffered by some. Those who fought the whole war on the Western Front certainly had it harder and more brutal than Bill Cowell, but what he saw and experienced was bad enough. When an individual soldier presses on with his duty when there is a high risk that it will lead to his being wounded or killed then he is a brave man, whether it be in Passchendaele or Palestine. It is to his great credit that he turned out such a civilised and decent man.

The army Bill Cowell was part of was possibly the finest fighting army that ever left the shores of Britain. The soldiers, whether part of the relatively small professional army from pre-war Britain, part of the Territorial Force as Bill Cowell was, or part of the millions who joined up in Kitchener's New Armies, were simply magnificent. During the Second World War, the British Army could not stand up to the German Army on level terms and were consistently beaten until either present in overwhelming numbers, as in Monty's Seventh Army in North Africa, or when shored up by the Americans, as was the case after D-Day. After the fall of Singapore in the Second World War, several people, including Winston Churchill and Sir John Kennedy, the then director of military operations at the War Office, were concerned that Britons might no longer have the martial spirit. Concerns were expressed as to whether modern civilisations, particularly democracies, could still produce fighting soldiers such as those of Japan and Russia. The 'soft' democracy that was seen as a problem by Second World War leaders had, scarcely thirty years earlier, produced a fighting force that could stand its ground against any foe, one that stood comparison with all of its great forebears. The British Army of 1914–18 fought the enemy for every day of the four and a half years of the war. It was the one constant factor in the Allied war effort and was one of the major factors in ensuring their eventual success. Mistakes were made early during the war years and the generals and their staff had much to learn but, contrary to the myth of 'lions led by donkeys', they did learn those lessons, and remarkably quickly, and by the end of the war a whole raft of new tactics of totally integrated, all-arms warfare was the norm rather than the exception.

One of the many things that made adjustment to civilian life difficult was a question none could totally dodge – 'Was all the suffering and death worth it?' The war was fought to stop German militarism and expansion, to save Belgium and France and because Britain was honour-bound by signed treaties, but

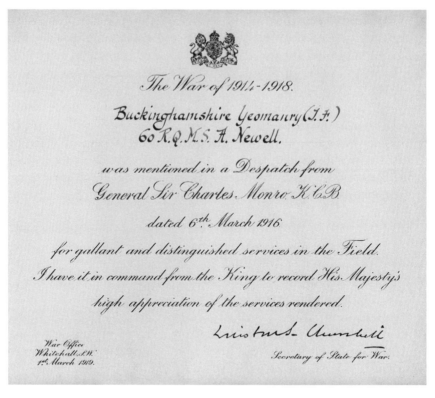

Mentioned in Despatches, Aubrey Newell's record signed by the then Secretary of State for War, Winston Churchill. (Mike Holland)

Europe was also going through traumatic change. The events of Sarajevo were merely the trigger for far greater forces which overwhelmed Europe during this period.

Whatever caused the war, it did not succeed in preventing German militarism. Indeed, it could be argued that it made things worse. It was not, by any stretch of the imagination, a war that ended all wars – the second half of the twentieth century saw enough war to satisfy even the most aggressive and warlike of people – nor did it end in a satisfactory peace.

In the last chapter of his accounts of life in the yeomanry (*The Yarn of a Yeoman*), S.F. Hatton writes:

> The peace has been much harder than the war. Most of us who went out in the full flush of young manhood came back to find ourselves thoroughly out of touch with life in England. Jobs were scarce, the pay was poor, there were vested interests at work to hang on to positions gained by the stay-at-homes whilst the boys had been out yonder. One crept back almost apologetically

into the daily round, and it was hard to knuckle under to regular hours, petty regulations, trivial jealousies, when one had slept for four years on the open desert beneath a canopy of stars.

To the ex-soldier the peace had been a sheer disillusionment and disappointment. In the first flush of victory we were promised a 'land fit for heroes' to live in. Never again should the ugliness of the slums, the blindness and brutality of ignorance, the vile evils of the overcrowding in our big cities retard the growth and progress of our young manhood. We would build the world anew. The peace-day hymn for thousands of our young children was the hopeful, stirring, progressive hymn of Blake. What was it they sang in such impassioned chorus?

> Bring me my bow of burning gold!
> Bring me my arrows of desire!
> Bring me my spear!
> O clouds, unfold!
> Bring me my chariot of fire!
> I will not cease from mental fight,
> Nor shall the sword sleep in my hand,
> Till we have built Jerusalem
> In England's green and pleasant land.

That was the spirit of the Nation in 1919. But the statesmen, the politicians, the business men, the financiers have let us down. Lloyd-George! You were the man with the greatest chance in history. We won the war, but the people of the nation believe that you did. You could have done almost anything you liked, the people would have risen to the greatest heights imaginable under your guidance. Such was the feeling of relief at the cessation of hostilities that had you even called for a 'burn your war bonds' campaign the people would have followed you. They would have given of their war profits freely and without stint had you shown the way, and thus had rid ourselves and our children of this terrible burden of taxation for all time.[106]

This is undoubtedly a naive view of the options open to the government following the war; the financial situation of the nation would not allow generous handouts, nor a lessening of the tax burden. However, it eloquently expresses what many of the soldiers thought of their wartime leaders whilst also expressing the difficulties of adjustment.

In his report to the House of Commons on the day of the Armistice, Lloyd George stated:

Quartermaster Sergeant Aubrey Newell, who joined the RBH in 1902. He served throughout the First World War and was Mentioned in Dispatches. In peacetime he ran an electrical shop in High Wycombe. (Mike Holland)

> Thus at eleven o'clock this morning came to an end the cruellest and most terrible war that has ever scourged mankind. I hope that we may say that thus, this fateful morning, came to an end all wars.[107]

Whether he truly believed this or not will never be known. Perhaps, on that day, it was a case of hope becoming belief, but surely of more significance are the words of one German corporal who recorded his thoughts in his book, *Mein Kampf*:

> Since the day that I stood at my mother's grave, I had not wept ... but now I could not help it. And so it had all been in vain ... Did all this happen only so that a gang of wretched criminals could lay hands on the Fatherland? In these nights hatred grew in me, hatred for those responsible for this deed. In the days that followed, my own fate became known to me ... I for my part, decided to go into politics.[108]

Thus, even as Lloyd George spoke to the British Parliament, the seeds were being sown for a second and even more terrible conflict. What would water those seeds and ensure that the hatred and resentment of the defeated would grow was being put together in the discussions, horse-trading and cutting up of Europe known as the Treaty of Versailles.

On 12 January 1919, David Lloyd George, Woodrow Wilson, Georges Clemenceau and Vittorio Orlando sat down in the French Foreign Ministry building on the Quai d'Orsay to begin the series of meetings which would culminate in the signing of the Treaty of Versailles on 28 June 1919 in the Hall of Mirrors at the Palace of Versailles. During these six months the victorious allies rewrote the map of Europe, the Middle East and Africa. As is always the way in international politics, the rhetoric, both prior to the conference and during the talks themselves, exceeded the international statesmen's ability to deliver. Woodrow Wilson, the first US President to travel to Europe whilst in office, came, in his own eyes, as a world arbiter, the man who could take a truly disinterested attitude to problems and could be relied on to be a fair and honest broker. He had always stressed that the US had entered the war for truly unselfish reasons with no territorial demands, no desire for revenge and no empire to protect.

Georges Clemenceau, on behalf of the French, wanted reparations. France had been desecrated and vast tracts of her sovereign territory laid waste by the most terrible war in history. In particular, Clemenceau wished to build in safeguards to ensure that his beloved France was never invaded by Germany again. He had fought against the Prussians in the Franco-Prussian war and now the Great War, and he reputedly told an American journalist shortly before his death that 'My life hatred has been for Germany because of what she has done to France.' He also asked that he be buried upright facing Germany as part of his lifelong obsession with guarding the borders against his eternal foe. His great triumph was to persuade the Allies that the peace conference be held in Paris as he wished the hour of the Germans' humiliation be in the capital of France.[109]

David Lloyd George arrived at the conference fresh from winning a general election which gave him his mandate to speak on behalf of the British people. His coalition, however, was mainly Conservative and the Conservative leader Bonar Law was there with him, riding shotgun and making sure that the mercurial Welshman protected British colonial interests, their mercantile pre-eminence and their world position.

These were the big three; also present at the first of the meetings was Vittorio Orlando, the Prime Minister of Italy. Italy had originally signed a treaty to form a triple alliance of Germany and Austro-Hungary in 1882. However, at the outbreak of the First World War they reneged on the treaty and joined the Allies in May 1915 with promises of land down the Adriatic coast and control over parts of the Ottoman Empire. In particular, the Italians approached the Paris talks with the objective of taking control of Fiume, a port with a predominantly

Italian population on the Dalmatian Coast. Orlando was handicapped during the conference by his inability to speak and understand English, the main language spoken at the sessions of the big four.

Above all of these, admittedly selfish, objectives were Woodrow Wilson's famous fourteen points which were designed to bring into being a new approach to international relationships and to create a 'League of Nations':

1. There should be no secret alliances between countries
2. Freedom of the seas in peace and war
3. The reduction of trade barriers among nations
4. The general reduction of armaments
5. The adjustment of colonial claims in the interest of the inhabitants as well as of the colonial powers
6. The evacuation of Russian territory and a welcome for its government to the society of nations
7. The restoration of Belgian territories in Germany
8. The evacuation of all French territory, including Alsace-Lorraine
9. The readjustment of Italian boundaries along clearly recognizable lines of nationality
10. Independence for various national groups in Austria-Hungary
11. The restoration of the Balkan nations and free access to the sea for Serbia
12. Protection for minorities in Turkey and the free passage of the ships of all nations through the Dardanelles
13. Independence for Poland, including access to the sea
14. A league of nations to protect 'mutual guarantees of political independence and territorial integrity to great and small nations alike'.

National delegations met over and over again; the leaders of nations also met for six months. The politicians and their civil servants argued, compromised and hacked up the pre-war map of Europe, the Middle East and Africa. There is a well-known saying in the military that the most dangerous thing on the battlefield is a subaltern with a map. There may be elements of truth in that, but once the battle is over and the peace needs to be negotiated, there is no doubt that a group of politicians with maps and pencils is far more dangerous.

The Treaty of Versailles was finally signed by both the defeated and the victors on 28 June 1919; the League of Nations came into being and various new national borders were created. The Ottoman Empire and the Austro-Hungarian Empire were no more. The Jewish homeland agenda was put firmly on the international agenda. But too many countries were left unsatisfied. In the end, it is too easy to say that the politicians let the soldiers

Bill Cowell in old age, back in his beloved North Bucks, outside the farmhouse in Swanbourne. (Bill Cowell)

down; no one could have been expected to see what was approaching over the horizon or to understand the evil regimes that would arise in Nazi Germany, in post-revolutionary Russia and in Italy. That the leaders of these regimes tried to use elements of the Treaty of Versailles as an excuse for their actions does not condemn the motives of those who sat at the table. Nor should the attribution of war blame and the imposition of war reparations be used as excuses; after all, many of the countries involved had been through the most horrific experiences it is possible to imagine. Millions of the most promising young men from around the world were sacrificed and it would have taken saints rather than human beings not to wish for some sort of recognition of that fact, and for financial compensation to rebuild their shattered countries.

This book was intended to be a tribute to both my grandfather, Bill Cowell, and to the other fighting men of Buckinghamshire. The county of Buckinghamshire is my part of England, somewhere I both love and understand, where I spent my early formative years. As described by Rudyard Kipling, it is my 'one spot – beloved over all'. For him it was Sussex; for me it was, and always will be, Buckinghamshire.

God gave all men all earth to love,
But since our hearts are small,
Ordained for each one spot shall prove
Belovèd over all …[110]

13

THOSE WHO FOUGHT WITH AND ALONGSIDE THE ROYAL BUCKS HUSSARS

Field Marshal Sir Edmund Allenby

By the standards of many British Army generals, General Sir Edmund Allenby had a good war. The popular line 'lions led by donkeys' has forever tarred the reputations of British senior commanders from the Great War, but Allenby was one of the few exceptions. Like most clichés, the saying only tells a partial truth. Allenby undoubtedly spent the majority of his war career in a theatre where he had a scope to affect the outcome which simply wasn't available to his colleagues in France. It is a truism, however, both on the sports field and the battle field, that you can only beat the opponent put in front of you. Judged on this basis, Allenby was a consistently effective and suc-

General Edmund Allenby.
(Wikimedia Commons)

cessful general who deserves the accolades which came his way following the Palestine campaign.

He was born in 1861 in Nottinghamshire, educated at Haileybury, and after leaving school applied to join the Indian Civil Service but failed the entrance exam. He was, however, successful in the entrance examination for officer training at Sandhurst. He was commissioned into the Inniskilling Dragoons and with the Dragoons went out to South Africa in 1882. He rapidly began to show promise as a field officer and, as if often the case during war, rapid promotion followed. Having returned to England, he was eventually successful in gaining entrance to Army Staff College where he met Douglas Haig for the first time. It was obviously not a meeting of minds as it marked the beginning of a rivalry which would persist through the First World War. At graduation, Allenby was not overwhelmed by the descriptions from his tutors when they described him as having 'much practical common sense' and being an 'active and good soldier'.

When the Second Boer War broke out in late 1899, Allenby returned to South Africa with the Dragoons. He was by now a major and was made second-in-command of the regiment. He further added to his reputation as a good battlefield commander and towards the end of the war was given command of one of the Cavalry Division's columns, tasked with protecting convoys and battling insurgents. He subsequently stated that his column never lost a convoy or battle during his time in charge; however, he found himself increasingly worn down by the pressure of constant campaigning, and needed some time to recuperate with his wife in Durban. By the end of the war, Allenby had been promoted to the rank of colonel and received the personal praise and thanks of Lord Kitchener. Following his return to the UK, he took over command of the 5th Irish Lancers and was promoted to brigadier general in 1905.

In 1909 Allenby was promoted to major general and made inspector general of cavalry. He rapidly established a reputation as a strict taskmaster with a volcanic temper and as such was not always popular with the officers who served immediately under his command, especially those he did not consider up to the job. During this period he began to refine some of his ideas on the use of cavalry in modern warfare and increasingly saw them as mounted infantry who would fight as foot soldiers or, if the situation warranted it, could mount and charge the enemy. These tactics were subsequently to serve him well in Palestine.

At the outbreak of the First World War, Allenby was given command of the British Expeditionary Force's Cavalry Division and sailed with the BEF to France. However, after the Battle of Mons, the battlefields settled down into stalemate and cavalry became increasingly irrelevant; by the beginning of the Second Battle of Ypres in late April 1915, Allenby was in command of V Corps, which eventually became the Third Army. He commanded the Third Army during the bloody Battle of the Somme and it was here that his differences with Haig's leadership began to grow, such that, by the time he led his troops into the Battle of Arras, he was beginning to be openly critical of Haig's tactics and it was only a matter of time before he was moved to another command.

Although Allenby was obviously a senior officer of some considerable talent, his initial efforts in France did little to enhance the reputation he had previously built up in South Africa. Not getting on with his senior officer, Field Marshal Haig, did nothing to help. He was always his own man and, perhaps uniquely amongst the British military hierarchy, he had a good opinion of Lloyd George. This alone would have made him suspect to Haig.

He was a man of wide interests and read extensively about the countries in which he fought. He was an amateur botanist and ornithologist and above all, so far as the horse soldiers of the EEF were concerned, he was a cavalry man with a knowledge and understanding of what cavalry could achieve and what was best suited to their particular talents. When he left his interview with Lloyd George, he had been presented with a book entitled *Historical Geography of the Holy Land*. Mischievously, Lloyd George claimed that it was a better guide to a military leader whose task was to reach Jerusalem than any survey to be found in the pigeon holes of the War Office.

Following the war, Allenby was appointed High Commissioner for Egypt from 1919 until 1925. Although he was probably not a natural diplomat he governed with tact, courage and fairness, and became a highly respected figure. On his retirement he became rector of Edinburgh University. He died in London in 1936.

In 1932, just four years before he died, Field Marshal Allenby addressed the British Legion with these prophetic words:

> It is good that we should meet each other often, recalling ancient memories and renewing old acquaintances. It is good for us and it is good for our children and all the younger generation. Over eighteen years have passed since you answered your country's call. It is difficult to realise that babies then in arms are now of men's estate – and those men and women who are just beginning to play an active part in the service of our country knew nothing about the war of their own experience. Those girls and boys have got to learn from you, lest the lesson you learnt with such suffering be wasted. True, they can read history, and should do so. But written history is no efficient substitute for the spoken word. On you who made history lies the duty of telling these young people how the war was fought and why, show those children what sacrifices were made, that the land of their fathers – this green pleasant land – might be saved, and Great Britain and the Empire secured to help them against the direct efforts of their enemies.
>
> Unless the rising generation learn now – and learn from you who know – they may have to pay again with pain and bitter tears the debt which you have already discharged.
>
> Let us be true to the principles which unite and guide the British Legion. Show kindness in others' trouble, courage in our own. Hold together. Trust in God; and keep your powder dry.[111]

Sir Randolf Littlehales Baker, 4th Battalion

Sir Randolph Baker was a major in the Dorset Yeomanry at the outbreak of the war, but soon achieved the temporary rank of lieutenant colonel and commanded the regiment which served in the 6th Mounted Brigade alongside the Royal Bucks Hussars. He was successfully nominated for the Distinguished

Service Order in 1917 thanks to his leadership of the regiment. The citation read, 'he has shown energy and devotion to duty since he took over the command of the Regiment. He handled the Regiment with ability and skill before Gaza on 26 March and 19 April 1917.'

He was born on 20 July 1879, the son of Reverend Sir Talbot Hastings Bendall Baker and his wife Amy Susan Marryat. At the age of 21, on the death of his father, he succeeded to the title. After the war, on 29 June 1920, he married Elsie Burrell, and after her death he married Mary Caroline Orlebar, daughter of Augustus Scobell Orlebar, on 8 October 1955. He died on 23 July 1959 at the age of 80. He played a full part in the life of Dorset, serving in the office of deputy lieutenant and on the bench as a Justice of the Peace for Dorset. He had one child, Selina Littlehales Baker, who was born on 26 October 1925 and died on 28 March 2010.

Captain J.C. Bulteel

John Crocker Bulteel came from a Devonian family which could trace its ancestry back to William the Conqueror. His father, John George Bulteel, married the exotically named Maraquita Musini Grenfell, the sister of the Commanding Officer of the Bucks Hussars, Lt Col John Grenfell. John Bulteel, however, seemed to have no need for nepotism to succeed and proved to be a brave and resourceful cavalry leader. He was extremely popular with his men and had the happy knack of leadership which inspired men under his command to acts of bravery of which they had thought themselves incapable.

Born in 1890 and educated at Eton, Bulteel proved himself a natural horseman and carried his expertise in fox hunting into the field of battle. He was successful in many of the point-to-point amateur races held by the troops whilst in Palestine; no doubt some of his popularity arose from the enthusiastic punters amongst his squadron.

Soon after the end of the war he married and had three daughters whilst carrying on an extremely successful career as Clerk of the Course at Ascot race course. During his tenure he inaugurated the King George VI and Queen Elizabeth Stakes, which is now probably the second richest race after the Derby. He was later knighted for his services to racing, and died in 1959.

Sergeant William ('Bill') Charles Cowell

It is difficult to write about Bill Cowell, and all the other heroes who figure in this book, and adequately explain their lives to a modern audience. Bill Cowell was not a man who would have fitted comfortably into the twenty-first century. He was a man born into the nineteenth century, during the reign of Queen Victoria, who was brought up, educated, trained and who adopted his views of life during the very early part of the twentieth century, during the reigns of King Edward VII, George V, Edward VIII and our present Queen's father, George VI.

On returning to North Bucks, after being demobbed having served in the army of occupation, he soon married his childhood sweetheart, Dorothy Midgley, an ironmonger's daughter from nearby Winslow. They went on to have four children, two girls and two boys, and eleven grandchildren, all of whom arrived before their grandfather died. He farmed Dodley Hill Farm in Swanbourne, land owned by Lord Cottesloe.

Bill Cowell and his wife never travelled outside the UK after the war. They took their holidays every year in Llandudno. (Bill Cowell)

Surely the marvel of his life was that the experiences of war, and indeed the anti-climactic nature of the society to which he returned, failed to embitter him. He remained a man with an essentially optimistic and cheerful outlook on life – someone who was fun to be with.

He never lost his love of riding and one of my earliest memories is of my grandfather mounting up on a hunter to ride around and inspect the farm. He was always ready to discuss his war experiences with me, often accompanying the talk with soft, asthmatic wheezing laughter as he explained the apparent stupidities and contradictions of governments. The brass plate on the Vickers machine gun which told the user that after two minutes of continuous firing the gun would stop and the fact that soldiers were provided with free cigarettes whereas now people are warned that smoking is harmful to their health were just two of the inconsistencies he seemed to find amusing. He was a lifelong smoker.

Lt Col The Hon Fred Cripps

Fred Cripps was the second eldest of four brothers born to Charles Alfred Cripps. The father was initially, probably through habit, a Conservative but soon modified his views and became a member of the Labour Party. Showing a rare impartiality, however, he was ennobled by Asquith's Liberal administration, mainly for his legal work. He took the title of Baron Parmoor from a small village in Buckinghamshire and during the war he headed a government committee determining compensation for damage caused by enemy air raids. The experience of the war changed his political views. He felt himself unable to support the war and strongly opposed conscription to the point of showing marked sympathy for conscientious objectors. Whatever his differences of belief with his son, however, he appears to have been a caring and loving father and Fred makes no reference in his autobiography to ever having been pressurised in any way to give up his military career.

Colonel (The Hon) Fred Cripps DSO.
(Bucks Military Museum)

After attending Winchester College, Fred Cripps joined the Royal Bucks Hussars in 1903 at the age of 18. In the same year he went up to New College, Oxford, but the lure of fox hunting, gambling and horse racing meant that he was unable to devote as much time to his studies as perhaps his tutors would have wished. A bad fall whilst steeple-chasing sealed his academic fate as the recuperation period meant that he took no exams; indeed when his father was frequently asked what Fred was doing at Oxford, he was known to reply, 'learning to do nothing gracefully'. Whatever else came out of his time at university, he did make a number of useful friends and business contacts which were to serve him well following his war service. He subsequently stated that he did not allow his academic shortcomings to dishearten him unduly as he became Master of the Oxford Draghounds, President of the Bullingdon Club and a member of the polo team.

Fred Cripps took over command of the RBH from Lt Col John Grenville, who had been sent back to England by a court martial for infringing the censorship regulations. He subsequently also commanded the joint regiment of Berks and Bucks Yeomen of the 101st Machine Gun Battalion in France. The general feeling amongst those who expressed them was that, as it was necessary to go to war, in doing so they were happiest under the command of an officer such as Fred Cripps. Comments from fellow officers suggest that a smile was never totally extinguished from his face and he was a man of matchless personal courage. He was a charismatic man to whom life seemed to come easily. Badly wounded during the assault on Chocolate Hill, he was evacuated back to the UK, but was passed fit in time to rejoin the regiment for the fight against the Senussi. He served with distinction during both the Palestine campaign and later in France, when the Berks Yeomanry and the Bucks Hussars were dismounted to serve as machine gunners.

It may be difficult to believe, but the buccaneering Fred Cripps' youngest brother was the rather more puritanical Stafford Cripps who achieved fame as the Chancellor of the Exchequer under the post-Second World War Labour administration. Fred, however, continued in his own inimitable fashion as a merchant banker with Boulton Brothers, where he spent a considerable part of his career dealing with their Russian interests. Conversations when the brothers met up must have made interesting listening! He continued to serve with the Bucks Hussars up until 1922, when he became embroiled in a trial at the Old Bailey involving bank fraud. He was found to be guiltless of any involvement in the scam, but felt obliged to resign from the regiment prior to the trial and, despite attempts by influential friends and military authorities to get him back, he never again took up his old post.

On the death of his eldest brother, Fred inherited the title of Lord Parmoor which still exists to this day, passed down through his son and grandson.

Lt Cols John, Arthur and Cecil Grenfell

The Grenfell family are surely one of the most curious and multi-talented families in English history. They seemed to be born to fight and, if their own country was not fighting anyone, they were willing to travel to other countries to join in their fights. One of the early members of the family fought in the American Civil War on the side of the confederacy. George St Leger Grenfell (1808–68) was a soldier of fortune, which is perhaps a nice way of calling him a mercenary. He was born in London, the son of George Bevil Granville Grenfell, but was mainly brought up in Penzance, and seemed to be destined for the family's business of banking and metal dealing.

He moved to Paris in 1830, where some financial irregularities led to his father's ruin and he left France in 1837. The outbreak of the Crimean war gave him an opportunity to fight and he served under the command of fellow Cornishman Major General Hussey Vivian. After the war Grenfell went to live in South America, where he was involved in further fighting in several local revolutions.

The outbreak of the American Civil War gave him the major opportunity that he had been waiting for. He joined the Confederacy with an introduction to General Robert E. Lee, but subsequently served under Colonel John Hunt

Morgan who made him his adjutant general. Grenfell soon became a renowned fighter on behalf of the South and, together with Morgan, successfully harassed the Federal Army throughout Kentucky. In 1863 he joined Bragg's Army in Tennessee and subsequently served in Virginia with General 'Jeb' Stuart.

He was not classified as an American citizen and thus was able to travel to the north where he was interviewed by Edwin H. Stanton the Secretary of War, and allowed to live freely. Nevertheless, he became involved in Confederacy conspiracies, as a result of which he was tried by court martial, found guilty and sentenced to death. Following a plea for clemency from the British Parliament his sentence was commuted to life imprisonment by President Andrew Johnson.

Grenfell was sent to Dry Tortugas, a hellish prison camp off the coast of Florida. He tried to escape during a storm, but after breaking out of the camp was never heard of again.

Another exceptional member of the family was William, the 1st Baron of Desborough, who brought the Olympics to London in 1908. He was a distinguished athlete himself who had rowed for Oxford twice in the Boat Race and won a silver medal for fencing. He also enjoyed mountaineering, swimming, fishing and big-game hunting. He swam the Niagara rapids twice, climbed the Matterhorn three times, rowed across the English Channel and was Amateur Punting Champion of the Upper Thames. He was President of the Amateur Fencing Association, Marylebone Cricket Club and the Lawn Tennis Association.

At the outbreak of the Great War it was therefore inevitable that the Grenfells would be well represented in the British Army. The Royal Bucks Hussars had three members of the family: John, Arthur and Cecil Grenfell, all sons of Pascoe du Pré Grenfell and Sophia Grenfell, and three of a total of thirteen children. Prior to the Great War, John married Adeline Octavia Lambart, daughter of Gustavus William Lambart and Lady Frances Caroline Maria Conyngham. Their maternal grandfather was Admiral John Pascoe Grenfell and their uncle was Field Marshal Francis Grenfell, 1st Baron Grenfell.

An older brother, Lieutenant Robert Septimus Grenfell, 21st Lancers, was killed in a cavalry charge during the Battle of Omdurman in 1898. Three other brothers, Cecil Grenfell, Howard Maxwell Grenfell and Arthur Morton Grenfell all reached the rank of lieutenant colonel in the British Army. A cousin, Lieutenant Claude George Grenfell (Thorneycroft's Mounted Infantry) was killed at Spion Kop during the Boer War, and two other cousins Julian Grenfell, the poet, and his brother, Gerald William Grenfell, were killed in the First World War.

The youngest of the thirteen children were twins – Francis and Riverdale. Both were killed in the Great War. Captain Francis Octavius Grenfell was killed in action on 24 May 1915 at the age of 34. He was decorated with the Victoria Cross. On 24 August 1914 at Audregnies, Belgium, Captain Grenfell rode with the regiment in a charge against a large body of unbroken German infantry.

The casualties were very heavy and the captain was left as the senior officer. He was rallying part of the regiment behind a railway embankment when he was hit twice and severely wounded. In spite of his injuries, however, he and some volunteers responded to a request for help saving the guns by the Royal Field Artillery and, under a hail of bullets, helped to manhandle and push the guns out of range of enemy fire. The citation was gazetted on 16 September 1914 and read, 'For gallantry in action against unbroken infantry at Audregnies, Belgium, on 24th August 1914, and for gallant conduct in assisting to save the guns of the 119th Battery, Royal Field Artillery, near Doubon the same day.'[112]

John, Arthur and Cecil Grenfell all survived the First World War. Cecil died in 1924, John in 1948 and Arthur in 1958.

General Sir Ian Hamilton

The First World War ruined the lives of countless good men. For some it was the physical effects of high explosives, poisonous gas or machine gun bullets. For others it was mental deterioration caused by prolonged exposure to inhuman conditions against which their minds rebelled. For a few, however, it was their reputations which were destroyed, their self-belief and self-regard. General Sir Ian Standish Monteith Hamilton, GCB, DSO, to give him his full title, was one who fell into this latter category.

It seemed as if he were born to be a soldier. Although he was a proud Scot he was actually born in Corfu on 16 January 1853, the eldest son of an army colonel and a mother who was a daughter of the third Viscount Gort, a member of a distinguished Irish family. He could trace his family on his father's side to a senior officer in the army of John Churchill, the first Duke of Marlborough. After the typical education at English public school, his father sent him to continue his education in Germany to learn the skills and science of warfare from the Prussian General von Dammers who, conveniently, was a family friend.

In 1873 he fulfilled his destiny and joined the army, serving as a young subaltern in the First Boer War. He saw action before being captured by the Boers in 1881, showing his strength of character when he refused to surrender his sword. General Joubert, Commander of the Boer forces, was obviously impressed by the defiance of this young British soldier. On learning that the sword had previously belonged to Hamilton's father, he allowed him to keep it. It was during the Boer War that he received the first of several severe wounds to his left arm which eventually resulted in him losing most of its use.

Following his release by the Boers and the end of that war, Hamilton saw active service in a number of imperial wars which figured so frequently in British history towards the end of the nineteenth century. Service in India, Egypt and Burma ensured rapid promotion for Hamilton so that by 1891 he was a full colonel who had made his name for being cool under fire and indeed had received several Mentions in Dispatches. He also received another severe wound to his left arm, which left him permanently, albeit not severely, disabled.

Returning to England, he was rescued from a series of staff posts by the outbreak of the South African War where again he served with great distinction and great physical courage. This led to his promotion to general and the award of a KCB, and finally to being appointed as Chief of Staff to Lord Kitchener. He was twice recommended for the Victoria Cross, and would undoubtedly have received it had it not been for his senior rank.

Again, the end of the war saw General Sir Ian Hamilton return to Britain to take up a number of staff posts until, in 1907, he was promoted

General Ian Hamilton. (Wikimedia Commons)

to full general. In 1910 he was appointed General Officer Commanding-in-Chief of the Mediterranean and Inspector General of the Overseas Forces. During this posting he naturally had a lot of contact with Australian and New Zealand troops, which stood him in good stead for his command of the operations on the Gallipoli Peninsula in April 1915.

At the outbreak of the First World War, therefore, there were few if any British generals with a more varied CV than General Hamilton. He had studied war in different theatres and had led troops under fire with great gallantry. His personal courage and his background knowledge of military science could not be bettered and he would have been justified in thinking at the outbreak of hostilities that this would set the seal on his career and reputation.

Sadly, as is evident, it all went wrong. His many friendships within the Liberal Government did not save him from the indignity of a Royal Commission which was called to look into the failures at Kut and at Gallipoli. As is the way with such enquiries, it served to spread as much disinformation as it cast light on matters. Sir Ian Hamilton felt vindicated to some degree although he spent the rest of his lengthy life rather on the defensive regarding his actions in Turkey and, unlike Allenby, went into print with his Gallipoli diaries, which were essentially an elongated rebuttal of his many critics.

In later life he became rather too closely associated with the far right of politics and indeed wrote admiringly of Adolf Hitler during his rise to power. He lived to see the error of his ways, however, dying at the age of 94 in 1947. Whatever the rights and wrongs of the military situation in the Dardanelles, General Hamilton was renowned as a gracious and charming man of many talents. A noted linguist, he wrote beautifully in the English language, an example of which was his thoughtful tribute to his troops on being relieved of his command in Gallipoli:

> On handing over the command of the Mediterranean Expeditionary Force to Sir Charles Monro, the Commander-in-Chief wishes to say a few farewell words to the allied troops, with many of whom he has now for so long been associated. First, he would like them to know his deep sense of the honour it has been to command so fine an army in one of the most arduous and difficult campaigns which have ever been undertaken; and, secondly, he must express to them his admiration at the noble response they have invariably given to the calls he has made upon them. No risk has been too desperate, no sacrifice too great. Sir Ian Hamilton thanks all ranks, from generals to private soldiers, for the wonderful way they seconded his efforts to lead them towards a decisive victory, which under their new chief he has the most implicit confidence they will achieve.[113]

Lt Col H. Lawson and Major Fred Lawson

The founding member of the Levy-Lawson family was Joseph Moses Levy, who had been sent by his father to Germany in the first half of the nineteenth century to learn the printing trade. On his return to the UK he founded a printing business in Fleet Street. He proved to be very successful and by 1855 he was chief proprietor of *The Times*. His company was also printing a newly formed newspaper called the *Daily Telegraph* and when the latter was unable to pay its printing bill, Joseph Levy took over the ailing paper and turned it around: within a year he had overtaken *The Times*' circulation and rapidly made the *Daily Telegraph* into the most successful of the 'serious' newspapers.

His son Edward Levy took over the newspaper and took it from strength to strength, along the way assuming the name Levy-Lawson. He rapidly became a pillar of society, especially in his native county of Buckinghamshire where he was created High Sheriff in 1886. In 1903 he was created Baron Burnham of Beaconsfield.

In 1862 Edward's eldest son was born, Harry Lawson Webster Levy-Lawson. The name Levy was changed to Levy-Lawson whilst he was still at school and from then on this was the name that the family would be known by. Educated at Eton and then Balliol College, Oxford, he gained a first-class degree in modern history. On leaving university he began a life-long career in public life, holding a number of appointments such as treasurer of the Free Land League and vice president of the Municipal Reform League, and was also a member of the Executive Committee of Municipal Federation League. During this period of his life he also met and married Olive de Bathe, daughter of General Sir Gerald Henry Perceval de Bathe. In 1891 he was admitted to the Inner Temple where he practised as a barrister.

Harry Lawson's interest in national politics was not to be satisfied by a career in law, however, and at the comparatively young age of 23 he was elected Member of Parliament for St Pancras West as a Liberal. As his father, the proprietor of the *Daily Telegraph*, was a staunch Conservative, this must have sparked some lively family debate. He subsequently lost the seat in the 1892 general election, but got back into Parliament by winning a by-election in 1893 in the Cirencester constituency. Again, however, it proved to be a short-lived triumph as he lost in the 1895 general election and was not to return to Parliament for another ten years, when again he won a by-election in Mile End in the East End of London. This tenure in the House was also short; he lost his seat in 1906 though he regained it in 1910. Throughout this period he also held a number of other public offices: he was a member of the London County Council and Mayor of Stepney for two years between 1907 and 1909.

During this rather hectic public life he was commissioned into the Royal Bucks Hussars in 1902 and rose to the rank of lieutenant-colonel, commanding the regiment before resigning shortly before the outbreak of the First World War, in 1913. He rejoined during the war to command the training regiment, which remained on home duties throughout the duration. It was during the war, in 1916, that his father died and he succeeded to the titles of Baron Burnham and the baronetcy and took his seat in the House of Lords. He also succeeded his father in the management and ownership of the *Daily Telegraph*. It was to Lord Burnham that Lt Col Grenfell wrote the fateful letter which resulted in his court martial.

His nephew, known to all as Fred Lawson, commanded A Squadron of the Bucks Hussars throughout their service in Gallipoli, Egypt and Palestine. He proved to be an excellent leader and was Mentioned in Dispatches three times and awarded the Military Cross. Throughout the war he wrote many times to his uncle, letters which, on the face of it, were in contravention of the strict censorship laws. Amazingly frank about the performance of his fellow officers and making few pretences at hiding his whereabouts from the newspaper magnate, he was lucky that Lt Col Grenfell was the only officer actually court-martialled. After the war he rose to the rank of major general in the Territorial Army and in 1943 he succeeded to the family title as 4th Baron of Burnham.

Thomas Pakenham, Brigadier General the Earl of Longford

Thomas Pakenham, the 5th Earl of Longford, was born on 19 October 1864. His father, the 4th Earl, died in 1887 and Thomas succeeded to the earldom aged 23. He had also been commissioned in the Life Guards in the same year. In 1899 he commanded the 45th Imperial Yeomanry who, within weeks of arriving in South Africa as part of the 13th Battalion, found themselves surrounded and taken prisoner by the Boers.

Following the signing of a peace treaty with the Boers, Lord Longford was repatriated and, having achieved the rank of colonel in the Life Guards, he left active service in the Army to take on the more ceremonial duties of Lord-Lieutenant of County Longford. In 1899 he married Lady Mary Julia Child Villiers, daughter of the Earl of Jersey. They went on to have two sons and four daughters.

At the outbreak of the First World War Lord Longford was called back to the Army and took command of the 2nd Mounted Division consisting of the Berks, Bucks and Oxon Yeomanry. He led them from their time on the east coast, through their deployment to Egypt, and during the disastrous march across Suvla Bay on 21 August 1916. It was on that day that he lost his life somewhere towards the summit of what was known as Green Hill. He was by any standards an extremely brave man.

The second of his two sons, Frank, became a prominent Labour politician and, having inherited the earldom from his elder brother, as the 7th Earl of Longford, he became famous for espousing the cause of rehabilitating prisoners. In particular, he supported the extremely unpopular cause of releasing the Moors Murderer, Myra Hindley. Like his father he was a man unconcerned about thrusting his head over the parapet.

Sir Everard Philip Digby Pauncefort-Duncombe

Major Sir Everard Pauncefort-Duncombe served as Adjutant of the 1/1st Royal Buckinghamshire Hussars (2nd South Midland Brigade, 2nd Mounted Division) in Egypt, July 1915, and as a staff officer at Gallipoli during the Bucks' time in Suvla Bay, from where he was subsequently invalided home with jaundice. He rejoined the regiment in Palestine, however, and served the war out with the regiment until demobilised in 1919.

Sir Everard Philip Digby Pauncefort-Duncombe was born on 6 December 1885, the son of Sir Henry Philip Pauncefort-Duncombe the second Baronet of

Great Brickhill in Buckinghamshire. He married Evelyn Elvira Denny, daughter of Frederick Anthony Denny and Maude Marion Quilter, on 16 November 1922 and subsequently had two children, Sophia Pauncefort-Duncombe, born in 1925 and a son, Philip Digby Pauncefort-Duncombe, born in 1927. Like so many of the Bucks Hussars officer corps he played a full part in county life following demobilisation, serving as High Sheriff for the county in 1949. He died on 8 December 1971, aged 86.

Lieutenant C.H. Perkins

Lieutenant C.H. Perkins was not a typical officer of the Royal Bucks Hussars; for a start he was not from one of Buckinghamshire's landed gentry, but had been born in 1896 to a father who was a Canadian oil man working in the oil fields in Carpathia for the Austrian Government. Indeed, one of his cousins by marriage went on to fight for the Central Powers in the Austrian Army and was killed on the Russian front. Cyrus Perkins had been educated at Charterhouse School and was living in St Albans at the outbreak of the First World War. Whilst staying with some of his old school chums who decided to enlist in the army, Cyrus decided to join up too, and went to the Duke of York's Barracks and joined the Royal Engineers as a motorbike dispatch rider.

His mother was extremely unhappy that he had joined the British Army as an enlisted man and subsequently pulled strings to have him transferred to the 7th Reserve Cavalry Regiment at Tidworth. It was there that he found himself training with members of the Royal Bucks Hussars. As his opportunity to go to war seemed to be slipping further and further away, he applied directly to Lord Burnham who was Colonel of the 3rd Line Regiment of the Royal Bucks Hussars.

It was by this rather convoluted path that he found himself joining the Royal Bucks Hussars in Egypt following their return from Gallipoli in January 1916. He first saw action in the campaign against the Senussi. Captain Perkins survived the war and on his return to England he resumed his studies, going to Trinity College Cambridge. He subsequently worked for General Motors.

Cyrus Perkins was probably the longest surviving member of the the First World War officers from the Royal Bucks Hussars and at some stage he started to write his memoirs although, as far as I can discover, they never got into print. Nevertheless, the beginnings of his account can be found in the archives of the Imperial War Museum. In these documents Perkins describes his impression of the regiment. He always found the regiment a happy band of brothers although we can see from other officers' accounts that this was not always the case. He describes the Metropolitan Police and members of the *Daily Telegraph* print room staff who found their way into the regiment, no doubt due to the active encouragement of Lord Burnham. The fact that the non-commissioned ranks came from such close-knit communities of workers seems to have contributed to their cohesiveness under the stresses of battle.

He comments less favourably on the officer replacements and remembers one in particular who arrived in Palestine as a non-drinking, non-smoking devout Christian and, if that wasn't bad enough, also appeared unable to ride. Of course, as the yeomanry looked outside the traditional farming background for replacement drafts, the lack of familiarity with horses became more and more a problem, though presumably manageable as the regiment seemed to spend as much time leading the horses as riding them.

Sadly, Lt Perkins lost all interest in the Royal Bucks Hussars following demobilisation and lost contact with most of his old colleagues.

Captain Neil Primrose

One of the most evocative images left from the Great War is that of the 'lost generation'. This was a feeling that Great Britain lost a significant part of the brightest and the best in a generation of leaders, and, like all such myths, there is an element of truth in it. In assessing such losses, Neil Primrose would be an eloquent example as, prior to the outbreak of war, he appeared to be destined for a stellar career in politics.

He was born into a life of privilege and leadership on 14 December 1882, the second son of Lord Rosebery who, when Neil Primrose was 12 years old, became Liberal Prime Minister in a short-lived administration from 1894 to 1895. He had come to power on the resignation of Gladstone, but the Liberals were a party split between the left wing under Sir William Harcourt and an imperialist wing under Rosebery. The

The memorial to the Right Honourable Captain Neil Primrose MP, MC. (Bill Cowell)

administration lasted just one year before Rosebery tendered his government's resignation following a lost vote in committee over defence budgets. The fact that he chose to interpret this as a vote of non-confidence says something about his state of mind. He resigned as leader of the Liberal Party a year later and was never to play a leading role in day-to-day politics again.

Neil Primrose's mother was Hannah de Rothschild and by marrying her Lord Rosebery fulfilled or at least heavily contributed to the achievement of all three of his self-confessed ambitions in life – to marry an heiress, to win the Derby and to become Prime Minister. Hannah de Rothschild brought to the marriage as her dowry Mentmore Towers, a beautiful house in Buckinghamshire, and Mentmore Stud, one of the most successful thoroughbred stud farms in the country.

Although Primrose's father was clearly disillusioned with politics, he obviously did not hand on this cynicism to his second son because at the age of 28 Primrose entered the House of Commons as MP for Wisbech and within five years he had started on the first rung of the ministerial ladder with his appointment as Parliamentary Under-Secretary of State in the Foreign Office and subsequently Parliamentary Secretary to the Treasury in Lloyd George's coalition administration.

Politics, however, was not Primrose's sole occupation as, prior to being selected as an MP, he had joined the Royal Bucks Hussars as a lieutenant, married Lady Victoria Stanley, daughter of the Earl of Derby, and started an affair with a 19 year-old girl, Eileen Graves. The latter subsequently married a Putney bus driver whom she left a few weeks after the marriage, which was widely interpreted as a cover for the birth of Neil Primrose's illegitimate child. Whatever the truth of that particular matter, it is undeniable that his wife gave birth to a daughter, Ruth Primrose in April 1916.

As a sitting MP Neil Primrose was exempted from military service, but he was obviously uncomfortable sitting at home whilst his yeomanry colleagues were fighting, so in 1916 he joined his regiment and thus fulfilled his destiny by fighting and dying with his colleagues in Palestine.

Following his death, Prime Minister Lloyd George paid the following generous tribute to Neil Primrose in the House of Commons:

> May I be permitted, before I sit down, to utter one word of another who held an inconspicuous position in the Army but who was well known to all Members of this House. I refer to Captain Neil Primrose. The House knew his bright and radiant spirit well. To his intimates he was one of the most loveable men we ever met. He had ability far above the average, and, in spite of the reserve and the shyness which held him back, his future was full of hope. He had already rendered distinguished service in the field and for that service he had been recognised at the suggestion of his Commanding Officer; and he might well, for he had many offers, have occupied positions where he could have rendered services to the public, positions honourable to him, but positions of personal safety, and the fact that he had been chosen by his constituents to serve in this House would have rendered his acceptance of these positions honourable to himself. He chose deliberately the path of danger. He fell charging at the head of his troops, at the very moment of victory, and

Members of this House will, I feel certain, join me in an expression of deepest sympathy with those whom he has left behind to mourn him.[114]

Lord Rosebery was surely another casualty of this terrible war for he never recovered from the loss of his son. His condition was further worsened by a stroke suffered prior to the signing of the Armistice. He never fully regained his movement, hearing or sight. His sister Constance described the last years of Lord Rosebery's life as, 'a life of weariness, of total inactivity and at the last of almost total blindness. Crushed by bodily weakness and sunk in sad and silent meditations.'[115]

Major Evelyn Achille de Rothschild and Captain Anthony Gustav de Rothschild

The brothers were born in London, the second and third of Leopold de Rothschild and Marie Perugia's three sons and as such were part of one of the wealthiest families, not just in England, but in the world. The Rothschild banking family had branches throughout Europe. They were brought up living in Ascot House in Buckinghamshire, one of several great houses owned by the Rothschild family in the county.

Despite being born into such wealth and privilege they were expected to play an active part in the family business N.M. Rothschild & Sons bank. However, at the outbreak of war, both joined the Royal Bucks Hussars. Both Anthony and Evelyn were wounded serving in Gallipoli and evacuated back to the UK to recuperate. Within a few months Evelyn was back with the regiment in Sinai/Egypt and during the fight with the Senussi was Mentioned in Dispatches. Sadly, he was critically wounded during the Battle of El Mughar on 13 November and died four days later. On 5 December 1920, his brother, Captain Anthony de Rothschild, unveiled the War Memorial in the churchyard of All Saints Church at Wing, Buckinghamshire honouring Evelyn and his other comrades from Wing who were killed in the war.

REFERENCES

Papers concerning the proposed reorganisation of the Imperial Yeomanry [Buckinghamshire Studies, Royal Bucks Hussars ...]

Correspondence of Major General Sir Edward Frederick Lawson, 4th Baron Burnham concerning the RBH Association and his position as Hon Colonel of 299th Field Regiment RA (TA). [Buckinghamshire Studies, Royal Bucks Hussars ...] Sir E.F. Lawson was Managing Director of the *Daily Telegraph*, which was founded by his great grandfather

Letter concerning the desert campaign written from Lemnos [Buckinghamshire Studies, Royal Bucks Hussars ...]

Newspaper cuttings, articles about desert campaign and unveiling of RBH War Memorial in Buckingham Church

Letters to Colonel the Hon. H.L.W. Lawson, 2nd Baron Burnham concerning the organisation of the territorial forces and the desert campaign including a statement about attack on the Turks at El Mughar. [Buckinghamshire Studies, Royal Bucks Hussars ...

Roll of horses A Squadron with list of officers and some other battered volumes, written in pencil, list not complete. [Buckinghamshire Studies, Royal Bucks Hussars ...]

Letter from J. Liddington enclosing a list of other ranks RBH still serving 11 Nov 1918 the list is dated 11 Nov 1919. [Buckinghamshire Studies, Royal Bucks Hussars ...]

Extract from 'The Official History' Chapter 24 about the desert campaign, concerning Lt Col E.F. Lawson [Buckinghamshire Studies, Royal Bucks Hussars ...] Major Edward Frederick Lawson 1890–1963, 4th Baron Burnham in 1943 served with 1/1st RBH.

Printed copy of letter from W.E. St John about desert campaign [Buckinghamshire Studies, Royal Bucks Hussars ...]

Two letters to Colonel W.A.W. Lawson from 'The Elephant' at Alexandria [Buckinghamshire Studies, Royal Bucks Hussars ...] William Arnold Webster Levy Lawson (1864–1943) commanded the 2/1st RBH and became 3rd Baron Burnham in 1933

'With Horses to Jerusalem' by Capt Cyrus H. Perkins 1/1st RBH. Typescript account of cavalry action against the Turks at El Mughar 1917 [Buckinghamshire Studies, Royal Bucks Hussars ...]

Orders to the Yeomanry, (mostly printed, mostly 1820s) from Richard Grenville, 5th Earl Temple, later Marquess of Chandos, Lt Col commandant, with some correspondence [Buckinghamshire Studies, Royal Bucks Hussars ...]. He became 2nd Duke of Buckingham and Chandos in 1839

Volume containing list of officers and men of 2/1st Regiment RBH with dates of service and regiments which they joined [Buckinghamshire Studies, Royal Bucks Hussars ...]

Correspondence with extracts from London Gazette and address to RBH on departure of Colonel the Hon. Harry Lawson Webster from command of the regiment [Buckinghamshire Studies, Royal Bucks Hussars ...] H.L.W. Lawson (1862–1933) became 2nd Baron Burnham in 1916. He had commanded the regiment 1902–13

Centre for Buckinghamshire Studies: Royal Bucks Hussars: records of or belonging to, the Lawson family, barons Burnham. These papers relating to the Royal Bucks Hussars are the property of the Lawson family, barons Burnham, several of whom served in the regiment. [Buckinghamshire Studies, Royal Bucks Hussars ...] Lawson family, barons Burnham; The collection includes papers

Works cited

Anglesey, T.M. (1994). *A History of British Cavalry Volume 5 1914–1919*. Leo Cooper.

Attlee, C. (1954). *As It Happened: The Memoirs of Clement Attlee*. Viking Press

Beckett, I.F. (1985). *Call to Arms*. Barracuda Books Ltd.

Broadbent, H. (2005). *Gallipoli – The Fatal Shore*. Penguin Books.

Buchan, J. (1920). *Francis and Riversdale Grenfell*. Thomas Nelson and Sons Ltd.

Bullock, D.L. (1988). *Allenby's War*. Blandford Press.

Burnham, M.G. (1987). *Private Papers of Major General Lord Burnham CB DSO MC*. Imperial War Museum Doc 2743.

Carlyon, L.A. (2001). *Gallipoli*. Doubleday.

Carter, D. (2010). *Aphrodite's Killers*. Downlow Productions.

Carver, F.M. (2003). *Turkish Front 1914–1918*. The National Army Museum with Sidgwick & Jackson.

Chambers, S. (2011). *Suvla August Offensive*. Pen and Sword.

Churchill, W.S. (1931). *The World Crisis 1911–1918*. Penguin.

Cripps, F.H. (1957). *Life's a Gamble*. Odhams.

Edmonds, B.G. (1945). *Official History of the Great War France and Belgium Volumes 4 and 5*. The Naval and Military Press Ltd.

Erickson, E.J. (2008). *Gallipoli and the Middle East 1914–1918*. Amber Books.

Falls, L.G. (1927). *Official History of the Great War Egypt and Palestine Volumes 1 & 2*. The Naval and Military Press Ltd.

Gilbert, M. (1994). *First World War*. Weidenfield & Nicolson.

Grainger, J.D. (2006). *The Battle for Palestine 1917*. The Boydell Press.

Haldane, R.B. (1908). *Regulations for the Territorial Force and County Associations 1908*. The Naval and Military Press Ltd.

Hamilton, G.S. (1920). *The Gallipoli Diary*. Edward Arnold.

Hart, C.B. (1930). *The Real War 1914–1918*. Boston: Little Brown and Co.

Hart, N.S. (1994). *Defeat at Gallipoli*. Macmillan.

Hatton, S.F. (n.d.). *The Yarn of a Yeoman*. The Naval and Military Press Ltd

Hibberd, D. (1992). *Wilfred Owen: The Last Year 1917–1918*. M.W. Books.

Hitler, A. (2009). *Mein Kampf – English Translation*. Elite Minds Inc.

Holmes, R. (2011). *Soldiers*. Harper Press.

Hughes, M. (2006). *Allenby in Palestine – The Middle East Correspondence of Field Marshal Viscount Allenby*. Sutton Publishing Ltd.

Hughes, M. (2004). *Allenby in Palestine*. Sutton Publishing Ltd for the Army Records Society.

Lefebvre, G. (1969). *Napoloeon Bonaparte*. Routledge and Columbia University Press.

Lloyd George, D. (1938). *War Memories of David Lloyd George*. Odhams Press Ltd.

Lunnon, F. (1978). Interview.

Macmillan, M. (2001). *Peacemakers.* John Murray.

Marshall, P. (n.d.) Personal recollections of Private Marshall. *Reproduced by kind permission of the Berks Yeomanry Museum.*

Massey, W.T. (1920). *How Jerusalem Was Won.* Charles Scribener's Sons.

Massey, W.T. (1918). *The Desert Campaigns.* Constable & Co Ltd.

Middlebrook, M. (2007). *The Kaiser's Battle.* Pen and Sword.

Mortlock, M.J. (2011). *The Egyptian Expeditionary Force in World War I.* McFarland & Co. Inc.

Mortlock, M.J. (2007). *The Landings at Suvla Bay, 1915.* McFarland & Co. Inc.

Newspaper, T.A.-A. (1918, January 4). *The Age,* p. 1.

Perkins, C. (1920). With horses to Jerusalem. *Collection of private papers of C.H. (Lt) Perkins.* Imperial War Museum Doc 8704–29(A).

Robinson, J.F.M. (2012). Extract from the Great War Forum.

Sheffield, G. (2011). *The Chief, Douglas Haig and the British Army.* Aurum Press.

Sutton, C. (n.d.). Personal recollections of Captain Sutton. *Reproduced by kind permission of the Berks Yeomanry Museum.*

Swann, M.G. (1930). *The Citizen Soldiers of Buckinghamshire.* Hazell, Watson and Viney Ltd.

Taylor, A.J. (1965). *A History of England Vol XV 1914–1945.* Oxford University Press.

Taylor, J. (2009). War letters from 1914–19 from *North Bucks Times, Bucks Standard* and *Wolverton Express. www.mkheritage.co.uk.*

Teichman, C.A. (1922). *Memories of a Woucestershire Yeomanry MO.*

Terraine, J. *Douglas Haig – The Educated Soldier.* Cassell & Co.

The War Diary Vol 18. (1918). *101st Machine Gun Battalion (RBH) War Diary, 18.*

Wavell, F.M. (1943). *Allenby in Egypt.* George G. Harrap & Co.

Westlake, R. (2011). *The Territorials 1908–1914.* Pen and Sword.

Woodward, D.R. (2007). *Forgotten Soldiers of the First World War.* Tempus Publishing Ltd.

NOTES

1 (Lloyd George, 1938) *War Memoirs of David Lloyd George*, published by Odhams Press Ltd, p. 32

2 (Houseman, 1896) *The Shropshire Lad*, published by K. Paul Trench Trubner

3 (Hibberd, 1992) *Wilfred Owen: The Last Year*, published by Constable Press

4 (Cripps, 1957) *Life's a Gamble*, published by Odhams Press Ltd, p. 62

5 (Holmes, 2011) *Soldiers*, published by Harper Press

6 Extracted from documents held by the Bucks Military Museum (document study pack for the 200th anniversary of the Bucks Yeomanry)

7 (Swann, 1930) *The Citizen Soldiers of Buckinghamshire 1795–1926*, published by Hazell, Watson and Viney

8 (Cripps, 1957) *Life's a Gamble*

9 (Cripps, 1957) *Life's a Gamble*, p. 63

10 (Cripps, 1957) *Life's a Gamble*, p. 68; (Holmes, 2011) *Soldiers*

11 (Sheffield, 2011) *The Chief*, published by Aurum Press, p. 60

12 (Haldane, 1908) Regulations for the Territorial Force and for County Associations, published by the Army Command

13 (Westlake, 2011) *The Territorials*, published by Pen and Sword

14 (Anglesey) *A History of the British Cavalry 1816–1819 Volume 5*, published by Leo Cooper

15 (Carter, 2010) *Aphrodite's Killers*, published by Downlow Productions, p. 34

16 (Gilbert, 1994) *First World War*, published by Weidenfeld and Nicolson

17 (Swann, 1930) *The Citizen Soldiers of Buckinghamshire 1795–1926*, p. 58; (Beckett, 1985) *Call to Arms*, published by Barracuda Books

18 (Burnham, 1987) *Private Papers of Major General Lord Burnham CB DSO MC*, held by the IWM Doc 2743

19 (Churchill, 1931) *The World Crisis 1911–1918*, published by Charles Scribner's Sons, republished by Penguin Classics 2007, p. 499

20 (Hamilton, 1920) *Gallipoli Diary*, published by George H. Doran Co., p. 61

21 (Hamilton, 1920) *Gallipoli Diary*, p. 100

22 (Gilbert, 1994) *First World War*, p. 185

23 (Lunnon, 1978) Memoirs of a Buckinghamshire Yeoman, never published and supplied courtesy of Mike Holland, p. 2

24 (Cripps, 1957) *Life's a Gamble*, p. 103

25 (Cripps, 1957) *Life's a Gamble*, p. 104

26 (Burnham, 1987) *Private Papers of Major General Lord Burnham CB DSO MC*

27 (Burnham, 1987) *Private Papers of Major General Lord Burnham CB DSO MC*

28 (Chambers, 2011) *Suvla August Offensive*, published by Pen and Sword, p. 178

29 (Hamilton, 1920) *Gallipoli Diary*

30 (Mortlock, 2007) *The Landings at Suvla Bay*, published by McFarland & Co. Inc., p. 113

31 (Mortlock, 2007) *The Landings at Suvla Bay*

32 (Mortlock 2007) *The Landings at Suvla Bay*

33 (Carlyon, 2001) *Gallipoli*, published by Bantam Books; (Broadbent, 2005) *Gallipoli: The Fatal Shore*, published by Penguin, p. 264

34 (Teichman, 1922) *The Diary of a Yeomanry Medical Officer*, published by T. Fisher Unwin Ltd

35 (Teichman, 1922) *The Diary of a Yeomanry Medical Officer*

36 (Mortlock, 2007) *The Landings at Suvla Bay*, p. 112

37 (Mortlock, 2007) *The Landings at Suvla Bay*; (Hart & Steel, 1994) *Defeat at Gallipoli*, published by Macmillan

38 Centre for Buckingham Studies, 'Papers of J. Liddington'

39 (Hart & Steel, 1994) *Defeat at Gallipoli*, pp. 312–3

40 (Burnham, 1987) *Private Papers of Major General Lord Burnham CB DSO MC*

41 (Burnham, 1987) *Private Papers of Major General Lord Burnham CB DSO MC*

42 (Burnham, 1987) *Private Papers of Major General Lord Burnham CB DSO MC*

43 (Burnham, 1987) *Private Papers of Major General Lord Burnham CB DSO MC*

44 (Tennyson, 2007 edn) 'The Charge of the Light Brigade', in *England's Best Loved Poems*, edited by George Courtauld, published by Ebury Press

45 (Burnham, 1987) *Private Papers of Major General Lord Burnham CB DSO MC*

46 (Hart & Steel, 1994) *Defeat at Gallipoli*, p. 319

47 (Hamilton, 1920) *Gallipoli Diary*

48 (Hamilton, 1920) *Gallipoli Diary*

49 (Attlee, 1954) *As It Happened: The Memoirs of Clement Attlee*, published by William Heinemann

50 (Erickson, 2008) *Gallipoli and the Middle East 1914–1918*, published by Amber Books

51 (Hughes, 2006) *Allenby in Palestine – The Middle East Correspondence of Field Marshal Viscount*; (Woodward, 2006) *Hell in the Holy Land*, published by the University Press of Kentucky

52 (Hughes, 2006) *Allenby in Palestine – The Middle East Correspondence of Field Marshal Viscount*; (Woodward, 2006) *Hell in the Holy Land*, published by the University Press of Kentucky

53 (Taylor, 2009) Letter from trooper Arthur Mapley of the RBH 'War letters from North Bucks Times, Bucks Standard and Wolverton Express', www.mkheritage.co.uk

54 (Falls, 1927) *The Official History of the Great War Military Operations Egypt and Palestine Volume 1*, p. 99

55 (Massey, 1918) *The Desert Campaigns*, published by Constable and Co. Ltd

56 (Carver, 2003) *The National Army Museum Book of the Turkish Front 1914–18*, published by Pan Books in assc with NAM, p. 187

57 (Carver, 2003) *The National Army Museum Book of the Turkish Front 1914–18*, p. 188

58 (Taylor, 2009) Letter from Trooper A Chapman of the RBH 'War letters from North Bucks Times, Bucks Standard and Wolverton Express', www.mkheritage.co.uk

59 (Woodward, 2006) *Hell in the Holy Land*

60 (Woodward, 2007) *Forgotten Soldiers of the First World War*, published by Tempus, p. 34

61 (Falls, 1927) *The Official History of the Great War Military Operations Egypt and Palestine Volume 1*, Appendix 3

62 (Falls, 1927) *The Official History of the Great War Military Operations Egypt and Palestine Volume 1*, pp. 170–1

63 (Hughes, 2006) *Allenby in Palestine – The Middle East Correspondence of Field Marshal Viscount Allenby*; (Woodward, 2006) *Hell in the Holy Land*

64 (Anthony, 2002) *The Last Crusade*, published by John Murry, p. 36

65 (Hughes, 2006) *Allenby in Palestine – The Middle East Correspondence of Field Marshal Viscount Allenby*; (Woodward, 2006) *Hell in the Holy Land*

66 (Falls, 1927) *The Official History of the Great War Military Operations Egypt and Palestine Volume 1*, pp. 246–7

67 (Carver, 2003) *The National Army Museum Book of the Turkish Front 1914–18*, pp. 198–9

68 (Mortlock, 2011) *The Egyptian Expeditionary Force in World War I*, published by McFarland & Co. Inc., p. 77

69 (Falls, 1927) *The Official History of the Great War Military Operations Egypt and Palestine Volume 1*, p. 324

70 (Falls, 1927) *The Official History of the Great War Military Operations Egypt and Palestine Volume 1*, p. 348

71 (Teichman, 1922) *The Diary of a Yeomanry Medical Officer*

72 (Bullock, 1988) *Allenby's War*, published by Blandford Press, Chapter 9

73 (Carver, 2003) *The National Army Museum Book of the Turkish Front 1914–18*, p. 207

74 (Burnham, 1987) Records of or belonging to the Lawson family, Baron Burnham, Centre for Buckinghamshire Studies, ref. D206

75 (Burnham, 1987) Records of or belonging to the Lawson family, Baron Burnham, Centre for Buckinghamshire Studies, ref. D206/13

76 (Burnham, 1987) Records of or belonging to the Lawson family, Baron Burnham, Centre for Buckinghamshire Studies, ref. D206/13

77 (Cripps, 1957) *Life's a Gamble*, pp. 114–5

78 (Hughes, 2004) *Allenby in Palestine – The Middle East Correspondence of Field Marshal Allenby*, p. 88

79 (Hughes, 2004) *Allenby in Palestine – The Middle East Correspondence of Field Marshal Allenby*, pp. 45–6

80 (Lefebvre, 2009) *Napoleon*, published by Folio Society, pp. 209–10

81 (Grainger, 2006) *The Battle for Palestine 1917*, published by the Boydell Press

82 (Massey, 1920) *How Jerusalem Was Won*, published by Charles Scribner's Sons

83 (Grainger, 2006) *The Battle for Palestine 1917*, p. 121

84 (Falls, 1930) *Official History of the Great war Military Operations Egypt and Palestine Volume 2 Part I*, published by the Naval and Military Press Ltd, p. 168

85 (Perkins, 1920) Extracts from the memoirs of Lt Cyrus H. Perkins (Royal Bucks Hussars) entitled 'With Horses to Jerusalem', never published

86 (Perkins, 1920) Extracts from 'With Horses to Jerusalem'

87 (Carver, 2003) *The National Army Museum Book of the Turkish Front 1914–18*, pp. 219–20

88 (Teichman, 1922) *The Diary of a Yeomanry Medical Officer*

89 (Robinson, 2012) Extract from the Great War Forum imternet site and here reproduced with the kind permission of Thomas Robinson, grandson of Col J.F.M. Robinson MC OBE

90 (Perkins, 1920) Extracts from 'With Horses to Jerusalem'

91 (Woodward, 2007) *Forgotten Soldiers of the First World War*, published by Tempus, p. 195

92 *The Age*, 4 January 1918

93 (Perkins, 1920) Extracts from 'With Horses to Jerusalem'

94 (Swann, 1930) *The Citizen Soldiers of Buckinghamshire 1795–1926*, p. 73

95 (Massey, 1920) *How Jerusalem Was Won*, Appendix VIII

96 (Sutton) *Account of the sinking of the Leasowe Castle*, reproduced by the kind permission of the Berkshire Yeomanry Museum

97 (Marshall) *Account of the sinking of the Leasowe Castle*, reproduced by the kind permission of the Berkshire Yeomanry Museum

98 (Hart, 2008) *1918 – A Very British Victory*, published by Weidenfeld & Nicolson, p. 12

99 (Terraine, 1963) *Douglas Haig – The Educated Soldier*, published by Cassel & Co., p. 433

100 (Edmonds, 1945) *Official History of the Great War Military Operations France and Belgium 1918*, Appendix XX

101 (Sheffield, 2011) *The Chief*, p. 305

102 *The War Diary Vol 18*, 1918. The official war diaries of the Royal Bucks Hussars as part of the 101st Machine Gun Battalion

103 (Edmonds, 1945) *Official History of the Great War Military Operations France and Belgium 1918 Volume V*, Chapter VI

104 *The War Diary Vol 18*, 1918

105 (Taylor, 1965) *A History of England 1914–1945*, published by Oxford University Press, p. 1

106 (Hatton) *The Yarn of a Yeoman*, published by The Naval and Military Press in association with the National Army Museum, pp. 283–4

107 (Lloyd George, 1936) *War Memoirs Vol II*, published by Odhams Press, p. 1986

108 (Hitler, reprinted 2009) *Mein Kampf*

109 (Macmillan, 2001) *Peacemakers*, published by John Murray

110 (Kipling, 1988 edn) 'Sussex', in *The Coloured Counties – Poems of Place in England and Wales*, edited by John Arlott, published by T.M. Dent & Sons

111 (Wavell, 1943) *Allenby in Egypt*, published by George G. Harrap & Co. Ltd, p. 138

112 (Buchan, 1920) *Francis and Riversdale Grenfell*, published by Thomas Nelson and Sons, p. 221

113 (Hamilton, 1920) *Gallipoli Diary Vol 2*, published by George H. Doran Co., pp. 277–8

114 (Lloyd George, 1938) Hansard HC Deb, 19 Novembr 1917, Vol 99, cc. 865–7

115 (James, 1963) *Rosebery: A Biography of Archibald Philip, Fifth Earl of Rosebery*, published by Weidenfeld & Nicolson, p. 485

INDEX

101st Machine Gun Battalion 138, 146, 150–2,170

11th Division 53, 54

1st Mounted Brigade 57

22nd Mounted Brigade 111, 123, 124–6

29th Division 43, 48, 53–5, 57

2nd Mounted Brigade 41, 55, 177

2nd South Midland Mounted Division 48, 54, 55, 177

32nd Brigade 53–4

3rd mounted Brigade 57

4th Mounted Brigade 57

51st Highland Division 151

53rd Division 47, 70, 110–1

5th Mounted Brigade 84–5

6th Mounted Brigade 81, 87, 119, 124, 126–30, 132, 137, 167

86th Brigade 54

87th Brigade 54, 60

Addington 15

Agincourt, Battle of 36

Ahmed, Sayed 74–5, 80

Aire Klavak 53

Alexandria 42, 43, 66, 69, 72, 74, 82, 83, 99, 100, 137, 138, 140–3, 145–6

Allenby, General Sir Edmund 97–8, 100–7, 109–15, 127–8, 130, 132–6, 165–7

Anfarta Ridge 46

Anglesey, Marquess of 31

Anzac Cove 39–41, 44, 66

Armistice 16, 152–4, 159, 181

Arras 97, 151–2, 166

Ashmead-Bartlett, Ellis 46, 58, 60

Aspinall, Col 46

Asquith, H.H. 35, 40, 95, 170

Ataturk 67

Attlee, Clement 67

Australian Light Horse Brigade 76, 81, 85, 87, 94, 109, 113, 133

Avonmouth 42

Aylesbury 18, 41

Baker, Maj. Sir R.L. 167–8

Barker, Lt Percy 62, 64

Barron, Sgt William 83–4

Barrow, General 127, 129

Battine, Captain C.W. 101

Beersheba 86–8, 90–3, 95, 99, 102, 105, 107, 109–15, 134, 136

Beitunia 131–2

Bennett Captain C.H. 64, 141–2

Biache-Saint-Vaast 151

Blaksley, 2nd Lt J.H. 79

Blenheim, Battle of 36

Boer War 9, 12, 25, 36, 39, 44, 76, 166, 172, 173, 177

Bonaparte, Napoleon 12, 102, 103

Bowyer, Lt W.B. 76–7, 88, 120

British Expeditionary Force (BEF) 12, 36, 37, 69, 153, 166

Buckingham and Chandos, Duke of 25, 30

Buckingham 15, 41, 50

Buckingham, Marquess of 18, 24

Buckinghamshire 9, 15–8, 24–5, 42, 50, 70, 156, 163, 170, 175, 178, 180, 181

Bulteel, John Crocker 23, 30, 62, 77, 80, 89, 117–9, 121–2, 132, 168

Burnham, Lord 30, 62, 99, 100–2, 175, 176, 178

Bury St Edmunds 41

Byng, Lt-Gen. Julian 45, 46, 47

Cairo 43, 72, 73, 82, 83, 97, 98

Caledonia, HMT 145, 146

Campbell-Bannerman, Henry 27

Chapman, A. 78

Chauvel, General 10–109

Chaytor, Brig.-Gen. 85

Cheape, Captain L. 75

Chesham 41
Chesham, Lord 25
Chetwode, Lt-Gen. Sir Philip 87, 90, 98, 110
Chocolate Hill 47–8, 50, 56–7, 59–60, 171
Churchill, Jack 47
Churchill, John *see* Marlborough, Duke of
Churchill, Winston MP 30, 37, 38, 40, 47,
  149, 157, 158
Churn 41
Citadel Barracks 43
Clemenceau, Georges 147, 148, 161
County of London Yeomanry 115
Courtrai 152
Cowell, W.C. (Bill) 8–10, 15–6, 18, 25, 27,
  30–3, 42, 43, 49, 50, 51, 61, 62, 68, 70, 72,
  93, 94, 98, 103, 109, 149, 153, 155–7, 163,
  164, 168–9
Crecy, Battle of 36
Crimean War 36, 38, 69, 171
Cripps, Hon. Fred 16, 23, 25, 27, 41, 42,
  50–1, 64, 100, 115, 119, 132–3, 151, 169–71
Cromer 41
Cucq 150

Daily Telegraph 30, 42, 99, 101, 175, 176, 178
Dalmeny, Lord 98, 129
Dardanelles Committee 38, 40, 41, 64
Dardanelles 37, 38, 39, 44, 63, 66, 162, 175
Davis, Lt Harold 55–6
de Rothschild family 121, 180, 181
de Rothschild, Anthony Gustav 23, 181
de Rothschild, Evelyn Achille 62, 64, 122,
  126, 181
Dead Sea 114
Defence of the Realm Act 1798 24
Disraeli, Coningsby 30, 142
Dodley Hill Farm 15, 169
Dorset Yeomanry 48, 55, 58, 59, 78–80, 83,
  117, 118, 122, 128, 133, 167
Dreadnought battleships 12, 38

East Riding Yeomanry 123–5
Egypt 24, 38, 41–3, 48, 64–6, 68–87, 95,
  97–9, 101, 136, 137, 141, 146, 149, 167,
  173, 176–8, 181
Egyptian Expeditionary Force (EEF)
  69–71, 74, 77, 80–4, 97, 105, 166
El Arish 82–3, 85, 86
El Hassana 82
El Kossaima 82

El Medjel 134
El Mughar 115, 120, 122–3, 126–8, 131,
  132, 181
Etaples 145, 146, 150

Field Service Regulations 27–8
Fisher, Admiral 'Jackie' 12, 37, 38, 40
Fleet, John 60
Fortescue, J.W. 30
Fourteen Points (*see* Wilson Woodrow) 162
French, Sir John 69
Fuller, J.F.C. 45

Gallipoli 9–10, 35–70, 74, 75, 129, 133, 141,
  174–8, 181
Gaza 65, 81, 86–94
  battles of 65, 88–112
Gaza-Beersheba line 86, 91, 105, 114–5
George, Percy 50
Gillam, Maj. John 57
Gloucester Hussars 55
Godwin, Brig.-Gen. 101, 115, 119, 129, 137
Gore, Maj. St J. Bt 141
Great Saxham 41
Grenfell, Lt Col C.A. 23, 30, 41, 64, 76,
  171–3
Grenfell, Lt Col J. 23, 30, 62, 75, 76, 99,
  100–2, 168, 171–3, 176
Grenfell, Maj. A.M. 23, 30, 41, 171–3

Haig, Field Marshal Sir Douglas 12, 27, 28,
  38, 96, 97, 147–51, 165, 166
Haldane, Richard 12, 25, 27, 28, 36
Hamilton Camp 30
Hamilton, General Sir Ian 39–41, 45–8, 53,
  55, 57, 64–6, 173–5
Hammersley, General 48
Hampden, Brig.-Gen. Viscount 83
Hannibal, HMS 66
Hatton, S.F. 158–9
Helles Memorial 50
Helles 43, 48
Hetman Chair 53
High Wycombe 41, 160
Hill 100 55
Hill 112 53, 57
Hill 70 52, 53, 54, 57, 59, 60
Hodgson, Maj.-Gen. H.V. 81, 100
Holl, Captain 139–42
Horne, General Sir Henry 151

Horses 22, 28, 31, 33, 34, 42–3, 71, 72, 77, 80, 105, 111
Hotchkiss machine gun 31, 89, 125, 144
Houseman, A.E. 13
Huj 87, 88, 126

Imperial Mounted Division 81
Imperial Yeomanry 25, 36, 177
Ismail Oglu Tepe 53, 55
Ismet Bey, Col 107

Jaafar Pasha 79, 80
Jaffa 123, 135, 136
Jebel Medwa 75
Jerusalem 88, 91, 97–8, 105, 113–5, 123, 127, 128, 130, 132–5, 167
Judean Hills 114, 127, 128, 130, 132
Junction Station 114–5

Kantara 83, 84
Katrah 134
Kemal Pasha, Mustapha 67
Kenna, Brig.-Gen. P.A. 55
Khamsin wind 71, 110
Kinloss, Lady 30
Kiritch Tepe 46
Kitchener, Lord 6, 27, 35–40, 45, 47, 52, 64, 81, 157, 166, 174
Kress von Kressenstein, Col 85, 91, 93, 110
Krithia 39
Kut 65, 174

Lala Baba 44, 48, 49, 54, 55, 57, 59
Langtip, Sgt H. 109
Lawford, Maj.-Gen. S.T.B. 152
Lawson, Lt Col H. 30, 99, 100, 175–6
Lawson, Maj. Fred 23, 24, 42, 52, 62, 63, 115, 143, 175–6
League of Nations 162
Leasowe Castle, HMT 138–45
Liberal government 40, 174
Lindley, General 48
Lloyd George, David 11, 37, 38, 95–7, 113, 135, 159–61, 166, 167, 180
Longford, Lord 27, 48, 50, 52–5, 60, 177
Luddite Riots 18
Ludendorff, Quartermaster General 147, 148
Lunnon, Frank 23, 50
Lynden-Bell, Maj.-Gen. Sir Arthur 82

Machine Gun Corps 120, 137, 150
Magdhaba 86
Mahon, Lt-Gen. Sir Bryan 45, 47, 48
Mapley, Trooper Arthur 72–3
Marlborough, Duke of 30, 36, 49, 173
Marmaris, Sea of 37, 44
Marne, Battle of 37
Marne, River 147
Marshall, Private 143
Matruh 75–7
Maxwell, General Sir John 64, 74
Mediterranean Expeditionary Force (MEF) 39, 175
Menominee, SS 42
Mersa Matrus 99
Mesopotamia 69, 74, 137
Metropolitan Police 42, 178
Middlesex Yeomanry 85
Monchy-le-Preux 151
Money, Maj.-Gen. 97
Monro, Lt-Gen. Sir Charles 65, 67, 175
Mudros 62, 64, 66
Murray, General Sir Archibald 69, 70, 73–5, 81–3, 86, 90–4, 95–8

Nablus 130, 134
Nash 15
Nekhl 82
Newell, Aubrey 158, 160
Newmarket 41
Newport Pagnell 23, 25, 60
Niven, Lt William 53
Nottinghamshire Yeomanry 137

Occupation, Army of 156, 169
Orlando Vittorio 161, 162
Owen, Wilfred 13
Oxfordshire Yeomanry 27, 30, 43, 177

Palestine 26, 32, 33, 34, 65, 77, 80, 82–3, 89, 91, 96, 97, 99, 106–7, 113–4, 121, 129, 132, 136–7, 151, 157, 165–6, 171, 176
Pauncefort-Duncombe, Maj. Sir E.P.D. 177–8
Pelves 151
Perkins, Lt C.H. 115, 117, 119, 126, 129, 132, 133, 178–9
Peterloo Massacre 19, 21
Peyton, Maj.-Gen. W.E. 48, 60, 64, 83
Pitt, Brig.-Gen. T.M.S. 81, 99, 101

Pitt, William 17
Primrose, Neil 30, 80, 98, 120, 122, 128–30, 179–80

Qatiya 84, 85
Qatra 115
Queen Victoria 16, 25, 169

Ramallah 130
Ramleh 129
Rawlinson, Lt-Gen. Henry 45–7
Regulations for the Territorial Force and County Associations 1908 28–9
Robertson, Field Marshal Sir W. 73, 81, 91, 96, 97, 103, 105
Robinson, Col J.F.M. 123
Romani 84–6
Royal Buckinghamshire Yeomanry 17
Royal Bucks Regiment of Yeomanry 25
Royal Flying Corps 83, 92
Royal Latin School 50
Royal Navy 12, 37, 39, 106, 141, 145
Russia 38, 100, 147, 157, 162, 163, 171, 178

Sackville Carden, Vice Admiral 39
Saint-Laurent-Blagny 151
Salisbury Plain 18, 19, 30
Salt Lake 10, 48, 49, 52, 53, 55, 58–60
Scarpe, Battle of 151–2
Scarpe, River 151–2
Scimitar Hill 48, 52–5, 57
Senussi Tribe 74–80, 85, 120, 171, 178, 181
Senussi, Mohammed Ali el (Grand Senussi) 74, 75
Shellal 95, 109, 110, 114
Short Magazine Lee-Enfield Rifle 31
Sidi Bisr 137
Sinai Desert/Peninsula 32, 71, 80–3, 85–6, 104, 181
Smith, F.E. (Lord Birkenhead) 27, 30
Snow, Lt Col 75
Souter, Lt Col 79
South Africa 9, 34, 39, 79, 96, 98, 165, 166, 174, 177
St Peter's Field 20
Stopford, General Sir Frederick 45, 46, 48
Stowe House 18, 24, 30
Suez Canal 38, 39, 64, 69–70, 75, 80–1, 87
Susuk Kuyu 54
Sutton, Captain 143

Suvla Bay 10, 41, 43, 44–6, 60, 62, 66, 67, 129, 177
Swanbourne 15, 163, 169
Sweet Water Canal 84
Sword (1908 cavalry pattern) 10, 31, 33, 79, 117–9, 122, 124, 127, 129, 130, 156, 173

Teichman, Capt O. 57, 59, 95, 122
Tel el Khuweilfeh 110–1
Tel es Sheria 110, 111
Territorial and Reserve Forces Act 1907 28
Territorial Force 16, 25, 27–9, 36, 37, 136, 157
Thilloy-lès-Mofflaines 151
Turkey 37–9, 95, 162, 174
Turner, Dick 53, 156
Two Tree Hill 55

Verney Junction 15
Versailles, Treaty of 160–3
Vickers machine gun 31, 150, 169
Von Saunders, General Otto Liman 65

W Hill 48, 53
Wadi el Ghazze 87, 90
Wadi Imleih 110
Wadi Jamus 115
Wadi Majid 76
Wadi Senab 76
Wallace, Maj.-Gen. 75
Waterloo, Battle of 36
Wavell, Field Marshal Lord 65, 103
Wellesley, Arthur (Wellington, Duke of) 12, 36, 49
Western Frontier Force 75, 78, 83
Wilson, Sir Henry 70, 147
Wilson, Woodrow 161, 162
Wingfield-Digby, Maj. 128
Winslow 15, 169
Wood, Frank 50
Worcester Yeomanry 57, 58, 93, 122
Wyfold, Lord 16

Yeomanry Mounted Division 109, 114, 124, 129
Yibna 115
Yilghin Burnu 54
Young, Lt J.D. 52, 62, 76, 142
Ypres 146–8, 152, 154, 166